Praise for Viki King

"Viki King is a writer for the ages, all ages."
~ Ellen Sanders, Author and Co-Producer,
Everybody Loves Raymond.

"She shows me the empowering meaning and importance of my experiences great and small. In her presence, flat surfaces of life become dazzling holograms."
~ Dianne Skafte, Author, *Listening to the Oracle*

"These stories that make up her life are like gems falling from a vast treasure chest, each one gorgeous and priceless."
~ Joe Sichta, Producer, Director at Warner Bros, Disney, DreamWorks, VRI Studios

"This is a book like no other you have ever read. It is a life work, an autobiography, yet after reading the book you will feel you have been in it as an observer next to the heroine throughout her life from infancy to senior citizen."
~ Rick Ronvik, Chicago Board of Education

"Viki King's humor and gentle yet formidable strengths are invaluable."
~ Angela Moonan, Corporate Coach, Futurist, Forbes Coaches Council

"Viki King's wisdom and storytelling prowess is a beacon of inspiration, illuminating the path of aspiring writers to craft our own literary masterpieces."
~ MB Stevens, Private Client

"No matter what, she's undaunted. It's remarkable and inspiring."
~ Joey Sanderson, Private Client

How to Be the Hero of Your Own Life

A Guide on How to Go Forward from Here

You may have noticed lately that the world has gone rogue.
We all knew that being alive now was going to be a humdinger for humans. We knew it and that's what we're here for, to discover our talents that we came to contribute. What's your contributing talent? What's your piece of the puzzle that's going to help everybody out?

Very early on, Viki King knew *her* plan.

What if she wrote the story of her life as she was living it to show the how-to beats of a lifetime, such as

- how to let your heart do the talking,
- how to step into your own spotlight,
- how to get from surviving to thriving,
- and much later how to conduct a conscious death.

And what if she could encode wisdoms in each stage, phase and, age? The takeaway for the reader would illuminate something for their life they never considered before; that would be a big help to all of us. So, that's what she did, she chronicled her whole life from before birth to the last of everything and all the iterations in between.

She has a lot to say while hanging semi-sideways in the womb. Later she chronicles all 15 years it takes her to become an overnight sensation in Hollywood. Through it all, with wit and wisdom, she expands you as you read and changes any part of you that might be a victim into a victor. What is it that you came to do, be, and have? Now is the time to do, be, and have it.

How to Be the Hero of Your Own Life demonstrates **the high art and exacting skill** of becoming to use the stories of the author's life to inspire the reader to be the hero of their own life. ~

Books by Viki King

How to Write a Movie in 21 Days – The Inner Movie Method

Beyond Visualization

Feelization – Feel It in Your Heart, Have It in Your Life

Split-Second Stories – How to View the World with an Open Heart

How To Be the Hero of Your Own Life – A Unique Autobiography

How to Be the Hero of Your Own Life

A Unique Autobiography

It starts before birth, ends after life, and
addresses all the ages in between

Viki King

BOOK of LIFE
BOOKS

How to Be the Hero of Your Own Life

Cover art and design – Steve Hubbard
Graphic art – Gretchen Martin
Cover photo – Nicole Goddard Photography
Make-up – Elishah Urbaez
Interior book design – Judith Arnold
Tech production – Kathryn Linehan

Book of Life Books, LLC
1112 Montana Avenue
Suite 242
Santa Monica, CA 90403
www.bookoflifebooks.com
bookoflifebooks@gmail.com

ISBN: 979-8-9916322-0-1 (hardback)
ISBN: 979-8-9916322-2-5 (paperback)
ISBN: 979-8-9916322-1-8 (ebook)

Library of Congress Control Number
2025933756

Contents

Call to Earth

One to Nineteen

20s Passage

30s Passage

40s Passage

50s Passage

60s Passage

70s Passage

The Last Passage (Whenever That May Be)

"We're all born fully realized.
We just don't realize it."

~ Viki King

Call to Earth

Here's the Situation

I'VE JUST ARRIVED in eternity after a triumphant life on Earth. I'm basking in the sunlight because that's my idea of heaven. In honor of my arrival, there is a celebration. Just as I am reveling in this experience, I hear a voice boom out from the sunlight.

Voice: Would you like to go back for another lifetime?

Me: What? No! Didn't I do it? Haven't I done it?

Voice: There's more.

Me: You mean a do-over?

Voice: No, it's a gift.

Me: I appreciate the gift, but I'd like to, you know, Rest in Peace!

Voice: For eternity?

Me: Maybe not that long. At least for a little while, maybe just bask in the light, kind of juice up before I turn around and do it all again.

Voice: Most souls jump at the chance.

Me: I don't mean to be contrary. Well, I guess I do mean to be contrary. It's just that Earth can be a lot of trouble. People forget they are spirit beings having a human experience.

Voice: Isn't there wonder there?

Me: Yes, of course, there's wonder there. It's splendidly precious, but there's also the raggedy bits.

Voice: What are those?

Me: There's suffering; there's war and injustice and cruelty; there's pain and fear. People can get hurt.

Voice: Are you worried that you would suffer?

Me: Me? No. I can always make it out of suffering with some benefit from it. It's what others must endure that bothers me. I'm talking about people who just don't have a chance, someone who just can't get out of something they're caught in. From here it all seems so short a time and safe, but when you're there, on Earth, having a life, it can be a real predicament.

Voice: Suffering can show you to go another way.

Me: That's a really good use of suffering, but I don't think people know that.

Voice: Go tell them.

Me: You can't tell them; people want to do it themselves.

Voice: This is the most dynamic time to be alive on planet Earth.

Me: Yes, I know that time is coming up, that's why I'm excited to be here, as the perfect vantage point to watch it from this front-row seat.

Voice: Go be there in a human body—what better front-row seat than that?

Me: I was hoping for a nap first?

Voice: You are being asked to participate in the greatest transformation that has ever yet been on Earth. So many have worked for so long to bring Earth to this tipping point of change.

Me: Well, certainly I'm willing to do my part. I wouldn't want to go in just to have goony fun. That's not my style.

Voice: Somewhere between goony fun and transcendental elevation you might find plenty to fill up a lifetime.

Me: Are you talking about heaven on Earth? You know we've been working on that for millenniums. That's uphill all the way again.

Voice: Difficulty never stopped you before.

Me: No, it's never stopped me. It can kill me, but it's never stopped me.

Voice: Then don't do it that way.

Me: Why didn't I think of that? I'll tell you why . . . It's just, well . . . the thought of starting all over again . . .

Voice: Start from where you left off.

Me: Can I do that?

Voice: It's your choice.

Me: Because the thought of a learning curve . . .

Voice: I have a question for you. Is life worth the trouble?

Me: Of course, it's worth the trouble, but why does it have to be trouble?

Voice: It doesn't.

Me: So you're saying go in and let it not be trouble? Is that even possible? Earth is the conundrum planet. It can be crazy making, but there's also love and beauty and magic happening when you least expect it. I don't mean that it isn't worth the trouble. I guess

	you're saying we're free to just make it up as we go along?
Voice:	Whatever you like. You create your own reality.
Me:	I just thought that since you've got your finger on the pulse of everybody's pulse you could do something to help humans out.
Voice:	It was never meant for humans to suffer so.
Me:	Excuse me for saying, but there is definitely suffering going on there, and I think definitely a desire to know your path and get it right.
Voice:	Your soul knows your path.
Me:	But as humans, we don't know that our soul knows. Sooner or later somebody up here has got to put your foot down.
Voice:	There is no right way, or wrong way, just your way.
Me:	I know it's the opportunity for me to expand further. I know that. I'm happy to go back, but does it have to be now? Don't I need a chance to regroup, reconnoiter, rejuvenate? You know, gather wonder before I go back? I could get all wondered-up being here and then after a little quiet time, I could take wonder in with me. How about that?
Voice:	With all you accumulated from the last life what is the first thing that comes to mind that you learned about humans in that life?
Me:	People are under construction, wear a hard hat.
Voice:	Okay maybe something else.
Me:	Is there something unprecedented beyond our imaginings about to come on Earth that I don't know about?

Voice:	Go in now so you are ready for your part in the 21st century.
Me:	Okay sure, I'm happy to be ready. Ready for what?
Voice:	You'll see when you get there.
Me:	That sounds cryptic.
Voice:	It won't be cryptic when you get there. You'll know exactly what you want to do and be happy that you're there doing it.
Me:	Oh goodie, a surprise. Imagine how thrilled that makes me—not at all. Why do I have to leave the bliss that is here?
Voice:	That is the point—take it with you.

Well, that shuts me up. Meanwhile, the skies open and the heavens beam upon me. I am zapped with the brightness of ten thousand suns, and I am brim full. An angelic chorus can be heard.

Me:	Is this theater to get me to consent?
Voice:	Oh, is the choir too much?
Me:	No, I like the choir. The choir is good.
Voice:	I thought it might be too much.
Me:	Do you want to know what I think is my bottom-line truth in this matter?
Voice:	Yes, please.
Me:	If I go back now, I'll have to be made of galvanized steel and axle grease.
Voice:	That's not the kind of strength you are.
Me:	What kind of strength am I?
Voice:	You let your feelings feel all the way down to the deepest and your thoughts all the way up to the highest.
Me:	Okay, for a minute I was pretty sure I'd have to be somebody else.
Voice:	Not possible.
Me:	I just would like a little time to reflect on the enormity of what I'll be asking of myself.

Surprisingly, a beautiful beach appears in front of me with a splendid expanse of sunlit ocean.

Voice: Take a walk. Have a conversation with yourself. See how you feel. I'll meet you at the Department of N.O.B.U. when you're ready.

Me: Department of N.O.B.U. Will I know how to get there?

Voice: It will come to you.

The light of the grand Voice morphs into the magnificent beach. The sun gleams on the water, the sand, and the tide pools—all my very favorite elements of nature. I could be here for eternity.

As I glide along the surf, I have a conversation between me and myself.

Me: Was that Voice who I think it was?

Myself: I think so.

Me: I was rude. I should apologize. I think I just got scared and right away put up my dukes.

Myself: You spent a good part of your last lifetime learning to resist nothing, and here you are resisting everything.

Me: Well, you know any decision I make about anything has to come from inside me. I'm definitely not leaning in favor of being pulled along.

Myself: You can't be. Earth is not for the faint-hearted.

Me: I'm not faint-hearted and neither is anybody who is there now.

Myself: It's a place that's not as it seems. It's got war and disease and neighbors with barking pit bulls when it's ingeniously designed for our every expansion.

Me: Yes, ingeniously designed, and then there's the human condition.

Myself: Which particular human condition are you talking about?

Me: Humans are so sincere and want to love and be loved and do right and not fight and not eat the third piece of cake—that human condition. First, you don't know what you want, and then you do but you don't know how to get it, or you know what you want and what you have to do to get it, but you don't do it—that human condition.

Myself: Oh, are you afraid you're going to stop your own self?

Me: Well, what if I go in to be human and I'm . . . human?

Myself: Yeah, what if . . . You better go and find out.

Me: Actually . . . as I look out at the vastness of the ocean and feel it within me, I'm peaceful and rested and whole.

Myself: Maybe we're being asked to go back so fast for the very reason that we just came from there. We still have Earth Mind. Maybe having that kind of cumulative experience could be useful in the new life.

Me: But another lifespan? Already this puts me in a human frame of mind and makes me crabby. Besides . . .

Myself: Besides? You always say the important thing after you say besides . . . What is it?

Me: Well, while I'm here in eternity, I planned to write an account of 'How to Have a Life on Earth'—where humans can have a manual to view the world with an open heart so they can be inspired to be the hero of their own life.

Myself: Go in and write it there. You'll have a lot to say about being human and how to navigate life on Earth because you'll be a human navigating life on Earth. Go impart your wisdom. You know people have always said to you, 'I never thought of it that way.' Go give people another way to look at life.

Me: You mean while living a life, I'll be recording a guide for living a life? I'll have to be poly dexterous.

Myself: What's that?

Me: I don't know. I think I just made it up. I think it has to do with working overtime. Doesn't a person have to be well rested for that?

Myself: Energy is unlimited.

Me: Well, it's true now that I'm not resisting so much. I'm also not tired so much.

Myself: Just settle down and access what you really feel about Earth.

Me: Well . . . Earth is beautifully simple if you just let it be. What do you think, should we go back?

Myself: I think since we're offered the gift of life on Earth, we ought to damn well accept it.

And suddenly something appears at the end of the beach.

Me: What's that ahead? It says, "Department of . . ." Oh, that must be the Department of N.O.B.U. It did come to me.

A trailer has appeared on the beach. It looks like a makeup trailer on location for a movie. And suddenly I am inside, sitting in the chair looking into the makeup mirror. There are bulbs all around its frame. All the bulbs work. Oh, I see, that's how you can tell it is who I think it is that I'll be talking to.

As soon as the bulbs turn on, I blurt out that I agree to go back but under one condition: I have to have a sense of humor or the deal's off!

Voice: Yes, that is your essential nature.

Me: Okay then. I agree, but I'm really crabby about it.

Voice: I notice.

And so, we begin. ~

The Matter of N.O.B.U.

Me: Excuse me right away. Are you who I think you are? Everyone has their own ideas about you. I'm wondering if you have a name I could call you for short?

Voice: Yes, Natural Omnipresent Beauty Unlimited.

Me: That's for short? That about says it all, doesn't it? Natural Omnipresent Beauty Unlimited. ~

My Original Agreement

Me: What happens here?

NOBU: This is where you create your Sacred Contract; that is the Original Agreement that you make with yourself for this lifetime.

Me: I give myself my own guidelines to live the life I decide to live?

NOBU: Yes.

Me: Oh, I didn't know it worked that way.

NOBU: Yes, it's always up to you.

Me: Ask ten humans on Earth—at least nine of them don't even know they made a contract with themselves. Probably because there's no paperwork.

NOBU: You carry the records within you as a blueprint in your body.

Me: Wow, that's amazing.

NOBU: Do you have a feeling for what you'd like your life to be for?

Me: Oh, ten thousand things at least. I suppose, being a self-appointed Defender of the Cosmic Order, I would like to see more sure success for more people, and I'd like a plan with that in mind.

NOBU: That's doable. Would you like to start with your parents? What you inherit from them will give you a unique mix of both their ancestries. When you know that, you will know what you want to do with it.

Me: Okay good. That sounds like the place to start.

NOBU: After we finish with your contract here, you will have 'The Meeting of the Three.' That's when you meet your parents, who will create the right circumstances for you to develop as the human you need to be. They will have the perfect combination of character traits that you will inherit.

Me: Oh, what will some of those traits be?

NOBU: You need to know right away that you will be coming from a long line of people under the influence of alcohol. What do you think about that?

Me: Will I have the alcohol gene?

NOBU: You'll have a propensity.

Me: Will I have a choice in the matter?

NOBU: It's always your choice.

Me: Not that there's anything wrong with people who drink, except that they drink. I choose not to drink.

NOBU: As you say.

Me: I see that I'll be getting the appropriate emotional baggage from Mom and Dad. I guess this is where families put the fun in dysfunction.

NOBU: Yes, your trouble can be your miracle.

Me: My trouble can be my miracle! That's beautiful. Yes, let it be my miracle. Aren't you clever?

NOBU: Yes, omnipotent.

Me: Can we get to the clause on humor right away? You know I'm serious about requesting it. I need the humor gene because Earth is no laughing matter. I've got to be able to find the joke in the damn bad circumstance.

NOBU: You can't get away from wit; it's part of your eternal personality.

Me: Oh no, not my eternal personality again?

NOBU: Yes. How about being indomitable?

Me: Oh no, not that again too? Take a simple character trait and go too far with it, and it turns around and bites you in the behind.

NOBU: How about grit, courage, optimism, and the power to push uphill?

Me: Oh yes, all me. With all that huffing and puffing I'd like to get something accomplished.

NOBU: You have no idea what you'll accomplish.

Me: That's what I'm afraid of. Anymore tendencies to go over while we're at it?

NOBU: How about ultra-sensitive?

Me: That again, too?

NOBU: Yes.

Me: Okay. But this is not an easy life we're creating. When do I get the easy life?

NOBU: Whenever you decide to make it easy.

Me: Right.

The Freewill Clause

NOBU: One of my favorite topics is free will.

Me: I don't want to hurt your feelings, but don't you think that free will is kind of overrated?

NOBU: You think so?

Me: I'm just saying that humans have free will to choose with no clarity about the choices. It might work better if humans had a clearer view of the big picture, then maybe we could make educated choices.

NOBU: Your heart knows what to choose.

Me: Being human, sometimes the last thing you think to tap is your heart.

NOBU: It works best to be the first, always.

Me: Up here it's so clear. On Earth, all kinds of everything gets in the way.

NOBU: It's designed to be so simple.

Me: I can appreciate the work of art you made. It's genius. It's just that you set it up and then you gave it over to humans to live it.

NOBU: I hear your complaint. You're not the first one to voice it.

Me: Does this have something to do with the world cracking wide open sometime in the 21st century?

NOBU: Could be.

The Gift of Giving

Me: What about a clause about the gift I will be giving to the world?

NOBU: We'd rather you didn't.

Me: Didn't give a gift to the world?

NOBU: You are the gift. As far as what you give, you have already given too much.

Me: I didn't know there was such a thing as too much giving.

NOBU: That's why you need to go in and find out. You won't be rewarded if you go in and be the expert you have always been.

Me: What then?

NOBU: Go in and experience a New Soul program.

Me: What does that look like?

NOBU: That's what you can find out.

Me: You mean that's one of those things that it takes a lifetime to discover?

NOBU: Yes.

Me: Oh goodie, you're saying go in and hang by a thread?

NOBU: That would be perfect.

Me: But there's so much I want to offer. I can be a big help.

NOBU: You will naturally be a big help to others. You always have been. This time be a big help to yourself too.

Me: Man oh man, that's more challenging.

The Meaning of Life

Me: Apart from the astonishing miracle of it all, is there some specific point to life? Is there some sort of malaise you hope to eradicate?

NOBU: Yes. For you, in your life, you seem to have a concern for people's sorrows.

Me: That's been going on since the beginning of time. I'm learning from you; it's all part of the fun.

NOBU: Maybe it's time for a different kind of fun.

Me: Yes, please. I would be up for less suffering for humanity.

NOBU: Okay, go do that then.

Me: Do what? Eradicate sorrow for humankind?

NOBU: Yes.

Me: And how am I going to do that?

NOBU: I have every faith in you.

Me: That's funny you have faith in me. Isn't it supposed to be the other way around?

The Purpose Clause

NOBU: What do you suppose are the kinds of things a person needs on Earth?

Me: They need to have meaning, a reason to keep going, a purpose, even if it's just to seek out the best chili dog ever made.

NOBU: What is something that you will need?

Me: I'll need the very useful quality of joy. The ability to turn circumstances into happiness.

NOBU: And how about a talent for life on a daily basis?

Me: That too.

NOBU: Will you be willing to let what is be?

Me: Okay, I can do that. Actually, I can't do that. I've been known to fight what is.

NOBU: As you work to change circumstances, be willing to accept circumstances.

Me: Okay, that will be new.

Me: While we're on my reason for being—I understand that some humans feel their purpose is mostly unbeknown to them. What's my soul's reason to be there?

NOBU: You say.

Me: To shine my light so it inspires and invites everybody else to shine their light.

NOBU: Of course, you'll know the full nature of that more and more as you live.

Me: Oh, I guess that means you're not going to tell me.

NOBU: You'll see it as you live it.

The Before-Your-Time Clause

Me: Oh no, I'm going in before my time again? How about I stay here and rest up a while, and then go in?

NOBU: If you don't go in before your time, you won't be able to make it your time.

Me: That means heavy lifting again.

NOBU: You wouldn't want it any other way.

Me: I'm put in mind of a truth—when introducing a new concept, first the world rejects it as ridiculous, then they fight you on it, and eventually it's accepted as always being true.

NOBU: How about that you will be received and valued for what you have to offer.

Me: Wow, what a new world that would be. Imagine that.

NOBU: You won't have to imagine that; you can live it.

Me: Okay, I certainly welcome that. Thank you.

The Illusion-of-Separation Clause

NOBU: What do you think of betrayal?

Me: What about it?

NOBU: Do you want to experience betrayal in this lifetime?

Me: No, I'm not a fan of betrayal. It's kind of a waste of time. Humans get stuck in a story that someone has done something terrible to them, and then they keep playing that story repeatedly. It's not true. Whatever the transgression, it's always a gift to move you along. I know it's not there to keep you stuck.

NOBU: You do know that you had many lifetimes where you were bludgeoned or in some ways unfairly treated?

Me: Yes, I do know that. It always moved each life along even if that meant it ended. We just got on with it. Of course, when I'm physical and human, I might forget and be mad at someone's actions toward me.

NOBU: How about if all those who were your accusers will show up in this life and support you?

Me: No thanks. I have no tit-for-tat to play out with anyone. I don't carry any feelings that have to be rectified.

NOBU: Maybe they do. Maybe they need to rectify for themselves what they did. Would you deny them that?

Me: Oh. Okay, I suppose. You see how complicated it can get down there. P.S. I'd like to attach a law clause here. I don't want any lawsuits or trouble with the law, and while we're at it, let's have no need for hospitals and doctors either.

The Food Clause

Me: Oh goodie, the Food Clause.

NOBU: You've been known to eat everything, and often.

Me: One of the reasons I agree to go back to Earth is the food!

NOBU: You don't fool me. You know it's a sacred mission.

Me: That too, but the food is some of the best in the universe, and humans eat every day.

NOBU: I know you like the 'see-food' diet. When you see food, you eat it. Ha, ha, ha, ha, ha.

Me: Are you testing my tolerance for vaudeville?

NOBU: I thought it was funny.

Me: It's an old joke down there on Earth.

NOBU: Well, go make new ones.

Me: I'll be happy to, while I'm eating anything served on a bed of, on the half shell, in a tortilla, braised or marinated, smoked or even tartare. Pair it with arugula or polenta or risotto, and I'm happy.

NOBU: What about an issue with weight?

Me:	Doesn't weight sometimes appear to be an issue when underneath it's really meant to solve something else? I'd like my body and self to work together as a team. If my body needs something, we can communicate with each other and take care of the needs. I want the kind of life where I have the freedom to eat when I'm hungry and sleep when I'm tired. I'll be running on high-octane energy. Eating will be the fuel that supplies me.
NOBU:	Then it's a good thing you love to eat.
Me:	And excuse me for saying, I'm hungry now. I haven't eaten since my last life.

The door that wasn't there a minute ago flings open, and there is ambrosia, food of the gods, delivered immediately and piping hot in a delicate sauce.

Me:	I'm flabbergasted! Food anytime! Leaving this to go to that, I can't even bear the thought. See what I mean about staying up here to bask in the light of the source? Oh, and as a rider on the contract—'Let it be my birthright that I can always be able to eat. Non-negotiable.'

The Physical-Looks Clause and More on Characteristics

NOBU:	How do you want to look?
Me:	Presentable enough that I can be effective, maybe good posture or something that would inspire approachability.
NOBU:	Most people want to be beautiful or handsome.
Me:	Okay, you can make me beautiful and paid handsomely.
NOBU:	Ha. Ha. Always thinking.
Me:	Maybe not right away but could I acquire luminescence? I'd like my light to shine.

NOBU: Always. How about depression, insomnia, or thinning hair?

Me: No, no, and not even possible.

NOBU: How about dimples?

Me: As long as they're not on my thighs.

NOBU: Any requests?

Me: Pardon me if I'm being indelicate. One of the necessities of a happy body is that what goes in comes out effortlessly and on a regular basis, therefore I would like to respectfully request lifelong 'poop-ability'.

NOBU: Ah yes, an underrated quality.

Me: I'm in awe that my human body is designed to last my lifetime, however long that may be. It's ingenious.

NOBU: The human body is one of my greatest achievements.

Me: You've designed it brilliantly to have so much of it be automatic. All we have to do is change the oil on time and keep it maintained.

NOBU: Yes, multi-faceted, multi-conscious, multi-dimensional.

Me: May I have the ability to orchestrate, regulate, and dictate my body to be stable, balanced, focused, steady, sustainable, maintainable, retainable?

NOBU: Yes, that's how it can be delivered. You know you will be empathic. You're going to be sensitive to everybody's feelings. How would you like to manage that?

Me: It's always been my challenge to feel everything from everyone and then try not to carry everybody in my feelings.

NOBU: Here is a zap—the gift of discernment. You will have the ability to know what is going on within others, to feel it and even heal it, yet

	not take it on to yourself. You will have an uncanny combination of caring and not carrying others.

Me: I could have used that for the last many millenniums, give or take a few. That takes the pressure off. Thank you.

NOBU: It will still be a sensitive area for you, and you'll have to have extra vigilance in your care of yourself, and while we're at it, it wouldn't hurt for you to take an aspirin now and then and have good health insurance.

Me: How about a capacity for vitality and maybe mind over matter? That's always useful.

NOBU: I'd like to add a note to the face to create a slight beauty mark on your cheekbone just to the side of your eye.

Me: Oh, why is that?

NOBU: It indicates thoughtfulness and a wink to the supernatural.

Me: Thank you and I'd please like more than a wink to the supernatural. I'll need all the help I can get.

NOBU: Yes, that clause is coming up. First, would you like to see some more of your talents and tendencies?

Me: All my 'usuals'?

NOBU: Yes. You're independent and I see no reason why you need to back off from that.

Me: Good, that's always worked for me.

NOBU: And determined, resilient—you'll ignore physical strains, you can burn out, but you'll keep going.

Me: Yes, that all sounds familiar. Also, I'd like a knack for Earth—I want to be able to navigate being a human; to know that despite Earth's thorny nature, I can figure it out and arrange a good life for myself and others.

NOBU: Yes, that sounds reasonable.

Me: I'm going to be extremely sensitive again. Any suggestion about that?

NOBU: You'll have to ground your body very early.

Me: Okay, you'll show me how to manage that?

NOBU: It's already arranged.

The Money Clause

NOBU: You want a vow of poverty?

Me: No. Earth is a physical world; I want the ability to create physical success. I don't think I'll be distracted by shiny objects or have a need for amassing excess, but I'll like enough cash to at least manage a taco when I need one, or a five-star hotel. I'd love to see that everyone is supported and supplied so they can get on with developing the special something that only they can bring to the world. That would be a good use of money.

NOBU: In humans, there are infinite ways to access the vast source of talents that you're given. You needn't chase money; you can let it find you.

Me: That's a great idea. I'd like a talent for enterprise—no matter what, I can always tap my reservoir of abilities.

NOBU: The secret is to trust that there is always enough.

Me: You mean my resources can pay off in more resources?

NOBU: Yes. That and maintaining a high FICO score.

Me: Will I know what that is?

NOBU: It doesn't matter. It's just a random number.

Me: I trust that eventually my right livelihood will kick in, but to get there I'll need enough cash to carry on. I'll have to have some ability to build a platform and stand on it so I can be heard. I'd like leverage to deliver what I offer to the world. I definitely want the gene that gets stuff done. And I better be good at self-presentation; I have a feeling that the times I'm going into will have a lot of noise—everybody promoting something. I'd like to have the gift of a clear offering.

NOBU: Meanwhile, do you want a steady paycheck?

Me: What would that look like?

NOBU: You work for someone doing what they need done, and at the end of the week they pay you.

Me: How long does that go on?

NOBU: Your whole life.

Me: There must be another way.

NOBU: You could be freelance.

Me: That sounds good. I like being free.

NOBU: You'll have to rely on your own resourcefulness.

Me: Yes, of course, I will. Let it be up to me. I'll think a thing, I'll feel a thing, I'll materialize a thing. That's how it really works, isn't it?

NOBU: Yes.

Chimes Go Off

Me: What's that?

NOBU: That's your future self just here to ask a request.

Me: You mean I can do that?

NOBU: You can do anything you can think of.

Me: Wow! What's my request?

Me at forty-five giving a message now: When I am three years old, I need help, and I don't know anybody is there for me. Now at forty-five, I remember that time and I want to help that child. I want to be there for me. Could you please put that in the Original Agreement?

NOBU: Yes, just feel the love you want to give to your childhood self. Feel it at your current age, and you will envelop your child-self in love.

Me: That's so powerful. You can be there from another age of yourself!?

NOBU: All time is simultaneous.

Me: Wow, here's just another amazing application of that!

The Yes, Please. Thank You. Clause

Me: What does that mean?

NOBU: Just remember—Yes, please and thank you. Accept all the help and all the love and all the magic all around. You'll fight it. You'll want to do everything yourself, but it's there for you when you're finally willing to say . . .

Me: Yes, please. Thank you. Okay, I might forget. Would you like to remind me?

NOBU: Yes, please. Thank you.

Me: Very funny.

The Happiness Clause

Me: I'd also like to have a knack for happiness.

NOBU: Oh yes, always. Happiness is the style in which you go about having a life. You understand that Buddha is not laughing because he's happy, he's happy because he's laughing?

Me: Oh, I see, that puts everybody in the driver's seat of themselves.

The Alone Clause

NOBU: Would you like to feel lonely?

Me: Is this a trick question?

NOBU: It can be.

Me: I don't ever feel alone, but I do think that Earth can be a lonely place for humans. They can feel profoundly hurled out into deep space. Many flounder around seeking connection. Can I do something to help?

NOBU: Yes, we can arrange for that. We did talk about your independence, but you do realize that you're fiercely independent?

Me: Is that bad?

NOBU: No, it works for you.

Me: Good.

NOBU: You're the Lone Ranger.

Me: What's that?

NOBU: I just recently put it in the zeitgeist. It's an archetype helper who rides into town, takes care of the problem, then rides out again. You're not the type to stay around for the barn dance. Anybody else might think that's a lonely life, but you'll thrive on it. Besides, you'll always have a Tonto.

Me: What's a Tonto?

NOBU: I'm developing that. It's a loving force that continually demonstrates to you that you are always witnessed and supported.

Me: Sounds ingenious. I can hardly wait.

The Love Clause

NOBU: You'll be the Lone Ranger, and would you also like to have a Beloved?

Me: Yes, thank you, but not too early. I have work to do before we meet.

NOBU: When you keep love simple, you'll always be ready for it.

Me: Do I pick out the love of my life?

NOBU: You'll know him when you see him.

Me: Sounds good to me.

NOBU: You will have great love.

Me: Oh, thank you. I'm so grateful to be independent and yet feel connected all at once.

The Children Clause

NOBU: Scanning here to see if there's any soul that you need to bring in as a child, to teach, to learn from, to love, to enjoy, to value, and to cherish. No babies this time around.

Me: Oh.

NOBU: How do you feel about that?

Me: Well, I guess I'll see how I feel when I get there. I don't want to wake up when I'm fifty and think, "Oh, I forgot to have kids."

NOBU: Will it be all right with you if you don't?

Me: Yes, I understand my calling does not call for children. Yes, that fits. I know I'm not going in to be a mom.

NOBU: There will be lots of young ones who will come to you to be their mentor, teacher, and guide.

Me: That appeals to me—plenty of dear ones to love along the way. They don't have to be mine. That's good.

The Intuition Clause

Me: Oh good, finally the second-sight clause. I'd like to be born with insight, foresight, hindsight, and all sight.

NOBU: To what end?

Me: I'll need specific tools with me. Certain qualities. I'd like all the Clairs.

NOBU: The Clairs?

Me: Yes. Clairvoyant, clairaudient, clairsentient, claircognizant. You know, a sixth sense, extrasensory, all-around knowing.

NOBU: I see. you are requesting full remembrance.

Me: Yes, please—to know myself as a spirit being coming to have a human experience. I know others will roll their eyes at this idea.

NOBU: To each his own.

Me: It would be a privilege to be able to offer insights to people.

NOBU: You do know that everybody's got their way of doing things and after all, it is their life. Unless somebody asks, it's not up to you to tell them anything about themselves.

Me: If I see someone is about to zig, I can't pull him or her off the curb and insist they zag?

NOBU: Nope.

Me: Well, what can I do about that?

NOBU: You'll be able to see their reasons for what they do and see that it's always a brilliant choice.

Me: Even if it looks a little rickety on the surface?

NOBU: Especially when it doesn't make any sense to anybody, yet it makes perfect sense to the person.

Me: Okay, I can do that. I can point out where the light is but not be attached to their outcomes. I get it—their business is none of my business.

NOBU: The choices any human makes are right for them and are going to put them in their right place. Always.

The How-to-Be-the-Hero-of-Your-Own-Life Clause

NOBU: Tell me about that.

Me: It's my guidebook for humans to look up any age they are. Something will be illuminated for the reader for their life at each age. I would love to do that. I'm happy to do that. It is my honor to do that. Can I do that?

NOBU: How are you going to do that?

Me: I'm going to live each year, amass notes on the events of the whole year, then pick out the essential scene that is the metaphoric passage for that year, and write it as a split-second story for that age. My story, although completely different from the reader's life story, will be written in such a way as to invoke specific wisdoms that will illuminate the reader's story for them. They can look up any age and reflect on themselves.

NOBU: That's a pretty big bite.

Me: Yes, big bite, that would be me. To state it clearly: It would be my honor to inspire. To write a book about my life that offers illumination for the readers to clarify their way. I would love for that to be my world contribution—my piece of the big picture. Is that possible? Can I?

NOBU: You have already begun it. You are on page 30.

Me: Glory be.

~~~

Dear Reader,

You might be remembering bits of your Sacred Contract. It really helps your happiness to know your reason for being.

The Meeting of the Three

Bright lights appear and come right to me.

Me: What's this?

NOBU: It's The Meeting of the Three. This is where you meet your parents.

Three lights radiate. They form a channel together. A bandwidth encodes as the family.

NOBU: You don't have to talk to them; this is more an opportunity to familiarize each other with your particular vibrational blueprint. You determine your frequency and what that creates as the story your family lives together.

Me: This is astonishing. This feeling is so much bigger than I could ever have imagined. I feel completely knowing of them and known to them.

NOBU: Do you have any questions before you accept this lineage as yours?

Me: I understand that my father drinks. Will that be all right? I know what that can cost a family.

NOBU: Some circumstances might seem bad, and some circumstances might seem good, yet all circumstances are for you.

Me: I understand . . . I accept.

The Closing of the Clauses

NOBU: Do you have any last questions?

Me: Will I complete my destiny?

NOBU: That's up to you.

Me: I'd like a moment to be with my contract. What is it that I am asking of myself? Is this the best and highest way to fulfill it?

Suddenly, I find myself back at the oceanfront basking in the sunshine.

I unite with my plan. I feel the full impact of what I ordered for my life. I see my whole life before me, and I accept. I feel it in my heart; I will create it in my life.

Me: Let it be known I take with me the ability to be who I am where I am, to love—not judge, to let fear expand me—not limit me. To be understanding and compassionate. To laugh, to be able to do, be, and have, and know the difference and know which when. To allow what is and let people be who they are. To be free to have what I need and what I want for the miracle in every moment. To contribute what is mine to give and receive what is mine to accept—as my world service. And so, I declare my intentions for my life.

I sign the agreement as it flutters up into the sunlight.

When I leave the beach, a line of bright lights shines as far as it's possible to see. Souls hoping for another lifetime. There are 999,999 of them. Oh, I see, you're showing me I am one-in-a-million, and so is everyone who is there on Earth now—one-in-a-million each. ~

Conception

NOBU: Do you want to be at your conception?

Me: Wait, what? Do you mean do I want to be around for my parents having sex? No, thank you very much. I'll hover over here and watch the sperms race to the egg. I can handle that.

Colors swirl. There is an explosion of energy. I am in awe.

Me: Wow, here's my mom the egg. She's dazzling! What a bright light. She's beautiful and powerful, and you can just tell she's smart and wise and funny too.

Here come the sperm. I see her magnetizing the right one to her. It's her call! There are sperm that are vital and grand, but they aren't the one. I'll be getting my power, my talents, and my strengths from her for sure. I'm glad I picked her to be my mom. I love her so much.

Here's my dad; here he comes now! I can pick him out of the crowd. Oh, I love him too. It's a different love for him. All his feelings are deep. My feelings will be deep too, but I hope I will know to manage them.

Here are three things I feel right away about him: I know I want to protect him from sadness; I'm going to be getting a strong work ethic from him; because of him, I'll learn to take care of myself early and always.

I feel a gasp as my eternal Self sparks into fire. I am a pilot light that just got lit in the me that is becoming. I feel my lineage pass to me to heal and come to fruition.

Me: This is pretty emotional. These are my parents. I love them so. ~

In the Womb

Me: Hello . . . I'm in! I am the one cell dividing! Now two, now four, now eight, now a million things happening! I am! Life begins! Is this when life begins?

NOBU: Life is eternally ongoing.

First Trimester–Week One

Me: Did I just go from a beam of light to a clump of matter?

NOBU: Yes, you are that, but you are not that mostly.

Me: So many sparks. I am a pinball machine pinging. Everything, all of me coming to life. It is at once spectacular and simple. I am the explosion of creation!

NOBU: All your major organs and body systems are started and will be coming right along.

Me: It's more of a gift than I can comprehend.

Week Two

Me: I feel the genetic combination of my mother and my father now creating my life. I already seem to have decided what from each I will come in with. The caution of one, the permission of the other, the steadfast, and the carefree, the yes and the no, the strength and the softness, the saver and the spender. Now they are one and I am it.

Weeks Three, Four, and Five

Me: It's all moving so fast I can hardly keep up. You can't see it yet, but my arms and legs are forming.

       I'm moving around in here. My bones are developing. I have structure. Hands will be coming along and fingers and toes. I'll get to wiggle them.

Several More Weeks Later

NOBU: What's going on in there this week?

Me: I have a brain, therefore . . . I don't know. I have a thought then another. which leads to another and pretty immediately I'm in here with Monkey Mind.

NOBU: Yes, your mind has a mind of its own.

Me: It just goes at it all by itself. I am the mind that knows I am thinking. See, right there, that's an example of my mind talking to itself. Can I turn this thing off?

NOBU: Probably not.

Me: I just had another thought—maybe I forgot to apply for membership in the human race. Don't I have to pass for human?

NOBU: No one will notice; they're all just worrying about themselves.

Later Still

Me: This is so great; I have access to anyone and everyone, living or dead, right here right now in my consciousness?

NOBU: Yes.

Me: Will I have this access once I'm born?

NOBU: Yes, that would be the library.

Another Week Later

Me: I've been meaning to ask you, what's this about no two snowflakes being alike? Is that true or is it just spin or what?

NOBU: It's true. Every living thing is a completely unique essence. And yet, all snowflakes are snowflakes. They each contain what is essentially true of snowflakes and what is the essential nature of each.

Me: That's enormous. It makes me tear up at the scale of how the same and how different we are from each other.

NOBU: Yes. All are unique.

Me: Our common humanity unites us, or does our diversity unite us?

NOBU: Both. You need the eagle and the condor to embrace the experience of one another.

And the Next Week

Me: Oh, something just happened. Something is all-encompassing. It's big beyond anything. What is this?

NOBU: It's your heart. It beats now in syncopation with your mother. From now forward it beats a hundred thousand beats a day for the span of your lifetime.

Me: My heart beats! I am feeling all the infinite feelings there are to feel. The enormity is enormous.

NOBU: Yes, that's your life force.

That Same Week

NOBU: Hello. What have you learned so far?

Me: It's not my mind's business what my feelings are feeling.

NOBU: That's quite advanced for the womb.

Me: There's a phrase that keeps repeating in the ethers ta eph'henvin ta ouk eph'heni, something like that. What does it mean?

NOBU: It's a stoic saying from two-thousand years ago, it means what is up to us, what is not up to us.

Me: Oh, you mean what I can control and what I can't control?

NOBU: Yes.

Me: So, whatever is going on in my family, it's best to stick to my own part?

NOBU: Yes.

Me: Do no harm, and be done no harm?

NOBU: Yes.

Me: Will this be in my hard wiring?

NOBU: Good, then it's decided.

Me: What's decided? Hello?

The Next Week

Me: My hands are formed. On the one hand, on the other hand, I'm just starting to have hands. I hold them over my heart.

NOBU: Now that your brain is fully formed, how are you managing it in there?

Me: I'm thinking there are some fundamental qualities of being a human that no matter what else, I need.

NOBU: Like what?

Me: A human being should be able to smile and want to readily, should have the capacity to enjoy gathering, preparing, and eating good food, should have an enthusiasm for life in general and some things in particular, and a knack for getting along with other humans.

We should be able to take care of ourselves. We should have curiosity about what we don't know and an ability to learn. And a willingness to be bigger than any fear that wants to overtake us. We need to adapt, apply, arrange, and adjust to having a healthy balance of giving and receiving. I'd like a sense of my own inner powers, and the courage to act on them. We need to know how to pay the bills, unclog the drain, color outside of the lines, and find joy in every moment . . . Hello, NOBU? . . . Are you there? . . . Hello?

Second Trimester

Me: I can kick, and I do. I can put my hand to my mouth. I can hear. I am five ounces. I'm speaking although probably nobody hears me.

I am one pound.

Fingers, toes, fingerprints fully formed. I can swallow. I hiccup. I am happy to be conscious of my own life developing.

Brain, nervous system, spinal cord, thinking, feeling. I smile. I cry. I yawn.

I recognize voices.

My eyes open and close.

Signal my mother to be sure to stay pregnant full term.

After No Sleep

Me: There are questions floating around me.
NOBU: Like what?

Me: My destiny is __? I am __? I want __? I need __?

What is all that? Am I supposed to fill in the blanks? Do I have homework, and I'm not even born yet?

NOBU: It sounds like what you plan to work on once you get born.

Me: Does this mean I'm being too much of a smarty-pants thinking that I'll avoid obstacles?

NOBU: Something like that.

Weeks Later

Me: This is fascinating. Not only are my baby teeth in place, my adult teeth are here too, ready when their time comes.

Oh, here come my ears into development. The sound of my breath with my mother's. The sound of my heart with my mother's. Not just the rhythmic beat but now the sound. This gives me the understanding of how to live in my body, now that I have one.

NOBU: Since you can hear, what are you picking up from your family?

Me: I'm hearing music.

NOBU: Will you create music?

Me: No, I don't think so. I won't create music, but I will be with some of the major music makers of our time. That's interesting. Why do I know that?

Another Week Later

NOBU: All systems coming right along. Where they all began rudimentarily, they are now developing fully.

Me: I don't yet see details, but my eyes do feel the light.

NOBU: What insight are you getting?

Me: People have their reasons for doing something for no reason.

NOBU: Tell me about that.

Me: Humans know if they eat a gallon of ice cream, they're going to get Häagen-Dazs thighs, and yet they eat the gallon of ice cream. They know better, but still, they do the same old thing and get the same old result.

NOBU: Häagen-Dazs?

Me: You mean you don't know Häagen-Dazs ICE CREAM? You mean you aren't all-knowing?

NOBU: How do you know about Häagen-Dazs ice cream?

Me: Oh please, I'm hanging semi-sideways in the body of a pregnant woman. Of course, I know about Häagen-Dazs ice cream.

NOBU: Bingo! That's it.

Me: Bingo? How come you know bingo, but you don't know Häagen-Dazs?

NOBU: Häagen-Dazs isn't scheduled to appear for some years to come. Bingo because you just demonstrated that you see beyond your timeline.

Me: Is that a good thing?

NOBU: I can then see and witness through you.

Me: Did you just explain the meaning of life?

Later That Week

Me: Oops I kicked my mom. It's just getting so small in here.

Week Twenty-Four

Me: Ah—I take my first breath in here. I breathe my lungs alive. Pasta in marinara sauce—I can taste! I have lips! I can smack them!

NOBU: What have you learned about Earth this week?

Me: I'll be in food heaven on Earth. I'm glad I didn't sign on for a weight problem because this is where it would begin.

I view my life now from inside a physical body. When I get out of the womb and into life, am I going to know how to operate this body I'm in?

NOBU: You'll figure it out.

Me: But we aren't delivered with an instruction manual.

NOBU: No one ever reads the manual anyway.

Me: So we get all the mechanics built in with none of the ability to operate them? We just go in and start pushing all the buttons until something turns the thing on?

NOBU: Pretty much.

Third Trimester

Me: It seems all systems are coming fully alive.

NOBU: Yes, at the twenty-eighth week the fetus has an excellent chance of survival.

Me: What! I didn't know there was a question about my survival! You mean I might have been turned around and headed in the other direction?

NOBU: Would you have?

Me: Are you kidding? I wouldn't miss this for anything. You knew that or you wouldn't have asked me to come in.

NOBU: Yes. I knew that.

NOBU: Now that you are listening in on your family all of the time, what are you learning?

Me: Never pay retail.

Week Thirty-Two

Me: What do you think of this letter I just wrote to my mom?

Dear Mom,

Thanks for this baby party. Getting all these things—a buggy and clothes—really helps me to understand that I'm coming into a physical world. I'm getting really strong to be born. I pretty much have the gene pool handled. I know I'll have your bone structure and Dad's eye color. I don't know yet about my nose.

Week Thirty-Six

NOBU: Everything is looking good.

Me: Excuse me for saying, but my skull bone is still soft. When is that going to harden?

NOBU: It needs to stay soft to squeeze through the birth canal.

Me: What! It collapses? Hello?

The Last Week Before Birth

Me: Wow, going from fetus to actual human—I'll have to start to think, to learn, to feel, to be physical. I see I must be encoded and embedded with what I worked out from my Original Agreement. The records are within my DNA. They are lodged in my body and there will be trigger responses throughout my life. Ingenious of you, NOBU, to design it that way.

NOBU: It's the Owner's Manual you requested.

Me: Wait, is this a kind of Life Map to go by? Because the first thing I'll do is not go by it

NOBU: Well, that's typical. It's Earth.

The Next Day

NOBU: Hello. You seem to be sorting.

Me: Since I'm moving out of this womb in the next week, I'm sorting through what actually belongs to me as my desires and what needs to be left behind.

NOBU: Travel light to be the light?

Me: Yes, that's it exactly, thank you. I create my imprint now from my inheritance. In my bloodline is my history, my ancestry, their history, their illnesses, and what made them happy. I'm about to take what's mine from that supply. I'm clear to be empowered, not deterred. What I bring in I bring in to heal and to be free.

NOBU: Sounds like a plan.

Later That Same Day

Me: (humming a happy tune)

NOBU: I hear you humming a happy tune in there.

Me: I just overheard my family. 'Joy' is my middle name, so I'm practicing. And besides, I realize . . . on Earth, there's chocolate.

Later Still That Same Day

Me: While I'm here between nothing and something, are there any last instructions I could be studying?

NOBU: Everything you need to know about having a life you'll learn by having a life.

Another Hour Later

Me: Hello . . .

NOBU: Yes.

Me: I'm reflecting on my contract, and I'm confused. All of this made sense when you were telling me this when we were talking over my Original Agreement, but as I get further from there and closer to Earth life it doesn't make Earth sense.

NOBU: Like what?

Me: My destiny is to live my destiny. Love myself enough to love myself enough. What!?

NOBU: You can take your lifetime to muse over those ideas.

And Another Hour

Me: Remind me—what is life on Earth for anyway? What did I come here to do, and will I do it?

NOBU: All anybody must do is show up. You have a piece of the puzzle; without your piece, there's a hole in the big picture. Show up and include yourself.

Me: Yes, I see, this is a planet where you get to make your own miracles.

Later Still

Me: Once I go in, how will I know how to come back out?

NOBU: Your body is encoded with the knowledge of how to be born. Your soul knows how to ascend into the higher dimensions when the time comes for that.

Just Days Before Birth

Me: Any time now I'll be hurled out into open space hoping somebody of my species is going to catch me.

NOBU: They're standing by.

Me:	After I'm born, will I still be me?
NOBU:	Of course. What would constitute success for you?
Me:	I must be what I can be.
NOBU:	And you shall.
Me:	That's a load off.

Forty-Eight Hours Before Birth

Me:	Hello. Are you there? What's happening? Is it time? Will I be getting born soon? Hello?
NOBU:	Yes, you're getting ready. Just two more days and you'll be born.
Me:	Is there anything more you can tell me about getting born?
NOBU:	We will be with you.
Me:	I don't get the part about being completely in the baby body. How will I breathe and think?
NOBU:	As you experience each moment it will take you to the next moment, and each moment will awaken an understanding that advances your actions. You will be able to breathe and think and feel on your own.
Me:	That's it? Automatic?
NOBU:	We'll help you.
Me:	Okay . . . Hello?
NOBU:	Yes.
Me:	What about this cord thing? How's that going to work?
NOBU:	Once you come through the birth canal the cord will be cut, and you'll be on your own.
Me:	Cut . . .! Hello? How do I know when birth is?
NOBU:	You'll know. It's a dawning.
Me:	A dawning. Okay . . . Hello?
NOBU:	You might want to get some rest.
Me:	But . . . I'm upside down in here . . . Hello?

A Few Hours Later

Me: NOBU.

NOBU: Yes, dear one.

Me: Even though I was crabby while creating my Original Agreement, I'm not really a crabby person.

NOBU: I know who you are, sweetie.

A Day and a Half Before Birth

Me: What's taking so long.

NOBU: You're waiting for the planets to align.

Me: What?

NOBU: Your Saturn needs to be in the sixth house—Capricorn rising.

Me: What does that mean?

NOBU: It means you'll have the ability to get things done.

Me: That's good to know. How about we get this birth done?

And Another Two Hours

Me: I don't know if I'm feeling for sure. Deep down I do know, but I don't know that I know.

NOBU: Your heart knows. Take it on faith—that's the point of life on Earth. Earth is subtle; it gives you the opportunity to be uncertain.

Me: You mean go ahead and be knocked off my ideas about what I think is the straight line of things?

NOBU: Yes, let yourself be surprised by life.

Me: What is the benefit in that?

NOBU: There are gifts in it. There is more. More than you know.

Me: Okay, I'm feeling the love.

NOBU: Yes, my lovely.

Me: I'm ready to get born.

Later

Me: Is this it. Is it time? Am I worthy? Can I do this?

NOBU: That's what this lifetime is for. You are given the gift of answering that for yourself.

And Finally, Hours Later, Reporting In

Me: Hello. Reporting turmoil in the womb. Eruptions, evacuations, and hot and cold sensations. I'm upside down! Could you give me a clue here—what the heck is going on?

NOBU: You're about to be born.

Me: That's it? That's the explanation—You're about to be born? That covers everything?

NOBU: Yes.

Me: I suppose if you help me to get born, it won't help me to get born.

NOBU: Yes.

Contractions Begin

Me: Remind me again, what is the purpose of creation?

NOBU: Experience is the purpose of creation.

Me: That's fine but does it have to be an unpleasant experience? . . . Hello?

Contractions Continue

Me: I know that I get up to it and retreat. I don't want to hurt my mom.

And Continue

Me: Are we there yet?

Between Contractions

NOBU: Always know that you have everything you need.

Me: Even when I feel like I don't have what I need?

NOBU: Especially then.

More Contractions

Me: Excuse me for saying, but nobody likes this part.

NOBU: Which part is that?

Me: The part where my large head has to go through a small opening to get to the wide world.

And More

Me: My mom is exhausted. I'm exhausted. I'm sure she would like to get up off this table and go home. And I'd like to turn around and go back to the light. And we know that's not going to happen, so the only way out is through. We both have to see it through.

NOBU: You're working together. You're working out how to be mother and daughter together.

And More

NOBU: Just because it's painful doesn't mean it has to be.

Me: Now you tell me.

After More Contractions

NOBU: Birth is an opportunity to develop skills for other milestones to come.

Me: I signed up to be the light and help the world to open to the light. That might be challenging, that might require resilience and fortitude and focus and heart and love and joy—now I know it also requires PUSHING.

Birth as a Metaphor for Life

Me: I go up to it and then have to back off from it. Is there another method?

NOBU: Expand the light of who you are.

Me: What does that mean? How do I do that? Expand the light of who I am?

NOBU: You are the cosmic spark of light incarnate.

Me: Okay, I get the spark of light part, but now I'm working on the part of me that's also a clump of matter.

NOBU: This is your unique birth.

Me: Oh, my birth, my way?

NOBU: Yes, birth is an example of the life you are creating.

Me: Hmm. I'm willing to get born my way; what is my way? How do I . . .?

I am the beginning of one hundred million wonders. I emerge from womb to world, I become my life? I become alive. I meet it. My life is flashing before me.

NOBU: This is the life that you set in motion.

Me: I hear voices. Am I getting closer to the outside world?

NOBU: Not quite yet. You asked for a fortune cookie or some kind of motto to inform your life. You asked for quotes to live by—here they are now as you go through the birth canal. They come to set the tone for the life you are creating. As you come down the birth canal you will hear them send you on your way.

Me: Do all babies get this?

NOBU: All babies can. You just happened to ask for it.

Moving Way Faster Now

Me: Wow. As I move faster down the birth canal, quotes are coming to me.

           "It don't mean a thing if it ain't got that swing." Duke Ellington

           "It's a wonderful world." Louis Armstrong

           "Know thyself." Oracle at Delphi

           "If you want to know the future, invent it." R. Buckminster Fuller

           "A little dab'll do you." An ad campaign that will appear in the 50s.

           And here now very rapidly, "Obstacles are only there in case you care to stop."

           "The only heart that doesn't break is an open heart."

           "You're only alive when you're living your dream; all the rest is make-believe."

NOBU: Those last quotes are from you from the life you're about to have.

My Birth, My Way

Me: Thrown open in awe I go forth in light. I can, I will, I do, I am. I am the body reaching. I cross the threshold. I dive through into life. I breathe life to me. Owwahhhhhhhh!

My head is a little bit twisted and pulled.

Me: I can do this, people. You're rushing; you can let it be natural. I can get my shoulders free of the birth canal myself.

I am whisked out. I am here.

Me: Where's Mom? Is she all right? So loud their voices. Holding my ankle too tight. My footprint is sticky on my feet. No time to stay balanced. I feel apart from where I came from. I'm here I'm not there. Where is here? So heavy, so dark here yet too bright for my new eyes.

      Here is Mom. Here is her warm skin, here she is. I feel the love.

      We have our private time together. We say hello. She counts my fingers and my toes. She welcomes me to the world.

My heart must be so big to be able to hold this love feeling I feel for Mom. Can my heart hold it? It is beyond my size. I am an infinite being in a tiny baby body. I come in as pure light shining. This begins me.

One Hour Old

In the nursery, there are lots of brand-new babies in separate cribs, crying and crying.

Me: You, little baby over there, it's okay. Even though you're forgetting who you are, try to remember. We'll just keep reminding each other, okay babies? ~

Day One

From Spirit Being to Human Being

Practically one hundred trillion new circuits are firing at once. This business of coming from nothing to being is an astonishing explosion of lifeforce, and yet it's all so natural.

I'm talking to you while I sleep. I check in on Earth to eat and bond with my family and then come back out to integrate it all. There are lots of movable parts to being an old soul in a human baby body. As organs function on autopilot I'm morphing into a physical life; into the tender feelings of what it means to be human.

You know how a baby jerks and kicks and misses its mouth with its fists, and cries with unbearable frustration? What a big deal it is to come in and settle in as a grand being now being human. Do you remember that feeling when you came in? What a precious treasure. ~

First Week

At Home on Earth

Me: NOBU?

NOBU: Yes, my dear.

Me: Did I come to the right planet?

NOBU: Yes. Why do you ask?

Me: Well, I'm feeling everybody's feelings and thoughts. It's just all floating in the air all over the place. Just today, a boy from the neighborhood, Lenny Bonetti, saw me in my buggy and decided to pinch my arm. (These things happen when moms look away for a minute.) I hope he doesn't want to do that to his baby brother when he gets born soon. If you come around my street, you better stay away from the Bonetti brothers because they are for sure going to be up to big trouble for their whole lives.

Not all the people around here are like that. Our milkman, Sweet Earl, saw Lenny by my buggy and shooed him away. Earl is good-hearted. Just now he's thinking about how many more bottles of milk he needs to deliver before he can take his family fishing at the lake.

I can tell you about every thought and feeling of every person and every dog and most of the cats on this side of the block all the way down to Narragansett.

NOBU: Yes. That's Earth.

Me: I thought humans felt separate from each other and they kept all those thoughts and feelings a secret from each other.

NOBU: They do. You just happen to be picking everything up telepathically.

Me: Like a radio with all the stations on at once?

NOBU: Yes. You can be overcome by it all, or you can find a way to organize it and have it be useful.

Me: Okay, I'm glad you're telling me this.

I decide right now I better know who I am so I can know the difference between my thoughts in my head and other people's thoughts in my head. If I can do that, I can be a help in the world, so I'll do that. Thanks. ~

Being Three Months Old

A New Baby's Story Starts Right Away

IT'S JUST AFTER Dad's birthday party in our new home.

Mom is putting away the cake dishes while Dad drives his mom, my grandma, home.

My brother is three. He's playing. I'm in my crib practicing language. Babies are born with certain universal sounds useful for our fundamental needs—oh, err, uh, ger.

Mom finishes the dishes and sits on the porch. It's a good warm night and she is feeling peaceful about this new home, two kids, and our new life. All is right with the world.

Just as Dad turns the corner at Grandma's street, she slumps over and then dies in Dad's arms . . . on his birthday.

Later, when Mom talks about this moment, she will say, "He was never the same after that." ~

One to Nineteen

1 Year Old

The Importance of Sounding Our Note

IT'S EASTER. WE have four chicks.

They are in a box in front of the heat register to keep them warm.

I can walk now so I walk over to them, and they each hop out of a different side of the box.

The chick that hops out the side by the register falls through the holes and down the furnace shaft into the basement. He chirps.

I run out to the porch where Dad is drinking beer. I chirp. He doesn't understand.

I hear the chick chirp. I chirp. Dad looks blank. Families don't understand kids.

I take Dad's hand and pull him to the basement door. We go downstairs so he can hear the chick chirping in the furnace.

He opens the big heavy furnace door. The hinges squeak. There is the chick! It hops out into my arms. Now there are four chicks again. One has lots of soot on him.

While it's still Eastertime the other chicks die. My favorite, with the soot, is going to live to be a happy grown-up chicken because I'll tell you why. The Vitali family, around the corner, have a whole bunch of kids and a great big chicken yard. Chirp goes over there to live.

Here's what I wonder: If he didn't chirp in the furnace, what then? ~

2 Years Old

Knowing All There Is to Know

Every night Mom makes supper at the stove. Dad looks out the kitchen door and talks about work. He says "bull*h*t" many times. I see his soul wanting to lift out of his body and be free, but he holds himself in. I see his heart breaking.

Mom is quiet—not a listening kind of quiet, more like a sit-on-your-mouth kind of quiet. She burns herself on the pan. She doesn't say anything, but I see there is more going on behind her face. Mom has her eyes on possible solutions but doesn't see any.

They don't notice I'm there too, with my turtle. He lives in his turtle bowl that has a green plastic palm tree sticking up in the middle. I have a wooden spoon from the kitchen. I see the sunshine on the floor and scoop it up and put it in the turtle bowl for later.

Mom doesn't say anything to Dad, but I see her stirring her feelings into our supper. Later when we eat, I can taste it, and later still in the night, I feel it in my body trying to get digested with the food. ~

3 Years Old

Why I Can't Go Out to Play

I'M STANDING AT the door to Dad's bedroom. I am three. He tells me to come into the room. This is just like always.

I love Dad more than anything in the whole wide world, but something decides me. I won't go in there. Not again, not ever.

Everything goes fast in my head now. I know to not go in there even if this means that no one will ever love me. I turn and walk away from the door, and I sit on the telephone chair in the hallway.

All of a sudden, I don't know what to do. These are such big feelings. I'm just three. I don't know what to do with these feelings. I start going up, up out of my body. An angel lady catches me and holds me. I don't see her, but I feel her holding me. She says, "Remember who you are." I am back in my body on the telephone chair. I don't know how this is decided but I know I am all right.

Dad comes out of the bedroom. He loses his balance. I run into the bathroom and hide behind the door. He comes in. I climb up on the sink and stretch into the medicine cabinet to get medicine for Dad. He comes toward me. I hand him the medicine. He drops it on the floor and slumps down. I know he won't wake up until tomorrow. I run to my bedroom and sit on my bed. I wish Mom would get home from work, but she'd just wonder why I wasn't out playing. I can't go out to play. I have to sit here and think what to do. ~

4 Years Old

Dear Santa Claus

*T*HANK YOU FOR *being Santa Claus. Will you please bring a toolbox for my big brother?*

Just before I mail my letter to the North Pole, Mom reads it. "That's very nice that you asked for something for your brother."

Maybe I'm not such a good girl for Christmas because I wanted Santa to bring the toolbox so that I could give it to my brother. ~

4 Years and 6 Months

Solitaire

WHEN I'M AT Nana and Papa's house, Nana plays Solitaire on her sun porch. She's okay when she shuffles and lays out the cards, but when it gets to the end of the game and she can't go any further piling the black ones on the red ones, she looks out the window really sad-like and says, "It's Jack's game." I don't know who Jack is. Then she goes to the pantry for a visit with Johnnie Walker—maybe he's Jack.

One time when she came out of the pantry, I had moved the cards around so there was more she could play but she didn't like that.

She just sits in her rocking chair and shuffles out another game. She has a big soft bosom and cushy arms. I imagine it would be nice for a kid to sit on her lap for a hug, but I don't know for sure. ~

4 Years and 9 Months

Smarter Than the Average Bear

My BROTHER'S BIRTHDAY party is going on in the dining room. He's seven.

Joey is the boy who lives on the corner. He's here and his mom is too. Mrs. Rockweiler is over there with the adults, having too good of a time. She has on her party voice but it's for a bigger party than this one. This is a kids' party. Joey should be the one having the good time. Mrs. Rockweiler tries to put everybody in their place. She tried that with me once, but she can't put me in my place because she has no place in me.

I know that Joey is smarter than the average bear. I'm showing him the game where you fit the pegs into the square holes and the round holes. He can't do it. With his mom around it's hard for him to be his real self. He doesn't want to play and throws the game in the air and runs outside. He's just a kid.

I notice that Papa has seen me wanting to help Joey. He says to Nana, "That kid's got horse sense." Just then Mom brings the birthday cake in and puts it on the table while everybody sings "Happy Birthday" to my brother. I suddenly know to look at the birthday candles and then back at Papa, then back at the cake, so now Papa will be on the alert. I know he sees what other people don't look at. I can do that too. Something is about to happen that he needs to know. Emily Dilly skips up to the table and is spinning round and round to make herself dizzy. Her long hair brushes across the good luck candle and she gets on fire.

Papa is looking right there. He cups his big hands over Emily's hair and claps the fire out before she even knows to be scared. The party goes on uninjured.

Papa and I look at each other. He says to Nana, "That kid's got more than horse sense." ~

4 Years Old and Practically Grown

Almost 5

HERE'S THE CONVERSATION I just had with Petey Blatt in Sunday School. His father is the minister, so he thinks he's the appointed one.

Our teacher Mrs. Baltimore asks us, "Where does God live?"

I say, "Inside me."

Petey says, "He does not. He lives in heaven; you don't know anything."

I say, "Yes, I do—I know everything."

Petey says, "That's blasphemy. My dad's the minister and you're going to hell."

I say, "There's no such thing as hell."

He says, "Boy are you in trouble."

The teacher—she's a little hard of hearing—says, "That's nice, children." Then she asks, "Why are some people good and some people bad?"

Mrs. Baltimore is kind of stuck on the evil thing. So, I make up a story for her. "In the beginning God put people on the Earth, and he told some that this is heaven, and he told others that this is hell and that's how they act."

She looks at me like she needs to pray for my salvation. I better say something because Mrs. Baltimore looks a little pale, like she might faint.

Here's what I tell her hell is because maybe she will understand: "When you die, you have to listen to what people say about your life. If you lived right and had good ideas, what you hear is heavenly. If you think you lived wrong in some way, it will be hell to hear what you and others think of your life. P.S. Your pets can say what they think, too."

Poor Mrs. Baltimore looks at me long and hard like she for sure has no faith in my future. She doesn't know what to do with me, and Sunday School is just about over when she says,

"Dear, what do you think you're going to be when you grow up?"

As I go out the door I say, "I'm going to be me." ~

5 Years Old for Sure

Kindergarten!

THIS IS MY very first day of school! Oh, I'm so excited.

I'm getting dressed under the covers. I run into the kitchen to get warm in front of the oven. The weatherman said there would be a record for the inches of snow, and there it is! The stairs out the back are covered all the way up. We could walk right out and walk right on top of the fence into Mr. Strobb's backyard. Mom and I bundle up and go.

School is way down below the hill. I can get over the snowdrifts. Even when they cave in, I can climb over. Mom says I'm indomitable. I guess that's like the Indomitable Snowman.

It's not very warm in kindergarten, and it's dark and there's lots of wood that smells like the cans of varnish from the garage.

Mrs. Flaherty is very nice. She's a grandma-type lady. I like her lace collar. She has red cheeks, but I don't think she drinks. I think she's the one in the family who pretends it's not so.

Suddenly, BANG! It's such a loud noise all the kids jump.

And BANG! again. It's a boy. He's banging the lid of the window seat over and over and he's spit-shouting and his face is not breathing.

I look at Mrs. Flaherty but she's pretending like it's not so.

He's a big boy, almost six. Does he know something bad about kindergarten?

One of the other kids says it's a temper tantrum, but I don't think he's mad—I think he's scared.

Later we're coloring and the tantrum boy has calmed down. Oh, it's Chuckie Grabowski. I know Chuckie. He's a really good colorer. I know this because last year at the All-You-Can-Eat-Hot-Dog Festival he helped break in my 64-pack box of Crayola's. We were the only two left-handers.

Now I know why he was so scared of kindergarten. Since last year, every time Chuckie used his left hand his mom and dad and Grandpa Grabowski would slap his wrist and make him put the crayon in his right hand. They gave him until the time he started kindergarten to get himself switched over.

And here's why they did that: Chuckie's dad, Mr. Grabowski the second, is the butcher on Grand and Belmont. He was left-handed too, but one day when he was using the meat-slicing machine he accidentally cut off the tippy tip of his pinky finger into Mrs. Lieberman's lamb shank.

The family didn't want that happening to Chuckie when he is the third generation to take over the butcher business, so they figured being right-handed would help with operating the slicer.

So, for Chuckie, starting school meant starting his life as a right-hander. No wonder his feelings came out on the window seat. School will teach him to leave his real self behind.

I decide to learn something else from school. ~

6 Years Old

Chippie Ralston

CHIPPIE LIVES ON our block. He's Vernie's dad. Chippie was a medic in the war and came back changed by it. He doesn't work. He sits on the grass down below the hill and throws his baseball into his baseball glove over and over again.

The war is over, but not for Chippie. Somewhere deep inside his heart, he's still being the medic to wounded soldiers.

One day last week, I was watching him throw his ball over and over against the schoolyard wall. I could feel what he was thinking. He was playing catch with some of the soldiers who didn't make it home. And then I could feel one of the soldiers who had been blown up on the battlefield. His foot and his arm were blown away from his body. Chippie ran and picked up all the pieces of him and put them on the stretcher. When he did that, right away the soldier floated up into a bright light and was peaceful, but Chippie wasn't, and still isn't, and probably never will be. So now I think they play a kind of distant catch with one another.

Maybe Chippie thinks this is what he can do for the soldier since he could not save his life.

On television, I heard a professor man talk about noble service. I think this is Chippie's noble service.

As for the dead soldier, I think this is his noble service too.

~

6 Years and 2 Months

Higher Education

Yesterday, just before first grade is going to start, I have a talk with my mom. I wasn't for sure I liked the idea of going to school. It seemed like a place that stops you instead of a place you could bloom. She said she didn't like school either but maybe what I could learn at school was how to get along with all the things that happen in the world. I could learn that from school since things from the world happen there.

I thought that was a pretty good plan, so I decided to go to first grade and see how it goes. ~

6 Years and 3 Months

What to Do About Big Bully Billy

ON MONDAY I saw Big Billy, the class rascal, was really, really scared to cross the street without the patrol boy. I saw him trying not to cry. The next day he ganged up on me and Penny Keske in the cloakroom to act all big shot, like the cloakroom belonged just to him and we were trespassing. Penny ran out screaming, scared of him. I already know for sure that he's just scared but trying to be scary instead. I just shook my head back and forth like I'm saying no without saying it. By now I've got my hands on my hips, then I say, "Big Billy, stop it; you're not that scary." That was the end of that. ~

6 Years and 6 Months

Crusader Rabbit

My BEST FRIEND Libby and I ran out of school at lunchtime to get home to watch *Crusader Rabbit*. It's our favorite cartoon show.

We're at Libby's house because her TV is better—but she's got that jelly with the little seeds in it. I like my jelly better. It's in a jar with Jughead and Veronica painted on the side so you can have it as a glass when all the jelly is used up.

Just then we hear Libby's cat squealing in the backyard. We run out to see. Calico has something in his mouth. Ew, it's rabbit fur. He caught a rabbit and chewed it bad. Why did he have to do that? I'm a dog person. I'm not a cat person. I lift up the bushes and there's the rabbit. He looks right to me and through me. I can see his heart pound under his raw skin. I feel my own heart pound in the same beat with him. His whole back is torn apart and mostly gone.

Oh, I must be scaring him. I put the bush back down, so he is protected.

By then all the neighbors come around. Mr. Williams from across the street tells Libby and me to get a bucket from the basement and fill it with water. We run fast. We want to help the rabbit. Mr. Williams puts the rabbit in the bucket of water and holds his head down with a stick. "Mr. Williams, stop that!"

I see the rabbit fight to live. He has so much strength. He is so alive and then he is drowned.

He survived the cat. He couldn't survive Mr. Williams. I didn't like the cat until I didn't like Mr. Williams.

He was a little rabbit but there was something bigger that came out of him than was in him. Where did he get that? How did he have that? Something really, really big. My heart knows this now for itself. ~

6 Years and 9 Months

The Mercurial Nature of the Human Mind at Six and Three Quarters

WE GO TO the dentist, Dr. Chronomeyer. He wants to be a pal to kids, so he has toys in the waiting room. When I'm finished and don't cry, he's going to give me a prize.

Cry? Why should I?

Okay, so I don't cry, and I get the prize. He gives me a little wad of mercury to play with. Right away I say, "Put it away. It's not safe. You shouldn't be giving that to kids to play with."

He says, "It's safe. People have it in their mouths in fillings."

"Just because it's in people's mouths doesn't mean it's safe, and it sure isn't. So, keep it away from kids."

He laughs at me and says, "Where did you get that idea?"

I don't say this to him, but I can tell you. Sometimes something really smart takes over my mouth and uses it to say something that needs saying.

My mom hands the mercury back to him.

I say, "You should listen to kids. They can have good ideas, you know." ~

6 Years Old, Almost 7

Vested Interest

MOM AND I and Libby and her mom, Kaye, go to Goldblatt's annual bargain sale. There are piles of clothes in bins the length of the whole department store basement. I'm really good at picking out bin wear. Just because I'm shorter than the bins, I can still reach the good treasures. I do it this way: I dig into the huge piles and feel the fabrics. I pull out the ones that feel rich or silky or curl-up-sleepy soft. I know Dupioni silk at age six. Oh look, I pull out a vest that I love! It's twenty-four cents. It has little ties, the color of sunset. When I wear this, it will always remind me to feel the good feeling of the sun across my heart. I want it for sure.

My mom says I can't have it. Kaye says to my mom, "Why don't you get it for her?"

My mom says, "She has to learn that she can't always have what she wants."

What? Is that true? I'm not the kind of kid that whines or nags for stuff. What is she trying to teach me? I already know a lot about what I don't want. I know that she is not happy with how the family is going. I'm supposed to learn what here?

I'll have to have a talk with God about this. I go under the bin counter and start my talk right away. "Am I misbehaving to want something? What is this, God?" Why would there be bins of Goldblatt's' clothes, a vest that's wonderful, and then I can't get it? What is that for? This is the first time I wanted something since I decided that I couldn't be with Dad. It's just a vest for twenty-four cents, what am I supposed to know here? Umm, am I supposed to not want something, that way I won't be hurt or disappointed if I don't get it? That would just confuse myself. Besides I know that's not what God thinks is a good idea.

Oh, now I feel God telling me I can have what I want, everybody can. It's my mom. She's thinking she's not getting what she wants with Dad and her dream of how it's supposed to be for our family. I feel this in my body. I'm carrying Mom's heavy heart. She feels she can't have what *she* wants. Yes, yes, you can. Mom, yes, we all can. It's not about a vest, it's about the little ribbon ties that are the color of sunset. ~

7 Years Old

The Greatest Show on Earth

THIS IS MY first suit. It's checkered with pleats in the back. The sales lady called it "back interest." I have white gloves on and a straw hat with ribbon streamers and the elastic band goes around my chin. Mom bought it for me at Robert Hall. My brother got a suit too, with a vest and two pairs of pants. These are our Easter outfits. Dad didn't get to see them because he was sleeping when we wore them to Easter church.

My dad is taking me to the circus today, just the two of us. I don't really like circuses so much, but Dad does so here we are. We got here just in time. The lights are going down so Dad can't see the seat numbers, so we just take any seat, and it starts.

I'm so happy to be with Dad. He has such black shiny hair. It's very curly. Maybe that's where I get my curls. I have Dad's curls in my hair.

Here's why I don't like circuses: They are pretend. There's glitter and then it's really crummy underneath it all. I see the beautiful aerial lady in the spotlight but when she comes down from flying on her trapeze, I see her limp and her costume has some safety pins on the back. There's all that pretend happy music and clowns acting way too silly for it to be real joy. There aren't any windows in the Big Top. Sunshine is going on outside without us while we are in here. We're missing the sunshine. It's how it is when I'm with Dad at the tavern. When we finally would come out, the sun would blast, and I'd sneeze until my nose got used to feeling warm and smelling fresh air. The sun to me is like a hug from God.

Now the lion tamer is on, except that there are just tigers. It seems pretty corny—this man whipping at them and strutting around taking bows. Any one of those tigers, if he wanted to, could eat that man in one bite. They just don't, because the man is too puffed up to even bother eating.

Dad says, "I wonder why the lion tamer doesn't tame any lions?"

And I make a joke to Dad: "Because a 'Lionel bury more.'"

He groans. People always groan at puns. But I could tell he liked it. Lionel Barrymore was an old-time movie star in case you don't know.

After the aerial lady and before the tigers, I start to have to go to the bathroom. But I want to be a grown-up and not say. Finally, I just have to so bad, I tell Dad I have to go to the bathroom, and he says, "We'll just watch this. You can go at intermission." He doesn't know that when a kid says that they mean it. I really needed to, so I said it again and he said, "Just after this and we can find it then."

I was getting jittery and jumpy, and oh, I had to. "Dad!"

"In a minute."

Well, that's it. I pee right there. The wooden seat had slats, so it dripped down to a big puddle on the cement under my seat. I peed all over the back interest on my checkered suit from Robert Hall.

Oh. Here I was being a grown-up but now I take off my white gloves.

Dad knew what happened right away. He did something great. He said, "These aren't our real seats," so we moved.

By the time the show was over, and we were leaving, my pleated skirt was just a little damp and a little bit wrinkled. Nobody noticed. They just thought I was a little kid. ~

8 Years Old

We Leave

MOM TAKES US and we leave on the train as far away from Dad as possible. All the way across the country I feel her let go in more relief, but with each lurch of the train, I feel further from Dad.

The second day on the train when I wake up, Mom gives me a present from Dad. It's a Cinderella watch in a plastic slipper. Her arms are the watch hands; nine-fifteen her arms stretch out, six o'clock her arms are up and down. It's the best present I ever got. I run through all the train cars looking for Dad, but he isn't here—just the watch.

As we finally arrive at Union Station in California there is an announcement on the speakers. They call my name and my brother's to come to the ticket master. It's Dad! I get so excited at the same time I see Mom's face. She is unhappy-surprised. All the parts of her face that were getting moved together on the train just fall all down.

Dad took his part of the house money and flew out to meet our train. I am so happy to see him, but Mom isn't, so I don't know what to feel.

We stay at the really dumpy Clark Hotel, and Dad stays at the Statler Hilton. I never saw such a beautiful place as that before. There is even a whole pool just for wishing, and there are all kinds of coins in the wishing pool. I wonder how much it adds up to.

Mom had been counting pennies to get us to California, and now here was the Statler and all those coins just sitting there; all those wishes, and I don't know what to wish. I know my wish is different than what Mom would wish, so I just save my penny to give to her. I know that Mom has taken us away. I know she loves Dad. He drinks, and she had enough of drinking from her mom, my Nana. She couldn't do it anymore. She was seeing that my brother needed a dad.

If you have drinking in your family, you know how deep it goes inside yourself. I don't think Mom even knows about the other part, the part that happened when she was at work and Dad, and I were home alone together.

Anyway, he's gone. She sent him away. But you don't stop loving the drinker. I know because that's what I decided on the telephone chair when I was three. I didn't stop the love; I just stopped the part that wasn't love.

So now we are in the rented room at the Clark Hotel far away from Dad and home and everything.

It's way too humid, and the dirty windows are stuck closed tight. Our lungs feel like heavy, soggy sponges. We can't get a good deep breath. Mom has been in the bathroom with her period that won't stop bleeding. She doesn't tell me this, I just know. She comes out of the bathroom and sits on the end of the bed. I know that she is falling out the bottom of herself.

We sit on the bed in the rented room, and we have no place to go because we have left my father. I want to be a comfort to Mom, but I am eight years old, and she is protecting me from her feelings. I help by not letting her know that I know. We are helping each other so hard we are no help at all. We sit one inch from one another. All we have to do is reach out and have our feelings together, but we don't, we can't. That's how deep it goes. ~

8 Years and 6 Months

The Projects

SOMEHOW, WE GOT back home from California but now we're far from the north side. Now we live on the south side in the projects near the airport. This is different from what we knew about before. My brother and I go to the airport every day. He made a shoe-shine kit and so he is an entrepreneur. I check the coin return on all the phones up and down the main concourse of the airport. You'd really be surprised at how much money we make with these jobs. Mom is a waitress and also works for Traveler's Aid at the airport, too. Anyway, it's safer and a lot more wondrous at the airport than in our neighborhood.

Our project house is one room in a long wooden barracks. The room has a bathroom and a little kitchen up against one wall. The rest is our living room. Soon after we moved in they gave us a second room by breaking through the wall. Now we have a bedroom. We are very lucky to live anyplace.

My brother and I go to portable school—many grades are there all together. We only go to school from nine to noon so other grades can go in the afternoon.

I have one school dress. Mom calls it my uniform; that way when I wear it every day it's not like I don't have anything else to wear.

Miss Petrie is our teacher. She just finished teacher school. We are her first classroom. Miss Petrie is a saint lady. Ritchie Dougherty is a boy who cannot sit quietly. He has to climb all over and be a monkey in the classroom. Miss Petrie is very patient with Ritchie. We don't have much learning because Ritchie has to be looked after so he doesn't hurt himself, but I think we learn the best thing—to be kind to a boy who can't sit still.

I think Miss Petrie cries when she gets home after school. She thought it was going to be different than what it is. But it isn't different than what it is.

Whatever happens, my mom always says, "It's good experience."

So, I guess that's what's going on now for us. It's good experience. ~

9 Years Old

Kids' Courthouse

We take an elevator at the courthouse. When I was a little kid, I thought that an elevator is an Otis Box that you get into and look at the numbers that light up. An Otis Box is where you wait with strangers. Meanwhile, there are tiny little workmen in overalls who come out and change all the furniture, while you create the reality you want. If you are going to the dentist, then you can go into the elevator and stand in there and create the idea of the dentist's office. The little men in overalls hear your thoughts and run around to make the place look just like what you are expecting from making it up in your head. When you're ready, the doors open, and you go to the dentist.

Now we are at the kids' courthouse, and we take the elevator.

When we come out, I'll have a different name. It doesn't mean I belong to my stepdad; I guess it just means I have two dads. One cancels out the other. I was hoping I'd see my real dad, but he isn't here. Maybe he already signed a paper that gives us away.

Judge Stonehill is sitting way up high. He's got a graduation costume on, and he hits a hammer on the table. A lady is typing everything he says. He tells a policeman with a badge to have my brother and me approach the bench, which means we stand in front of him, and now he's up really high. We can't even see him up there very much. He asks us some questions that we can hardly hear because he's up there so high. Wow, don't they know anything about kids in this place? Everyone is too stiff to talk to us for real.

I do hear him say to my mom. "They are maturing nicely."

He's talking about us like we're not even here. I guess he doesn't have any kids of his own; he's too busy being the judge of kids' futures when he sees them for two minutes each.

Pretty soon he stamps some papers and hands them to the badge man who also approaches the bench, who hands them to somebody else who hands them to Mom and now my stepdad. They all seem very smiley like this is good. The judge hits his hammer again, and it's done.

We are in the elevator with many families and kids who don't have parents. I have two dads. I am feeling all the feelings of all the kids. There are gobs of feelings going on in the elevator. I know these feelings will explode me. People getting on and off each floor, more kids shuffled from here to there. When we arrive on the ground floor, the doors open, and I throw up all over the lobby floor.

This is kids' courthouse for kids, but it doesn't have anything here for kids. There are feelings all stuffed up in each one. So many waiting on benches. Can't they just give them some French fries or something? I liked when I thought the Otis Box was where you created any good thing you wanted instead of a lot of the kids sitting on benches outside of courtrooms where their futures are decided without them. ~

9 Years and 3 Months

How Our New Dad Became Our Pappy

WE ALREADY HAVE a dad even though we don't see him anymore.

Our new dad needed a new name for us to call him. We were riding in the car. Mom said that he could be our Pappy. Mom is clever—she slipped it in on our ride down the road. I could feel it: we rode right into it easily. He is Pap now and ever after—my brother will have a dad. ~

9 Years and 6 Months

Ginny McRaney

THIS YEAR, AS a new family, we moved to a newer, bigger housing project. I have my own room and so does my brother. Now we have a family life and we both have friends.

Ginny McRaney is my friend. Ginny is a lifer. She's never going to get out of the projects. I already know that my brother and I will.

This school year something happened that I want to tell you about.

I have money—way more than my friends. I have a bank account and money in the drawer of my dresser. I might have almost thirty-six dollars.

It's my mom and stepdad's first wedding anniversary, which is the Paper Anniversary. I bought a paper gift for them. Ginny was over when I was wrapping it. I got the idea to make a bow out of a dollar bill. I got out my money box from my dresser and made the bow, and I was all set with their present.

The next day Ginny came over with some girls from school, and I was surprised to see her with them because they weren't her usual pals. They all had candies and little trinkets from the little store in the neighborhood—the kind of stuff that has dust on it because no one really has any fun money to spare in the projects and these things were luxury items. The girls all came in after their shopping spree, and Ginny brought me something, too. I realized that she had treated the other girls to their trinkets. Two things ran through my thoughts. Ginny was trying to buy their friendship and anyway where did she get the money? After they left, I looked in my money box. It was empty.

I felt a "stabby" feeling in my stomach. Was this what betrayal felt like? I could decide what I wanted it to mean.

My mom gave me two good ideas. She suggested I ask Ginny if she took my money. She also pointed out that it's a good idea to keep your money to yourself.

Ginny, being a good Catholic girl, 'fessed up right away and started shaking all over in shame. I realized that she brought the other girls to me because she didn't feel that she was enough. Oh, dear Ginny, if only you knew how golden you are.

If someone does something that hurts you, it probably has more to do with them than with you. There's a lot that goes on in people's lives that you don't know about. But with Ginny there is something I do know about her.

Ginny's dad was estranged from her family. Every now and then he'd show up, mostly for money, and then disappear hours later. Not very long ago, Ginny and I came skipping up her front sidewalk; when we got to the front door, a gunshot fired at us. The bullet whisked through Ginny's bangs and past my ear and hit the doorframe. Splinters of wood spattered our faces. Ginny's father was drunk and from inside the house had fired the shot at us. There was a shock from the sound; it was really, really loud. There was a ringing in our ears and wood splatters were all over us, AND there was still the drunk man with a loaded gun in his hand, and it was still in his hand. He already shot at us, who knows what he would be doing next. But here's the part I want to tell you about: Ginny was just shot at—we weren't even sure if we had been hit—and the thing that stands out to me the most was that Ginny was happy to see her daddy.

I remember hearing our school janitor, Mr. Moses, once say, "People can be hurting so bad they don't know what they are doing."

So, Ginny taking the money had to do more with her than with me. See, you don't know what people are going through. ~

10 Years Old

Why I Kicked Kritzberg in the Shins

KRITZBERG WAS REALLY annoying me. This was going on now for a whole week. When was he going to get over it?

He'd come up from behind me and poke my head or pull my hair or yank on my sleeve. Finally, we were in line ready to go home for lunch, and I just turned around and kicked him in the shins.

Mr. Gresley was right there. He saw the whole thing. I did it on purpose. Maybe I could get some mercy from Mr. Gresley.

I know he didn't think it was a serious crime that I kicked Kritzberg. I think he got the idea to take us to the principal's office so he could flirt with Miss Allenberry.

If you ever get taken to the principal's office, it's good to go on Fridays because that's the day that Mr. Biles, the principal, isn't there because he leaves early so he can get to the lake and start kayaking. Everybody knows this about Mr. Biles. So that's when Miss Allenberry is in charge.

Miss Allenberry is so lovely, and she smells like lilacs.

Miss Allenberry is way nicer to Mr. Gresley than I am to Kritzberg. She probably would never kick Mr. Gresley in the shins. But I think she also hasn't gone to lunch with him yet either. I know he wants to court her and now me and Kritzberg are part of their courting.

So here it is Friday and me and Kritzberg are in the principal's office.

I could tell that Mr. Gresley and Miss Allenberry were both getting a real kick out of this.

Poor Kritzberg was so scared to be in the principal's office. He didn't see it was kind of funny. He was just a boy with his first crush. He has all those feelings coming out of him that he doesn't know what to do with them all. But a pretty good thing comes out of it. I think going to the principal's office made him be over having the crush on me. It was too much. He'll go back to playing sports with the boys, that's way easier.

Miss Allenberry has a talk with me. I guess somewhere down the line of my going from girl to woman "I can soften to the advances of the opposite sex," but now I'm just pestered by all this. Leave me alone. After we leave the office Kritzberg takes off and runs after the boys who are playing in the schoolyard. I notice that Mr. Gresley stays back with Miss Allenberry; maybe she gets something from her own speech that she told to me. ~

10 Years and 3 Months

The Little Girl in the New Neighborhood

WE MOVE FROM the second projects to a new neighborhood where the houses and the people look the same as each other. It seems like this neighborhood was going on while we were gone, and now—we are back.

I met Martha. She eats her vegetables and has her vaccinations, and probably the most traumatic thing that ever happened to her life was that she flushed before her mother looked at her poop.

She has the kind of dining room that isn't used except for Thanksgiving Day. I bet she plays hide-and-seek under the table, but no one comes to find her.

I'm eating a peach as it drips down my arm, juicy and luscious. My hair is shiny-copper curly; my skin is sunburst warm, and my sun shorts let me be free and happy. This is summer and I am fresh grass, and barefoot natural.

I can feel Martha's mother, behind my back, deciding I must be a wild Tarzan-type child raised in the jungle. She has no real idea about who I am.

Martha has a part in her hair and barrettes, and a dress with a bow and puffy sleeves. She is . . . untouchable, like the doll on the shelf in the box that it came in with the cellophane still around it. Martha has that same doll-like gaze kind of semi-lifelike.

Her house is real stifling, no air has gotten in there since before she was born, I'm pretty sure. What is this I'm feeling? Meeting Martha, who is my same age, I understand something about myself. I see that she's a little girl. She is "Mary had a little lamb" while I feel a full octave playing all through me. I guess she's having an innocent childhood. I'm glad I didn't have one of those. ~

10 Years and 6 Months

Bingo Night

My stepfather is a precinct captain. I know all about getting out the vote.

I am volunteered to fold and stamp and lick and deliver political brochures door-to-door before election morning. I'm really good at it, if you'd like to hire me.

As the precinct captain's daughter, I even attend every funeral in the neighborhood. I see as many dead people as my schoolmate Jamie Slaughter, whose dad owns Slaughter Funeral Home. (I think that's a pretty funny name for a funeral family.)

Just before the election there is a bingo night planned for all the ladies in the precinct. This is a big deal. The ladies are serious about their bingo.

I am on the team to decorate the hall, pile up the prizes, and do anything it takes to put on an "Election Bingo Extravaganza."

Mrs. Griffin, the assemblywoman for the district, is in charge. I kind of look up to her. She is a woman in a man's world. Some of the men act fake important while Mrs. Griffin acts like herself and gets the job done. I think she has what power really is, not pretend power. Everybody knows she handles the hardest problems with good results. She has lots of kids, and her husband is in a wheelchair and doesn't work. There probably isn't one thing that is easy in her life and here she is running for Congress besides it all. Her first name is Grace, and I think I understand something from her about using grace in her methods to get things done.

Here's what's happening just one hour before Bingo Night is supposed to start.

The bingo people with all the equipment broke down in their bingo truck on the expressway and can't show up. "Beadie and Max's Bingo Extravaganza" will not be performing tonight.

What is Mrs. Griffin going to do?

I watch her. She just keeps decorating. She is calm. *She is not doing anything about it.*

What! I watch her.

Mrs. Griffin! Do something!

No. Nothing. She just uses the staple gun and puts up streamers.

How is she going to get into Congress this way?

Doesn't she know—the ladies are *very serious* about their bingo!

The hour goes by. All the ladies of the precinct arrive. *NO BINGO!*

Mrs. Griffin starts calling names for ladies to win door prizes. One after the other wins something. All night long, no bingo, just winning without bingo. The evening is filled with endless door prizes. The ladies are HAPPY.

They are *winners.* And no one had to play bingo to get a prize.

It is an extremely successful evening. They all win something.

Now I wonder how we would have even had time for bingo. We were lucky the "Beadie and Max's Bingo Extravaganza" equipment truck never arrived.

And besides, speaking of winning—Mrs. Griffin won the election.

See what I mean about grace. ~

11 Years Old

P.F. Flyers

I HAVE NEW shoes—P.F. Flyers—so I can fly.

It's the all-schools picnic, and the race is about to start. I can feel the energy in my shoes. I am being one with the morning. I am feeling the texture of the course. Together, my P.F. Flyers and I are going to run with the wind.

We line up— "Get on your mark, get set, go!"

The girl in the blue sweater bolts out in front. She wins before any of us even get going. How did she do that? I'm flabbergasted. I was so sure my P.F. Flyers and I would fly to the finish. I'm amazed.

I hear Mr. Ratz, the boys coach. He says, "She's a natural athlete, already six feet tall and competitive."

I think, Competitive?

He says, "She's got a killer instinct."

I think, Killer?

I don't know anything about killer instinct. You mean humans set up races to win *against* someone else? Why? I want to ask the coach, but he is off taking photos, taking credit for the girl in the blue sweater. He might not understand the nature of my question.

Sometimes I would like to make a documentary and call it *What Goes into the Finish Line*. I always thought that you run for your personal best, just to get yourself more, so that way you always win if that's something you have to do. Maybe the girl in the blue sweater was running a different race then the one I was running. Maybe everybody running the race is running their own race for all their own reasons. ~

12 Years Old

My First Last Will and Testament

I JUST GOT the world as a birthday present.

My Aunt Millie works at Replogle globe, and I got a deluxe globe that *lights up,* with a world atlas in the base, for my birthday.

I think she got an employee discount on it because it has a little spot between New Zealand and the Antarctic where the paper is nicked off a tiny bit so you can see the light through it. I think of it as an island of light that hasn't been discovered yet.

I got it yesterday. I have this big feeling of ownership. Really, I can have this? I can have the world?

All last night I looked all over the world and picked out places for me to go in my whole life. I can go to so many places. *All* the places. And you know what? No matter where you go on the globe, you can keep going and you'll circle back home. It makes me think that the whole world can be my home.

After I looked at my globe for a long time, I went to bed to dream of all the places there are, but instead I dreamed that my globe fell over and broke into a lot of pieces. Oh, I never want anything to happen to it. This is a new feeling for me. It's like getting a dog to take care of—you're happy-excited but scared to make sure you take care of it right.

Our neighbor Joey Pescarillo is a new dad. I saw him when he brought his wife and little baby home from the hospital. His shoulders were hunched up holding the weight of the world instead of little Ronnie, who's just six pounds. I feel that way about my globe. It's something that is mine that's special that is my responsibility to take care of. I always want to.

I just got the idea that a last will and testament would be good just in case I do die before I wake, like the prayer says.

1) I leave my Replogle deluxe globe, that lights up with a world atlas in its base, to any little brother or sister I might get. I'd want them to know the world is vast and they can explore it. I'd want them to feel this feeling of something that has value

that belongs to them. I like the feeling that I can have it and nothing's going to happen to it that's bad.

Now that I'm making out my First Last Will and Testament, I have to leave my dolls to someone.

2) Amelia has her doll, Monica, who can do no wrong. She just plays with Monica and doesn't even hear when anybody says anything to her. I know I'm jealous of Monica even though she's just a doll with a kind of stupid look on her face, but I give Amelia my doll, Clementine, because I know Amelia will take care of her. I don't think Clementine likes Monica very much, but they can learn to get along if I die and they have to. I don't think that's so hard for dolls to pretend.

3) I hope I don't die soon, not because I'm scared or anything, I just don't think it would be healthy for Mom. I think she'd feel really bad if I died. So, I'm not planning to die until way later.

But in case I do die sooner than later, I'd say to her, "I'm sorry I had to leave early. I hope you won't be too sad. Thank you for being my mom. I love you so much. I hope I wasn't too much trouble."

4) Libby is my very best friend. She has a whole bunch of good toys and books and art stuff. I'd give her my turtle bowl with the plastic palm tree in the middle. I'd like her mom to get her a turtle, but it's not a good idea because they have cats at her house. To Libby—P.S. Thank you for being my very best friend. I'm sorry I got mad when you drank your cocoa too fast and threw up on my face.

5) I have some coins in my piggy bank, except I don't know how much is really in there. I give it to my big brother. He's real smart about enterprise. He can have a business same as his bike repair business he had last week, even though nobody came over with their bikes because nobody knew he was sitting in the basement waiting.

6) You don't have to get sad, writing my will isn't about being dead. It's about what is alive in me. My globe gives me the feeling that I can have something that's a big deal to have. Just

because you love something doesn't mean it'll go away. You can love something or someone and it can turn out all right. ~

13 Years Old

Mothers Should Be Seen and Not Heard
LEAVE ME ALONE. I want to do it myself.

Today I had feelings that I was sorting through. Miss Gilhooly said, "You look pensive."

My mother said, "She's in love."

I didn't like that. They were private feelings—so private I didn't even know what they were yet, and my mother not only knew I had feelings, she identified them and broadcast them to the *librarian*.

I know that was her way of helping—her way of gaining access to me when I was not available to her. I know she wants to give help that I didn't ask to get. Well leave me alone; this is my life. If you want to live a life, live yours. Like once when she didn't like what I was doing for some reason—it was when I was eleven—and she said, "Behave yourself."

I was so surprised. I said, "I am behaving myself—this *is* myself."

And then I was even more surprised when I said, "You don't want me to behave *myself*, you want me to behave *yourself*."

If we match, we're fine, but if I come to my own conclusions then that separates us. I mostly agree with her way of doing things, but there are two lives going on here. Two—and the one I'll be living is my own. A little privacy please—let me have the feelings that I don't even know what they are yet.

And anyway, I'm *not* in love. You can't mean Nicolas Cooper—have you seen the inside of his locker? It's a mess. ~

14 Years Old

The Art of Making Art

I'M ON MY WAY downtown to the art institute. One of my art projects won me a scholarship there. I love my art teacher, Bert Amherst. She's not an official teacher; she's an artist who happens to have a quick job in the school district for this semester. She lives in her art studio, and she's flamboyant and an excellent artist. I see the big, grand picture of her and the no-steady-income part. It must be hard for her to be in the school district. Last year my art teacher was Miss Proust—I wouldn't recommend her. She used to write, in ink, across our beautiful sketches so that we couldn't turn them in again. She thought art was a school assignment that students would cheat on. Bert Amherst knows that art is an expression of your very soul.

Now that I know Bert, I am thrilled. She sees my creations and she's the one who submitted my work for the scholarship. She's the difference between someone who's telling you what to do and someone who is doing it and inspires you to let your own light shine. Her favorite phrase is "Wham into it."

It's December, nearing Christmas. I'm wearing one red long sock and one green long sock. People on the bus seem so perturbed about this. I wonder if it makes them feel like they forgot to think of something joyful for themselves.

Here's what I created today: "The Plot to Overthrow Self-Suppression."

Most of my art pieces have very elaborate titles. They tend to tell a whole detailed story. Bert says she feels jealous because I'm such a good artist and I spend time as editor of the school paper and writing stories, and she'd like to see me do just my art and no other expression. She says I'm a free spirit.

But isn't the point of a free spirit to be free?

Bert Amherst was the first one to see so much of me. There is even more of me than even she sees.

One of my art pieces went to the Louvre! It's a collage mosaic of shards of mirror. You look at it and see ten thousand reflections of yourself.

The title is "Signs from God Are Not Few and Far Between. Signs from God Are in Every Moment. It's Only Few and Far Between That We Choose to See Them. Trust That They Are There and You Will Wake Up and Live." See what I mean about really long titles? I do that so I get the idea clear for me. Afterward I'm able to say things with a few words because then I know what I want to talk about. Actually, when my mirror mosaic was shipped, it went without a title because by then it spoke for itself.

Bert's motto, "Wham into it," teaches me to boldly go and let the creation create. My art, my titles, my stories all come to life to heal an emotional issue that the viewer or reader might be having. Bert would like me to spend less time as editor of the paper and my own writing and more time with paint. To me they are all the same healing art. Because Bert pursues her art, that helps me to see that each one's art has its own reason. Mine is my own and I have my unique voice to express that. Bert is a great artist and a great influence on me. She's the one who knew about the worldwide contest that I won to have my work in the Louvre. But mostly, she's the one that showed me what reflection of myself to see in the mirror. That's Bert for you—she's a work of art. ~

15 Years Old

Cheers

It's CHEERLEADER TRYOUTS and I'm here cheering on the girls. Claudine is already a cheerleader, and she's going through one of those girl-hazing phases where all the other girls have frozen her out of their clique and shunned her. I don't know the reason, if there even is one. Girls at fifteen play this sort of drama and cast one among them outside the group. I befriended Claudine because I felt she was getting a raw deal. I don't really care for her very much, she always seemed kind of "not nice" but now she was getting treatment that was not so nice for her. Because I befriended her, she has been very nice to me and appreciates my kindness to her, but that's not why I am nice to her. I'm just leveling the field to be fair. I'm not looking for her devotion. I know that she will find her own heart; it's in there somewhere. She hands me a note—she says in it that she realizes she was a nasty person until she was treated like that herself, then she didn't know how to be kind until she was treated that way by me. Her note comes with kisses and little circles over the i's. In fact, lately, I did see the other girls including her. I guess the freeze is over.

Anyway, it's cheerleader tryouts and I've come to cheer on the girls. When I walk into the gym, they are all lined up against the wall showing their fear instead of their confidence. It's cold and they are in their dreary, swamp-green gym suits. They all look so pale. I've just rushed in from painting a mural outside with my art class. I have good warm clothes on under my paint overalls that have every splashed color on them, while my face is red, kind of rash-like from the weather. I've dashed in from a technicolor world and now see a gray atmosphere. The whole gym is kind of shivering and quiet, like the team is losing. So, I start cheering them on. One of the gym teachers, Miss Janglemen, who will judge the tryouts, seems to be relieved that the mood is changing up.

I am cheering them on and—surprise! —*I* get picked as a cheerleader. Me, of all people.

Do I accept this position? I do see something here. Even though it appears to be completely out of character for me to be a cheerleader, the one true thing I have always been *is* a cheerleader—not one with the popular clique or the highest kick, but rather the one who cheerleads people to their best self.

It's true. Ask Claudine.

That Afternoon

Hmm. Some things are an opportunity even if you didn't think of them yourself. I don't know where this will be leading. I do know that the way to find out is to accept what has been presented to me and go.

So, at the assembly this afternoon they announce the new cheerleaders' squad, and they announce me. I go up to the stage while the assembly applauds. I see Peggy Schragel in the audience—not picked. She wanted it so badly, yet she didn't show up at the tryouts. As I join the new squad on stage, I notice right away the boys are sizing us up, scoring us among themselves.

A microphone is awaiting our responses, but the other "winners" are tearing up and are unable to step up to the moment. I speak for the squad—impromptu, quickly, just enough to express gratitude, inspire the student body to support their team, and then close with a cheer. After all isn't that the job?

When I leave the stage to go back to my seat, I overhear two young girls say, "Look, she's crying," which I was not.

Another girl says, "She should fix her hair."

My seat was no longer available for me to go back to. Now I am a public figure.

After school, my friends and I are going to Cup a Joe and Josie's Soda Counter for my favorite, a vanilla coke. But here outside of school is my mother waiting to pick me up. I run over to the car to tell her the news that I am now a cheerleader of all things, and that I had intended to go with my friends. She happened to just come from shopping and is excited to show me clothes that she has just bought for me. Wow, what a day of plenty. I say, "I'll tell my friends that I'll see them tomorrow."

She says, "No, no, go with your friends." She would see me when I got home. And then she drives off.

I yell to my friends to go ahead, that I'll catch up to them and then I stand at the curb and watch my mother drive away. Growing pains go both ways. ~

15 Years and 6 Months

Different

As you can see, I'm on the city bus. I'm on buses a lot and the elevated train too. It's a big city and I get around all over it very, very well.

Being the editor-in-chief of the school paper, I can take myself downtown to lots of interesting celebrity interviews of movie actors and actresses promoting their films, or scientists presenting their latest data, or musicians in town to play their music.

I am more out of school than in it. My education is coming from the world at large. Yesterday, for the first time, I heard Fats Waller's song "Her Feet's Too Big." That's how I feel, my feet's too big for the school world. So, I am stepping out.

One really exciting invitation for this week was from the actual mayor of the city of Zamboanga in the Philippines. I met him at the travel show at the convention center. He read a travel article I wrote and invited me to come to Zamboanga and stay in a tree house they have there for the purpose of promoting tourism. He had the idea I could write an article about it for them. Flying out to Zamboanga, what a great idea, but I didn't go because I had a test at school this week.

It's a good thing I didn't go because as editor of the paper I got a call from the printer who needed a last-minute piece for the paper to add before going to press. The part that he needed was locked up at school, but I knew right where it was. It was on the table by the window. I called Rick Peterman. He's the faculty sponsor for the paper. He's the teacher for gifted students, but if you ask me, he's the gifted teacher. He got everybody in English class to recite the *Canterbury Tales* in Middle English, guaranteeing they will be a big hit at any school party.

Here's the plan I had: We'll just go over to school, open the window, get out the needed papers, and take them over to the printer. Nothing to it.

It turned out that the window was a little higher and I'm a little shorter than I thought. After lots of tries, we become the inept team of Laurel and Hardy. Finally, R.P. boosted me up, so I was now standing on his shoulders to get the window open. Meanwhile, he is an esteemed and responsible faculty member with a student now on his shoulders as we break into the school in the dark on a late Saturday night. I'm sure this will be one of our fondest laughing memories.

I know we will have Christmas cards from one another long into our old age, and I'll stay at his house when I come back into town for the forty-year reunion. It's that kind of teacher-student bond. I'm kind of glad the Zamboanga treehouse thing didn't work out.

Anyway, besides being editor-in-chief and cheerleading, I go to every other event and expo I'm invited to in the city, and that's just about something every day.

Even a monsignor, of all people, invites me to his salons that are held in his beautiful book-lined library. He invites doctors, and sports figures, and atheists, and prominent leaders, and mostly interesting people. I think he gets a kick out of me because I'm full of philosophical questions that have no answers. He says I can always be counted on to have a fresh way of looking at the suffering in the world. Oh yeah, that's me. I can do that on a regular basis. But one time, when the dean of religious studies from the university was speaking, I fell asleep. It was a cold blizzard outside and over warm in the library and the Dean—well, to use his own words— "lacked verve." He was saying "alas," and "nevertheless," and "indeed," so I fell asleep. When I woke up, I wasn't too embarrassed because I noticed that practically everybody fell asleep too.

Monsignor McClure has his salons every week. For me, this is way beyond school, which I'm happy about because I don't think that much of school.

I think the salons are the monsignor's way to enjoy a glass of sacramental wine. Mrs. Doyle, his housekeeper, pours him the one glassful then she disappears into the kitchen to put the decanter under lock and key.

Coming from my background, I'm a person who likes to know that the liquor bottle is locked up. I'm sure the right good monsignor would love a second glassful, but even he knows not to mess with Mrs. Doyle.

(Liquor in the hands of an Irish priest high on the food chain of the Church, or in the hands of my father and his father and my maternal grandmother, or the entire Sabatini family on the corner of my street—all six of the brothers and four cousins, liquor in the hands of anybody can be an equal opportunity disrupter. Just to let you know, I'm not going to be the one in my family to inherit a drinking habit. I'm the one in the family who doesn't pass it on.)

As I started to tell you, before I fell asleep, the salons are held in this beautiful old brownstone, in the stately library that's lined with leather-bound books that nobody seems to read. The Catholic Church has very expensive real estate. The church my family sometimes goes to doesn't even have heat. A wealthy collector of books, upon his death, willed this property to the church, that's why the monsignor lives here. When I'm in this grand library, I think of the man who put it all together. He was Ambrose Cornwall Mayweather. He was called the Colonel. I don't know what he was a colonel of. But he sure was a bibliophile—a collector of rare first-edition volumes. I wonder if he visits, as a ghost, and reads his books. It's a pretty nice library. Since he's in eternity, I would imagine that this could be his idea of heaven.

Sometimes I rush out of there to get to A Taste of Jazz, where I recite some of my poetry at night to live jazz music.

Or I rush to do improv in a workshop at the local improv theater, Bite Your Tongue. A friend said to me, "Aren't you scared to do improv and have to make it up on the spot?" I tell her that's just like life, we make *that* up on the spot."

Sometimes I rush out of there, too. Since I'm a cheerleader, I bring my cheering uniform and I meet the cheering squad and the basketball team at the away games. That's the only time I don't like bus transportation because it's dark early, and cold, and you're just on the bus to get from one place to another— that's not the way to have your life. Experiencing the adventure of being *on* the way *is* the way to have your life.

On Tuesdays and Thursdays and every other weekend, I'm at the art institute—another reality to be in. There are a lot of parts of myself. I'm all of them.

I've got my journal with me today. Every page has gold stars and clock faces and eyes glued in from magazines and smiling mouths. There's such energy on the pages. Life is coming right out of it.

Here are some things I just wrote in it this month. Once I write down a dilemma, it usually gets solved right there on the page. You can read some of the entries. They will give you an idea of what I'm experiencing now that I'm soon to be sixteen. You'll see that I'm full speed ahead since I wrote these.

Here's a piece called *Different*.

> *I don't see anyone around who has all the same parts as me.*
> *I was not sure yet which parts of me to be. I went to the school advisor to sift away the lump in my throat and make my heart surefooted.*
> *But as I tell her what I didn't want to be—what I was up against—she was that. She was conforming, habitual, ducks in a rigid row. Her message, her life, was, don't be different—fit in.*
> *I left her office and went on to become myself.*

See what I mean? That's what I'm being now.

There's a saying in Asia: "If your child is a nail sticking up, hammer it down." I'm definitely the nail sticking up. This I know about myself: I will definitely never be hammered down.

See, there's a kind of a theme that's running through this year for me. Actually, it's probably going to be running through my whole life—different, that's me.

Here's some comments I wrote down about some of my teachers:

Mr. Hammerspiel wears a pocket protector in the top pocket of his shirt. I think that if he's afraid of ballpoint ink, what else is he afraid of? One day he said to me, "You better learn how to be a good little wifey." That's not what he should be telling a kid like me. The school district should pay more attention to who they hire.

Last week we had a substitute. He was having a hard time managing second period. I told the kids to stop acting out and give the guy a chance, and they did. At the end of the school day, he thanked me for visiting the class and helping. I think he didn't know that I was one of the kids in the class.

One teacher, Miss Glory, whom I loved, left quickly. She might have gotten fired for being wonderful. As a goodbye, she said to me, "Stay extraordinary."

Okay, I will.

I feel myself pulling away from my fellow students, mostly Dora Normann. Her only focus is that her dad won't let her talk on the family phone for more than one minute. They have an egg timer set up next to the phone. Her dad tries to keep the line free in case someone calls for his business. He sells vacuum cleaners, but nobody ever wants one, so the phone sits there unused while Dora is traumatized, and her father is underselling his product line. Their garage is full of vacuums—mostly the premium, deluxe models. I'm thinking that between Dora and her dad, they are sitting there creating a vacuum. Ha, ha, except it's not so funny. I think her whole life is going to be affected by this. Meanwhile, there are a million possible lives going on beyond the egg timer on their table.

I think if you want to measure time, then measure time to be in the whole wide world. Time is not to waste.

When I see Dora's life and I see mine, I see that others just aren't cultivating the same capabilities that are there all around.

I feel Dora hoping for what? From whom? To go where?

I tell her, "Be who you are, where you are." Well, she is being who she is where she is. She's being blank.

So, you get the idea I'm kind of different than the other kids. But I'm not different like Lester Pulaski.

The kids in our grade call Lester Pulaski a creep and he's not. He just kind of scrunches up his shoulders and smells a little funny from his science experiments.

The label "creep" just keeps the kids away from experiencing his great mind.

They can't keep *up* with Lester, so they put him *down*.

I'm different but not an ostracized kind of different like Lester. Nobody would bully me, they wouldn't dare. The kids don't understand Lester because he is really, really, really smart. That's what scares them, so they call him Lester Fester.

I have talked to Lester for long times. We don't really talk back and forth; it is more that Lester tells me all about his scientific ideas and experiments. When we read *20,000 Leagues Under the Sea* in class, it lit Lester up. He could change science fiction into science for real, that's how smart he is. He knows what science stuff to put together to create the Nautilus and all the inventions on board.

(*20,000 Leagues Under the Sea* inspired me too, but I didn't see what Lester saw. When I read it, I could just see that Captain Nemo had some social issues.)

I tell Lester, "Lester, you are so smart you're going to make an impact on the world. You're going to help the world get through the future."

For me, I'm happy to be different from others and different from Lester. I want to offer inspiration to the other kids so that they can get good ideas for themselves. I'd like to make my impact on the world too.

Oh, look! The man that limped onto the bus about ten stops ago is now getting off, and he's not limping. Yes. Perfect.

That's the part about me being different that I didn't tell you yet.

But here's my stop. I'll tell you about that part later. ~

16 Years Old

Concept Car

Whew! At sixteen, on any given day, there's a lot going on. A lot of life choices coming up right and left.

Here's how it looks this afternoon: I have a weekend job at the auto show downtown at the convention center. I stand and model a new concept car that is a prototype designed for the future.

There are some ideas in its design that are brilliant and inspiring that will drive forward the entire future for all of us. Other ideas will have to be adjusted, like the chrome strip that looks aerodynamic but interferes with the door hinge.

It's perfect that I'm the one who is modeling the car of the future since I am sixteen and I am designing myself for my *own* future. It's not just me; all of us at present are creating our future. We are all concept cars.

I wrote my own presentation speech for the show for me to deliver every half hour all day long. I point up all the visionary ideas designed into the car and close my speech by saying, "There are no limits in technology. Any limits are in legislation." I notice that the spectators don't seem to care about innovation; they just seem to be interested in the sexy factor.

The sexy factor is what seems to be rampant on the convention room floor.

There's a salesman here who has been cruising around me and being a salesman of himself to me. My jokes are so funny to him. My every move is complimented. He's fake suave. It can't lead anywhere good.

He keeps asking me to "coffee" (that being another word for something of a deeper brew). I swerve away from him. Today I discover he is married. Why does this feel so bad to me? I don't have anything to do with him, yet I feel splashed with mud.

Is this the work world?

I think all the salesmen have a bet—which one of the girl models will they "get" this season? This isn't the first car show for Gretchen, the model who is modeling the sports car. She acts familiar with the salesmen's behavior and rides right along with it. She's modeling the latest sports car that's already in production, if you get my meaning. *She* goes for "coffee."

One of the ideas that I bring up in my presentations is the fact that humans can reach way further than where they are now, but humans, being human, are held back by where they are now. When I wrote that to give in my talk, I meant that we are only limited by our choices that we choose to choose. Now that I am here at the show and experiencing the salesmen and the other models, I see their choices.

Since my car is the car of the future, I want to make choices that drive me to the high road.

The others here seem to be going to very different destinations.

After work, I usually take the bus from the convention center to the city train to go home. Tonight, I have the option of taking the commuter helicopter to the train. I've been saving it up special—this is the night to make that choice. It's a good way to sort out all my feelings about all the experiences that showed up today.

The city glimmers with millions of nightlights twinkling, while I feel the vastness of millions of choices that make up each life.

I see that this is my time to start being conscious of my choices that drive my future.

I decide to choose the best life design for myself. I'll be aerodynamic and have a good serviceable door hinge to get in and out.

When I arrive home, my mother has been waiting for me. I say I was using the travel time over the city to think and sort out my feelings about what I choose to create for my life. I tell her about the salesman, and as I say to her, "He says that his wife doesn't understand him," she says simultaneously to me, "He says that his wife doesn't understand him."

Oh, I see, just because he's the first one I've heard say this, doesn't mean it's the first time it's ever been said. Thanks, Mom. ~

16 Years and 6 Months

Genius

As I'VE BEEN telling you, I'm so privileged to be editor of the school paper, and I get invited downtown to meet celebrities, luminaries, and interesting people coming through town to talk about their lives and what they offer to the world. Besides it being so much fun, I'm starting to see greatness. This is when I am meeting my first geniuses.

I already recognize greatness around me. There's greatness in everyone, such as Aunt Izzie, who runs the cafeteria at school. The kids respond to her because she acknowledges each one of them when she's dishing out their mashed potatoes. And she makes a different flavor "Izzie pie" every day. That's her genius.

My mother has greatness to her, my teacher R.P. Peterman, Libby's mom—who can design and sew anything.

When I was twelve, I first read J.D. Salinger. I read *The Catcher in the Rye,* and I definitely knew from him how to express greatness in writing. Many with greatness have started showing themselves to me in music. Maybe because I know I just don't have the music gene in me, I can really appreciate that in someone else.

My first in-person genius not from my immediate life is Thelonious Monk. I came to Rush Street—the jazz hub of the city—to interview him about his album he just recorded. I walked into the Gate of Horn from the sun-blasted street into the no-windows, dark club with one lone light bulb on the stage, and there he was at the piano. If you know anything about Monk, you know that he plays brilliant dissonance. You might say he plays the wrong note in the right way. This is what it is to be an original. I felt like the piano was lifting its keys up to be played like that, and it was never going to be played like that again. That's why Monk was my first bona fide genius outside of my neighborhood.

This month I also met Sarah Vaughan, Ella Fitzgerald, Miles Davis, Dizzy Gillespie—so many. Not just musicians—this year I met Elaine May and Mike Nichols and Del Close; their genius is improvisation and a certain way to live life as improv. Ask Bill Murray. He'll tell you. He lives life as an improv.

I got to stand right next to all of them, lean on the piano at sound checks. They had such ease with their talents. I'd look and look deeply. Can you see the genius gene? What is the behavior—the sway of their arms, the beliefs and talk—to know that it's in there somewhere?

Monk was a valuable understanding for me. When I walked into that club that day, there had been some consternation—I don't know the details. Monk went from disagreement to beautiful music. I saw something about genius. It's an ability to catch a light beam that's brought from where we all come from, so we recognize it as a call from home. The task on Earth is to balance it, protect it, nurture it, keep it grounded, even-keeled, able to soar in the connectivity and then, when the gig is over, get on the elevated train and go home. I saw the value in releasing, rejoicing, celebrating your full-hearted expression and also having the sense to make sure you have socks on if it's snowing. There's the genius aspect and there's managing the human part. For me, the spirit being, and the human being somehow have to meld or maybe can't. I got a great gift from seeing Monk managing his major and minor chords. I don't yet know the enormity of how big I could go and then how to pull myself back in and put myself away for the night. I see that the people I was meeting who had genius could be way up and out of their bodies and then could figure out how to get back in the body and get some sleep. Some geniuses can't do it. Maybe that's Monk. They come to Earth in all their talents and burn up in beauty.

I know this about Earth—you need to honor being physical. Whatever high-flying frequency is the bandwidth of your genius, you must also come home to the body and live in there. I know to go up, up, and almost away then learn to come down, down, and be here now. I know that's required. I'm just beginning to know the depth of how to manage that. ~

17 Years Old

The Best Outside Place to Become the Best Inside of Me

I'M GRADUATING FROM high school—now what?

I love the quote from Archimedes "Give me a place to stand and a lever long enough and I can lift the world." Right now, I need to work out the place to stand.

I have my plan to finish this book that you are reading. I plan on getting it done and out in the world to you while I'm in my twenties. I figure that then I will have a platform on which to launch many other lasers of light into the world. So where is the best place for my particular self with my particular plan to develop?

Do I even go to college? Or do I get a backpack and a rail pass and drop into Europe or Indonesia or do a walkabout in the outback of Australia?

I think I can save traveling to the far reaches of the world for when I'll be lucky enough to be invited to world places to come and bring what I can best contribute. I don't have to travel now to find myself. I already know who myself is, and myself is excited about learning what I can as soon as I can.

I could go to a college that's all about writing with classes in literature and reflective thinking, and yet I know that I can read and do reflective thinking on my own. Besides, my book knows exactly what it wants to be, and we're in clear communication with each other for it to be that. If I discuss it with professors that could really mess it up. It just wants a sharp pencil and lots of paper and all my whole heart. I already have all that to give it.

I need a place like a cup where I can pour my content in, and come out four years later with a platform, you know, a place to stand and a lever long enough. Maybe I could go to a college where they offer an education about what I don't know, and then I could learn all that and add it to what I have already started.

So, here's a college that has a communications degree with hands-on access to a radio and television station. Maybe I could create shows and learn all there is to know about production since I don't know anything about it now. After graduating from there I can move on to California or New York and get going on accessing network television and then films. Hmmm. I'll just let this decision come to me and let my heart decide.

And here's what decides it:

I met the magnificent Mordecai Van den Mueller, the great Shakespearean director. I met him at the improv theater. He was presenting a workshop for seasoned directors, and he offered me a complimentary slot in the workshop. Me? I was amazed, and I right away said, "YES." And immediately got really scared about being with all those very talented and accomplished directors who came from all over the world to study with him. The class was for each director to choose a play and block it for production. (That means that the director interprets the play and stages it as in who stands where on the stage and does what, when.) Since I never blocked a play, before, I got the idea that if I *write* the play that I block, I'll know better how I want to block it. So that's what I did and handed it in.

The next class day Mordecai showed up and started in on saying that one person in the class *wrote her own play*. I started cringing in my seat, feeling that I hadn't done the assignment right. All the others were tackling Ibsen and Chekhov, and I was maybe taking a short cut. But no, it turned out that it was the other way—he was astonished that I wrote a play in a few days and apparently, according to Mordecai, a well-written play.

Oh, well, yeah. The writing part is a given for me. I can get it from my heart to the page. Content is my natural state. I know my true self. I don't have to become that. I am that.

The part about getting it onward out into the world, I could learn a thing or two. I can perfect those skills.

So, I decide.

I'll go to the school where I'll have access to all that I need to have my place to stand and my lever long enough to lift the world. And get a scholarship to go there. ~

18 Years Old

Boschka

I'LL CALL HER Boschka; named after her Bosch spark plugs. She's a classic Volkswagen convertible fresh from the junkyard bought for me by my stepfather for $60. I'm away at school while she's being spray painted an iridescent finish with a new top, questionable brakes, a loud muffler, and a wonderful throaty honking horn. Imagine my delight! I will be picking her up on my next weekend trip home after finals.

I have an apartment off campus. Independence is more than just not calling home collect.

Great works are starting to come out of me.

I broadcast my kids' show every day on the college FM radio station, and every day when I leave there, little kids are lined up to meet me and my "characters" that have been on the show. I have fan mail from six-year-olds.

To get Boschka, I take the train home. My mother picks me up. The fluorescent lights in the train station cast a cold shadow at the gate where the crowd awaits our arrival. When I spot my mother, my heart jangles in my body and my easy breathing feels heavy.

Here's that moment—the one when you see your parent as old . . . as mortal. One day she will die—maybe not for forty years, but she's mortal, waning.

I see it because I'm waxing. This is my time now to expand and go full throttle into *my* life. Because of that, her job of mom is done.

It's a fleeting moment—she sees me, steps out of the bad lighting and she's fresh, luscious as ever, and ever on the job of Mom and yet there it was, the split second that forewarns new directions to come.

When our visit is over, I get into Boschka and kiss my mother a new kind of goodbye. I'll be driving back to school and the new off-campus apartment, the new radio show, the new world of me. As I pull away, I'm looking ever forward with just a chance glance in the rear-view mirror and there she is, in the middle of the street, waving until I am long down the road. ~

19 Years Old

Redemption Stamps

WHEN THE RED light goes on, I'm on.

I love the radio station. I spend all my time here. From the muffled sensation of soundproofing to the close, close friendships, I love it so much. I think it's like extra-terrestrials must get along on board the spaceship—there's a camaraderie. We're all cruising along in the same atmosphere.

It's like having a family without ties that bind.

Do you remember redemption stamps? You would get them at the supermarket when you purchased your food. You would get them according to how much you spent. And then you'd save them in a booklet, licking them and sticking them. After a while, you could go to the redemption center and cash in your stamps for stuff such as a blender or TV trays or luggage or whatever you had enough stamps for.

Well today, having lived on my own in my college apartment long enough to have amassed a few books of stamps, I, as a major in the radio-television department, am going forward in broadcasting. So here on this Saturday of my college life, I commit my life to step up and deliver my offerings to the world.

I have a friend Zo Oz (short for Zohana Ozenkoetter). I really like Zo. She's a radio-television major too and we are going to the redemption center to trade in our stamp books for a stopwatch each. In broadcasting, you need your own stopwatch.

I go to Zo's to meet her and she's on the phone with Jasper Flatt, her boyfriend—I like Jasper too. They're both talented and funny and completely lovable. Jasper is a musician. Jas Flatt—that always knocks me out.

They're always talking about getting married.

Zo hangs up the phone, and we leave for the redemption center. She's so funny and in turmoil—should she marry Jasper, or shouldn't she? Is she Zo, the broadcaster, or does she want to be Mrs. Flatt with lots of little Flatts running around? She is mulling this over all the way down the street.

I'm not worried about her; Zo can do anything, everything. She only thinks she can just do either.

So, here's what happens when we get to the redemption center, this being our trek to affirm our commitment to ourselves affirming ourselves. I get my stopwatch. Zo gets a toaster.

P.S. They were married on the day the semester ended. The same day I got an award for my radio show. It was also the day I moved on to developing my new children's television show for PBS, *Warm World of Wumpas*. ~

20s Passage

Moccasin Avenue

As I'm crossing the railroad tracks on my way home from campus, I'm thinking about my pending move after college. I still have a while to decide how I go up from here but maybe it will need some planning.

Oh, it's starting to rain. It's starting to pour. I'm just running over the street that is all torn up ready to be asphalted. The under base of the street is exposed and the rain is making quicksand of it. I'm wearing the moccasins that I've had since high school. My motto for my moccasins has been "Walk in wisdom, have a brave heart—and a little humor wouldn't hurt."

As I trudge through the mud, my moccasins are sucked down off my feet. I try to retrieve them, but I sink in too. I run the rest of the way home barefoot.

The next morning, after the rain, I come back with a shovel to dig out my moccasins and the road has been paved over! My moccasins are now permanent artifacts embedded in the street (archeologists will dig them up years from now and think Native Americans lived here.)

I realize I have walked out of my past self and the new path is about to form.

Somewhere along my way up to now, I wrote down on a piece of torn paper, *Go Directly to Your Dream.*

I've always known that no matter how many twists in my road, if I follow it, that's the best way to where I am going. I think I'll get the next pair of moccasins and put my *Go-Directly-to-Your-Dream* paper in the sole of my new shoe, and that way I can step off into uncertainty and be certain. ~

20 Years Old

The Book of Life

HERE'S BREAKING NEWS. You know this book that you're reading that I've been writing to you since before I was born? The one I planned on finishing and getting out to you by my twenties? Well, here I am in my twenties, but it has come to me, just now, in my understanding, that it's not to be finished and put out now. I'm to write it *my whole life* and put it out *at the other end of my life.* Imagine my mortification at hearing this news. The book has a way of telling me what it wants to be and when it wants to be it, and this is what it conveyed to me just this minute, *loud and clear.*

You probably don't see why this means so much to me. Here's why: It's because, as a book of life, it was never meant to be about *my* life, it was meant for *you* to be able to look up your age at any age, and with my split-second story of that age you could have access to your *own* story that you are experiencing at each age. The idea was to give you the gift of *your* life illuminated, but now not until the other end of *my* life.

Where's the gift in that?

Is it that I don't have all the chops as a writer yet to tell it in the best way? I do know that it's a warrior task sometimes just to walk up to the desk each day to write it. I already have seven notebooks of notes on the shelf. At this rate, there will be over fifty feet of notebooks before I cull it down to the book in your hands. I do know that each year I make notes all year and then pick out the best and highest story for that age.

I've always known that I was not living a common-denominator kind of life. At fifteen I told you how I am different. But you're different too—not the same kind of different as me, different in your own uniqueness, and yet there's a thread that runs through it for us together.

I thought up until now that I was making it an illumination on being human. You, as the reader, could receive a clue for yourself to unlock any clarity you could use in your life about what you are experiencing.

That was the plan—to have it done now—and it's been going great. The irony is, can it be done with sixty or more years to complete it?

I probably don't have all my expertise yet as a writer to get the whole of what is in my heart on the page. It can feel so big in me. I've heard mothers say after giving birth that their baby felt so huge in them and is now so tiny in the crib.

I know that there are aspects of me as a writer that will develop in mastery. I know I'll get it. I know I will say it how it is to be said. I know that. Maybe some wizardry will take years to develop. I know I will develop it.

This new arrival date is going to require an adjustment, a course correction, a look at it with new eyes.

I so want to include it in the pot with everybody else's offering. I am willing and it belongs to me to give it. So, here's the new plan: I have to go all the way up to my eighties to get it out. Not only do I have to write it for eighty years I have to stay alive all that time. I can't die young.

And probably I'll have to *self-fund the project*. I knew this was going to take everything I've got, and now I see it will take even more.

P.S. You might not think this is such a big deal because it's *my* big deal. You have a big deal of your own. It's like that joke—what's the difference between a major operation and a minor operation? The operation you're having is major, everybody else's is minor.

So, this might seem minor to you, but it's major to me.

What's major for you is about that thing that you might not even know what it is yet, but you have the feeling that it means everything to you. What would you die for? That's the very thing that will keep you alive. ~

21 Years Old

How to Broadcast Your Brightest Light
IT's MY BIRTHDAY! I'm twenty-one.

I'm happy to be on the radio with my kids' show, *Storyland*, and developing my TV kids' show for PBS, *Warm World of Wumpas*.

All my broadcast pals spend every waking hour creating together. We are free to explore and discover untapped parts of ourselves. Life right now is about us expressing ourselves.

Tonight, we are all over at the college television station, and I am directing my first show. I'm sure I designed it to be harder than it could have been. At twenty-one it's my time to be overly ambitious—I have bigger ideas than I have the skills to pull off so that for my *Warm World of Wumpas* production, I balance the idea with the execution of the idea to make sure something gets produced. Gill Nelson, my professor and much-admired mentor for directing, has a favorite expression when it's late and the day's production runs into obstacles. He says, "We'll live with it." But I'm twenty-one. I'm uncompromising. I'm not willing to "live with it." I want it how I want it, and I go until I get there.

I'm sure Gill would prefer to go home and be with his family. All my college chums are free and unencumbered. We can stay up late because this is it for us. This is us setting ourselves on fire so that we can set the world on fire with our contributions. We are budding free-thinking and free-flowing sparks of light igniting. We freely let out what we didn't even know we had inside us and experience new resources yet untapped. Genius comes out because it isn't spooked to stay in.

So, we go until we get it right, even if we haven't got the experience to get it right.

Here it is in the very middle of the night and we're still in the control room, still at it. We still all have oxygen on the thing to complete it the way we want it to be. It's midnight and finally, it's done and yes, we will live with it. Because yes, it's the way we wanted it to turn out. On the high of that, we—*the young lions of the future in broadcasting*—are feeling our powers. At this moment, our talent possibilities are foregone conclusions. We're it.

No one is thinking that any one of us will fall by the wayside or get sidetracked to obscurity or get bogged down in life's challenges. We are it! The future.

Nothing stands between us and the brightest light of mighty success. Life is a cinch, a slam dunk, no problem, full speed ahead. Life couldn't possibly get in our way along the way.

Gill Nelson wants to teach me to compromise. I don't want to learn compromise; I want to learn triumph. There will be plenty of time in a whole lifetime to accept it how it is. Not now.

Since it is midnight and now officially my birthday, we go to our usual roadside inn where the proprietor stayed open for us, ready with hamburgers and schooners of beer for all, which I can now legally partake of except I happily don't like beer, so I choose not to have any.

As we toast one another and as they toast me, it's decided that they'll take up a collection from the change on the table to buy time on the local commercial radio station for a half hour in the morning at drive time to create a program—*The Viki King Hour* (even though it will be half an hour) and so they all go off to wonderful WINI Radio to produce the program. I, being twenty-one and not a beer drinker, go home to bed.

In the morning, I get a call to turn on the radio and there it is—*The Viki King Hour* (actually a half hour) with heavy use of the reverb.

My good friend Ron Barrett (we call him Bear) hosts the show in a proper golden-throated radio announcer voice. There are personal testimonials and group singing and sound excerpts from the TV show we just did, and splices from my kids' show that I air on the college station. My broadcast family of friends "gifting" me with their accolades and individual brilliance. It is very funny, very urban, and now broadcasting live over the airways of WINI Radio, a farm station in our college town. And here's what happens: The station switchboard floods with more calls than they have ever received! Here we are, *the young lions of the future of broadcasting,* while WINI broadcasts out to the farmland. (Not the demographic for witty and urban repartee of near-genius proportions.)

In the farmland *The Viki King Hour* (actually a half hour) has preempted the hog report! The listeners are outraged. I am in awe at this young age to be having an impact. I'm twenty-one and already I've preempted the hog report. What a great start to my twenty-first year. This is promising to be a great life. ~

22 Years Old

Hello, Hollywood. I've Come to Introduce Myself

I ASKED DREW Winkelmeyer, the dean of the communication broadcast department at my college, to write a letter of introduction for me that explains my capabilities and accomplishments, then I sent copies of the letter to four hundred production studios and moguls and independent producers and directors and every address I could find in Hollywood, and I asked for meetings with them for this summer before I graduate next year. The idea is for me to meet and learn about Hollywood and hopefully have a job waiting for me once I graduate and move out there next year. That is my plan.

The letter paid off even better than I hoped. I have many astonishing appointments to see moguls and directors and writers and whoever would talk to me about the amorphous being of Hollywood.

I didn't ask for a job directly; I asked to come and meet them and learn and maybe that's why they consented to see me. There are so many responses, I hardly have time to rush around and see them all on my two-week fact-finding mission in Hollywood this summer before graduation and moving there next year.

What Is a Clapper Loader?

A lovely and gracious high-powered gentleman executive from the "Black Tower" at the studios responded to my request with an invitation to tour Universal Studios with him. He is from the top floor corner office. Maybe his Hollywood climb started like mine with a heartfelt letter of request to be invited in, maybe he just wants to enjoy my audacity to remind him of himself when he was my age. He meets me, for our appointment, in the grand and echoing reception area of the administration building. This is where the business of show business takes place. I know that's not where my platform is.

Mr. Chancellor and I are immediately whisked off in a golf cart, and we're taken directly to a sound stage where there is a major feature film being shot. Just being in this atmosphere, I soak up so much knowledge. Here's where the show of show business gets created, and this is more the world I have in mind for myself. I see the value of being here. I see that the act of my being here will get me here.

We're not even five minutes onto the sound stage, and I decide that I must have any job in the business for next year when I move here. Eighty percent of success is showing up, the other twenty percent is what you decide to do with it once you're here. I know that being here will take me to where I'm going.

So here I am at my beginning with this man who is at his pinnacle. This is my time to ask all the questions. When you're in your novice stage, people love to be around you because they can help. They know things that they can impart to you. They give you unsolicited advice. You hear something in their manner, how they are with others, what about them got them here from there. I'm so appreciative. It's a glorious exchange.

This happens to be a closed set (Mr. Chancellor must be very powerful because a closed set means visitors are not allowed). They are shooting a love scene between a movie star and a leading lady for a high-budget picture. Universal is a big operation. This movie will have to bring in many millions just to keep the lights on and the guard at the gate. That's the business part of show business.

I won't mention here who the Hollywood heartthrob movie star is, or his leading lady, because, well . . . it's a closed set, and besides, I'm going to tell you something about him that might not flatter him.

As Mr. Chancellor and I are standing at the edge of the set, the movie star, who has just had his shirtless chest freshly dabbed with makeup, comes over to talk to us. Although there is all the sound stage as room to stand, he bumps up against me several times.

I say, "Oh sorry." And then I step away from him and then he bumps me again while I'm asking about the gaffing and noticing all the setup decisions that the director is making.

Finally, he's called back to the love scene, under the covers, with the leading lady.

While this is going on, I'm looking at the call sheet and notice a lot of the crew is called for 5:00 a.m. Here's another aspect of show business to know about. Also, on the call sheet is a call time for the second AC clapper loader. I ask Mr. Chancellor, "What is a second AC clapper loader?"

Since he doesn't know, he moves heaven and Earth and all the crew to find out. I notice that he has a lot of power on the set, and yet he handles it with grace. Everyone seems to fall all over themselves to get him his answer. We are two ends of the bookend—me just starting and he at the top of the food chain. In between is where I'm going and where he came from.

A clapper loader, in case you don't know like I didn't, is the person who claps the clapboard. You know, the little handheld blackboard with a hinged clapper arm on the top. The clapper loader writes the movie title in chalk on the board and keeps track of what take it is, and then he says, "*Star Light,* Scene 42, Take 2, then he claps the slate and the arm together to make a sound. The purpose of this is to identify the scene and then sync the sound and the picture together.

When we're back in the golf cart, Mr. Chancellor says to me, "You're going to do just fine in this town."

I say, "You think so? Why is that?"

He says, "A sex symbol movie star just strutted half-naked in front of you, *trying to seduce you,* and you were utterly unfazed."

Oh, I see—just keep your sound and your picture in sync. I can do that. ~

23 Years Old

Fourth of July, Union Station

HERE I AM arriving at Union Station in downtown Los Angeles on the Fourth of July. Hello, I've come to set the world on fire.

I didn't realize until I arrived that I have come on the same train as I got off at Union Station when I was eight years old, when my mother left my father. On that trip, on that train, we were putting distance between ourselves and our dad. We didn't know what was ahead of us. We didn't know where we were going to live or what was going to happen. It's remarkable how patterns repeat themselves. It's Independence Day—I get to choose my own way from here.

No one will be calling my name over the PA system this time. I know no one in Hollywood. And Hollywood doesn't know or care that I've come with what I want to contribute.

Last year when I came to Los Angeles to meet with anybody and everybody about Hollywood, I hoped that when I moved here now, I'd be coming to a job.

Well, that *did* happen. I did get two job offers. I took both. One is permanent; the other one is for a single project. The permanent one is as an assistant to the producer at a small production company in a bungalow adjacent to the Paramount lot. I start next week. The other is at the end of the month, and somehow I'll figure out how to do them together. That leaves the rest of this week to find an apartment close to everything, get settled, and be ready. I'll get a car when the paychecks come in on a steady basis and I can build up some cash.

I step out onto the street at Union Station. I've grabbed a box of Union Pacific matches. I want to strike a match, make a wish, and blow it out in the direction of Hollywood and the ocean beyond.

I am so far from the ocean that many people I ask for directions don't even know where the ocean is. I am that far away. Maybe if any of us knew how far we were from where we thought we were going, we just wouldn't go there. And yet it is the Fourth of July of my life, the perfect day of independence to begin getting from here to being there. It's my life to create any which way I can.

Here's the challenge: What will it take to get there from here? I have what I have to offer. It's up to me to make my way in this new world. I always take as my protocol Archimedes' great quote: "A place to stand and a lever long enough and I can lift the world." I'm twenty-three, and my heart's desire is to use my good talents to lift the world.

If I jump, will I catch me? I'm about to find out.

The Wish

I take the Union Pacific book of matches out of my pocket and make my own private Fourth of July fireworks—I strike a match and make my wish: "Hello, World. Welcome to my contribution to you. It's what I now put my heart into." In the best Humphrey-Bogart-Lauren-Bacall-*To-Have-and-Have-Not* Hollywood tradition, I put my lips together and blow. ~

24 Years Old

Digesting the Power Lunch

THE ACT OF becoming myself is not very becoming. It feels like whole parts of me are waiting in line to start living. No one is asking for my unique contribution. I think this is what you get the Oscar for—do the very best service as a waiter when serving the buffalo wings; be the very height of impeccability; receive minimum wage on a junk job for rent money. Eventually, your turn comes—or does it? Here's my mantra for this month: If I Can Find Out the Game, Maybe I Can Win It.

Let me catch you up. If you recall last summer when I came out to Hollywood to tour the studios, I did get two job offers that I accepted. One was with a questionable producer of independent films. I worked there for three weeks. Every time the phone rang, he ran out of the office saying, "I'm not here." All the calls were from people he owed money to. I figured I didn't have job security.

The other offer I got was from a wonderful fine art animator who recognized my talent from my children's show, *Warm World of Wumpas,* that I had on PBS while getting my degree in broadcasting. He valued my work. The whole creative team was like a great family, but when the shoot was over the job was over. I'm beginning to get the picture of how Hollywood functions. The actual steady job in Hollywood is the job of getting a job. Meanwhile, I have been meeting a lot of writers, directors, actors, and producers on all the studio lots and locations as I peddle my projects and they peddle theirs. At one point, during yet another industry-wide strike, I delivered telephone books door-to-door. I thought I had hit the bottom of the hiring pool until I saw a producer I had just pitched to last week, who was now hauling his own quota of phone books to deliver.

What was all this about? The best and the brightest come to Hollywood to make something useful of their talents, and it seems to be a place that disregards you until you're famous, then you are revered. Neither response has anything to do with your true worth.

My ever-flexing strategy for this week is this: Do what needs doing to keep myself going and get my dream gotten.

The other day I had lunch at a trendy Hollywood eatery by invitation of a head of the studio. This was one of the executives I met last year on my fact-finding trip out here. He was at a different studio last year. Apparently, everybody moves around from studio to studio and project to project, and you form your alliances with people not with companies. We were having a "power lunch" talking about a "go project." The waiter was very attentive, and then I realized that he wasn't attentive as a waiter, he was attentive as an out-of-work actor wanting to get the attention of the head of the studio, whom I noticed paid no attention to him. We finished our lunch. The head of the studio paid with his expense account. We were in the parking lot in line for our valet cars and the waiter ran out and shouted at the head of the studio for allegedly giving him a dismal tip, and the head of the studio shouted back at him, "You'll never work in this town again." I wondered if he meant as a waiter or as an actor.

Meanwhile, our "power lunch" didn't materialize into a job for me either. Apparently, the head of the studio was replaced, and now he also will never work in this town again, unless maybe as a waiter. Welcome to Hollywood. ~

24 Years Also

Lifetime Guarantee

I DID GET a car because Los Angeles is the car capital of the world. You can't do business without one. I didn't get a Hollywood car such as a Ferrari or Bentley. I got a car that gets me from here to there and eventually to the next car. Meanwhile, the car that I got knows to follow signs to yard sales, which today is a charming nineteen-twenties bungalow. I pull over and park.

I discover that neighbors are selling everything for Ms. Evelyn, a ninety-two-year-old lady who is now in a nursing home. She won't be coming back. All her possessions are out here on the lawn. Her husband and family are all deceased; there's no next of kin, no grandkids—no one. She was the last of the family. Now it's the neighbors who are helping to clear her house and finish her life on this street.

I've always loved to get a tool at a yard sale. I can feel the patina on the handle of a good sturdy screwdriver as I imagine all the clockwise and counterclockwise twists on its barrel. It's always the owners' dearest and trustiest tool—the one always reached for. Those are the ones that I always reach for at yard sales.

As I look through Ms. Evelyn's things, a butterfly lights on this and that of her possessions. What can you tell about a lady's life? I wonder about her joys and accomplishments. Everyone puts into the world, and everyone receives back from the world. What was the put-in and take-out for her? How is she feeling about being at the nursing home while all her things are spread all over the ground for strangers to pick through? Does she even know or care?

The butterfly now lights on a pile of her kitchen gadgets. I'm going to assume, because of them, that Ms. Evelyn loved to cook. Oh, here it is. This is what I choose—a small paring knife with its wood handle a little bit split. There is definitely time-in on this knife. I think every meal started with this in her hand.

It's a Henckels; that's a brand that is known to have a lifetime guarantee and now her lifetime is coming to its close. With Henckels, you can show up at the store with your old knife, and they'll replace it. Ms. Evelyn could have easily returned it for a new one, but she didn't. She must have loved it just this way—with this split in the wooden handle. And now, I love it just this way too.

In all my ambition in my twenties, I'm not thinking yet about being ninety-two. I haven't thought of how my dying will go. Currently, I'm so grateful to be at the other end, the starting end; the part where I'm full of life and possibilities and eager to serve and contribute. If all goes well on this end of my life, that end of my life will take care of itself.

The butterfly lands on a book about a mountain hiker. In the photo, on the cover, the hiker shows such joy, such sure-footedness in his first confident steps onto the mountain. You know just by looking at him that he will have a successful climb.

I feel surefooted in my first steps out in the world. There's a me that is already so alive, and I have the task and the privilege to bring more of me to life.

This lady—did she know to make a fulfilling life for herself? As she is ending at ninety-two, I wish for her to be gratified for having lived her life, and now I'll make my way and wish to be gratified for having lived mine.

As I get back into my car and drive away from the yard sale, I'm happy to give witness to Ms. Evelyn's life.

As the butterfly flutters its wings in the yard, it affects the cosmos. Ms. Evelyn lived and put her flutter into the world. As I turn down the street, I give myself a lifetime guarantee that I'll put my flutter into the world too. ~

25 Years Old

Intrusion

IT WAS A police lineup. I was asked to come and identify the intruder who had broken into my house last Sunday night.

I wasn't the only woman asked here. Apparently, this was a serial rapist and we young women here now have in common a slight body type, same age range, same color hair. So, for him, we were all the same.

No one was really identifying him easily. They must have all been blindfolded too.

The lineup was not easy on the others. They were not faring well. They all had their entourage of family and friends, and a deep abyss hung over each group. I hadn't been happy about the whole ordeal, but why was I doing better? Was I doing better? Did I forget to be mortified, or did I just choose not to be victimized?

Just now I am in awe of being alive. Amazed at the experience of being narrowly close to dead, instead I'm feeling the phenomena of my life that still belongs to me to have.

If you're ever lucky enough to almost die, you know that feeling of euphoria at being alive. You feel the miracle—or you don't. That's what seems to be going on for the others here at the lineup.

I'm brimful, walking in gratitude. I was proud of how I had conducted myself. I was there for myself. I wasn't going to be knocked off my track. Maybe that's what the others are feeling, knocked off their track. Where am I when I need myself the most? I was there for me. I did not give myself up.

Now I understand a corny thing I said just after it happened, and friends asked if I was going to be all right. I said, "Winter has its birthday," meaning that there's always great benefit in bad occurrences. I'm just beginning to reap the gifts in this.

Meanwhile, people have their own reactions to the news.

My landlord said, "Why didn't you hit him with a golf club?"

I said, "Because the stores were closed."

If it hasn't happened to you, you don't know how it could happen.

Such as, "Why didn't you get away? Why didn't you kill him?" This is from a friend of mine who has been going to karate class hoping for a mugger so she can try out her new skills. She has no idea.

I could see that my family was on the lookout, watching me for long-term effects. As far as I know, so far, the experience did not diminish me; it deepened me. I feel that I was shaken, but not stirred.

That night I was in the kitchen making midnight pancakes, dancing to music I had on. It was a pretty noisy night of thunder and pouring rain, so I wasn't sure what that sound was that I thought I heard. I came through the kitchen door with my tray of power cakes and syrup and blueberries and a lit candle ready to enjoy, when BAM!—he grabbed me from behind and had me in a power hold before my pancakes hit the floor.

He was experienced at this. His tactics of surprise and leverage seemed military to me. This is what soldiers do in hand-to-hand combat.

My first instinct was rather than resist to lean into the force so that would disarm it, but he had tactics to combat that too, so I went all out in a full-on fight. I used my best authority voice, "Get out of my house. You weren't invited."

I don't like violence. I don't even like loud noises. But apparently, when push comes to shove, I'm going to push and shove back. More than push and shove. I decided pretty much immediately that "You will not behave in this manner. I will not relinquish."

It's so easy to be killed. I know that because he pushed his thumb into my windpipe until I was a centimeter away from blacking out. He did it repeatedly. Is this all it takes? A kink in the garden hose and you're cut off and life is over? There's a bone at the base of your throat; if you rest your thumb there and exert even the slightest pressure, you can feel the ease with which your whole life force could be cut off.

So, I had to think of something: If I could get us across the room, my television is on a tall pedestal—maybe I could get it pulled down on him. We twisted and lurched over there. I heaved my torso forward against the TV to get it to topple onto him—and hooray!—it did. The impact of it falling and crashing made for more violence in the room, but I was learning quickly to match his force with any of my own that I could possibly muster. I felt blood trickle down my back. I didn't know if I was cut from his knife or if he was cut by the television crashing. It didn't seem to stop either one of us.

He clearly had the upper hand in physical strength. No doubt this was someone who could bench press a hundred without breaking a sweat.

As I gasped for air, any ability to scream was cut off. I didn't know if it was the frequent strangulation or the knife that he now pressed hard against my vocal cords, but I discovered that I couldn't scream or shout for the neighbors. It was clear to me that no one was going to hear and come with help. It was up to me to save my own life.

He knew exactly how long, with how much pressure, to yank my arm behind my back before he could let it go and it wouldn't, couldn't move—unable to help me defend myself no matter how valiantly I commanded it to move.

I *did* feel that miracle strength a mother feels to lift a car off her toddler. I knew it was my life force fighting for me. I also knew that fighting was just going to tire me out; it wasn't going to stop him. I needed smarter, more efficient strategies.

What did I have to fight with that would out-strengthen his physical strength? I already was using triple sets of rapid-fire words to unnerve him.

In my best stern, booming voice, when I wasn't being choked or gasping to get air in, I said, "Leave now! Run!"

Now, what else could I come up with to leverage?

I knew that when a car comes down my street at a certain speed, in the rain, it sounds just like it's driving right into my driveway. That night it was certainly raining. Between bouts of strangulation when I *could* get air in, I set up a warning to him. "Someone is coming any minute. You're going to get caught. You better run. Run now."

At one point he said, "Stop this psychological warfare." This was encouraging so I continued.

And then as I was kicking and scratching, I used a scolding voice. "I didn't come all the way to Hollywood for this! Get out of my house Mister Green Beret Smarty-pants." I don't know where that came from, but it seemed to be so off-topic that it actually unnerved him.

~~~

For a moment back here at the lineup, they are asking me to approach him. The other young women cannot, will not.

He looks so frightened, so . . . caught. He is in army fatigues. I remember him saying, "Stop this psychological warfare." What is that war within him? What atrocities had befallen him in his life to compel him to spend his time in this manner?

~~~

Claps of thunder continued outside. I was utterly end-time exhausted. All my afterburners were burned with all my might, which continued to spark my brain but could not summon any more force from my body. My arm dangled unable to move, but ha-ha, he must have thought I was right-handed. Now I did everything I could to use my left hand for precision pinching and pulling and poking. I was down to specific, small assaults. A hairpin fell out of my hair. I caught it and hoped to use it to do lethal damage, and I continued to threaten him (that's funny, I threatened him).

And then we had come to that moment he was awaiting. Finally, the moment when my energy was expended. My mind still strategizing, ever fighting yet now unable to will my body into any strength. Still doing everything I could do to deter him. Just when he thought he was about to get to do what he came to do, just then, in the rain, a car came down the street at the perfect speed and sounded just like it was turning into my driveway, and once more I boomed, "Run. Now." And he did.

~~~

And P.S. This is the part of the story that makes me cry.

When my brother heard what happened, he built an ingenious homemade alarm system, got on an airplane, and came and installed it in my house. He made the buzzer so loud that if it ever went off, I think he would be able to hear it at his house three thousand miles away.

This was his fear for me, his protection of me, and his love. This was because when I was three and he was five, and I needed him to help keep Dad from me, what could he do? He was five. What he could do is be here now, and he is.

You can always find the miracle that is delivered in the startling package. Life events always come to expand us. ~

26 Years Old

Ooh, He's a Man

Dear Cupid,

I guess I forgot to say, don't bring me love right now. I've got to have a good job first. Don't aim your arrow at me. I'm not a target for love today. I'm not looking for love because I have my work to do. I'm on the verge of a delicate balance between junk jobs and time ticking until next month's rent is due. I am wrestling my genius to hurry up and bloom so I can make it before the bills catch up to me. So please get the message, I am not a love candidate. If Jesus himself wanted a date with me, I would reject him because he was wearing Birkenstocks.

See this neon sign I wear: Closed until further notice. I need to be let alone to become myself. I'll tell you when I'll be worthy to receive the Arrow of Cupid. Once I'm in my full capacities then you can come calling.

But no, you couldn't wait. You had to drop in front of me while I was in an earnest sprint to where I was going. You couldn't wait for me to do it myself. You had to send him. You had to have him come in and mix with my methods and derail and prevail and include himself in my forward movement. At least that's what I'm thinking love means—a distraction from focus.

Not now, please. I'm on my way through the rigors of personal challenge. Let me get to that then bring love. Thank you very much.

Signed,

Me.

Well, that sounds clear to me, but here's what happened:

There was a birthday party. All the revelers somehow managed to come and then go before the party got going. It was a birthday party for a one-year-old but there weren't any other kids at the party. The birthday boy's mom invited one hundred people from show business. It was an adult party for a kid. Maybe everybody was confused about that so that's why they left early. The only ones remaining were about seven or eight friends and immediate family and me, while I consoled the one-year-old's mom. She was crying because the party was a flop. The one-year-old, Toby, didn't care. He was happily chewing on the cardboard box that his rocking horse came in.

Jillian, the mom, grew up around adults in show business so those are the ones she invited for her son. But as far as I know, Toby is not yet in show business.

Jillian is inconsolable, so I stop consoling her and head out the door. As I'm about to walk out, the doorbell rings, and in walks . . . *him*. The first thought I have is, Oh, he's a man. My immediate next thought is, Oh, he's . . . *my* man.

I back up, sit down on the floor, and take my shoes off! Apparently, I am staying.

Here is a lovely individual coming into a stranger's house (invited by a partygoer who had already left). There were just a few people still here, including the mom, the child crawling around, and me—the mystery person sitting invisibly at the edge of the goings-on. Uncharacteristically, I did not say a word.

Within moments the caterer has gotten him a plate of food, which he now balances on one knee as the birthday toddler is being bounced in great glee on his other knee, while he simultaneously entertains the rest of us with his genuine presence and sheer light of life. Jillian is now aglow that her birthday party is a great success. I still haven't said a word. Can you imagine—me? Not a word. We all knew something was up with that.

He came into an awkward situation, but he doesn't seem to be bothered. He handles it beautifully and comfortably and elegantly. I see everyone in the room being changed by him. They all visibly go up a notch because of his presence. I see the power of it. A light comes out of him, naturally.

We learn that he has just come over directly from the taping of a show at CBS. He's a musician—saxophone, flute, clarinet, and piccolo.

Jillian jumps up and finds one of his records in her collection and plays it for all of us to hear. We all recognize his talent. Jillian is trying to think of the word virtuoso, but she can't think of it, so I say, "World-class."

He says, "That's the first thing you've said."

I say back, "Ahh." And then an actual electrical spark ignites between us across the room.

Everyone notices.

Hmm. Gracious, confident, wise, caring, powerful, gentle, talented, accomplished, grounded, sincere, relaxed, a leader. Did I mention handsome?

Then I remember where I have seen him before. In my art class ten years ago in high school, for my art teacher, Bert Amherst, I painted a musician playing saxophone with the flute, piccolo, and clarinet on a music stand in the picture. I had painted *him* right down to the color of the shirt he is wearing tonight. That painting was the one that won my art scholarship at the art institute and went on with my other work to the Louvre in Paris, and now here is the man himself that I had conjured up ten years ago in my painting. This is the gods' way of saying, "Yo, pay attention here."

I feel a shift in my heart that I am about to drop through to more love than I know, and I'll be getting to find out.

Yet being me, I just went home. I don't think he even caught my name.

A week later I get a call from Jillian. "Guess who's here! He wonders where you are, and who you are. He thought you lived here." (Probably because I took off my shoes.) "He came looking for you. Come over right away."

I've just washed my hair. I'm in my pajamas. I'm ready for an evening working on this book. Instead, I surprise myself as I leap up. *Something in us has arranged an appointment with one another for important life purposes.* All I have to do is get in the car and go there. All I have to do is manage my mindful resistance and *get in the car and go*. I throw on clothes and run out to the car, my wet hair will have to dry in the breeze with the windows down. It's far to get to Jillian's house, but I don't seem to care. I *have to* get there.

So, here's the conversation I have with myself as I wade through red lights and traffic and thrillingly speed through green lights and clear lanes.

Me: "Look at yourself. What's going on here? You know you're not casual about love. You know you're not a jump-in-with-both-feet-just-for-the-heck-of-it-type-of-person."

Myself: "Here in the car with mad abandon does not mean I'm rushing every which way into something random. This is a love for a lifetime. We will slow dance this into being."

Me: "Did you just say *love for a lifetime*?"

Myself: "Even though I didn't want it now, I didn't ask for it, I wasn't looking for it—here it is."

It's not how I thought love would appear. I thought that when I was ready, I would present myself as a full-out, fully loaded, full-throttle package in my own good time. Of course, love is what *gets* you fully loaded. You can't really *get anyplace* without including love, and so it must have been on my to-do list all along, but I wasn't noticing while I was busy perfecting the other parts of my equation.

And so, without looking for it, without seeking it, without thinking about it—as it was the furthest thing from my plan—he walked in, and I knew immediately. I'll have to make room in myself for such a sudden open heart as this.

I pull into Jillian's driveway. All the lights come on. My hair has dried perfectly. I ascend the stairs and ring the bell.

Me to Me: "I haven't longed to have anyone, and here it has come to me. My heart knows this. If I'm smart, I'll know it too and be willing to accept the gift." ~

27 Years Old

The Tonight Show

It's REMARKABLE THAt love has come to me so easily and elegantly.

Now I need to get a job so I can stop working so hard.

And just now there happens to be a writers' strike. Not only am I out of a job I couldn't get, I'm also out of a job that no one can have while the strike is on. I need to make a lateral move quickly and put my technical skills back to work. (If you remember, I'm well-taught in all things broadcasting from my college days. I even worked my way through several years of school as master control director for my local college TV station.) I'm not a techie at heart, but I do enjoy eating and paying my rent on a regular basis. I called on a summer relief position at NBC in the production department as studio engineer. Surprise, surprise, just when I called, they needed a swing person experienced and proficient on audio, camera (TK60s), and general cable-kicking. I can do all of that!

God love Reba Martinelli in personnel, I was the first and only female hired on for the summer to replace the permanent crew who would be taking much-needed time off.

Within days I was crewing on the news, the soap operas, the game shows, the sitcoms, all the one-hour musical specials, and then my continual position on *The Tonight Show*.

Why is it that this impossible-to-get-dream-job for anybody else came to me? I think because the shortest distance between where you are and where you want to be is always a path you wouldn't think to take yourself. It's certainly worked for me acquiring my Beloved, and now the life gift keeps giving along the Hollywood track.

Also, I know this: If an easy step comes, take it because that helps you to keep going through all the hard parts. You just need to have whatever helps along the way, whatever is going to give you the boost up.

I'll talk to you about it later. Right now, we're live. "Heeeerrre's Johnny!"

Just because this opportunity came easily to me, my position did not come easily to my coworkers on the show. I know that there is hazing for the new crew member on the team. You have to run the gauntlet, so everybody knows you have the right stuff—it's part of the job. When the new crew member is the lone female joining the group, there tends to be an extra flavor to the hazing.

On my first day on *The Tonight Show*, I was on the boom. The boom is a very precarious piece of studio equipment. It's a six-foot-high platform on huge air tires. The boom operator stands way up there and hangs on for dear life to the one post that comes up the center. On that center post is attached a fifteen-foot arm with the mic at the end of the arm. The whole thing is far beyond wobbly. It's designed for quietly picking up audio, not for the secure and grounded feeling for the boom operator. If I ever fall off, I suppose in the tradition of being a good audio person, I'll have to do it silently and try to land with a thud rather than a crash. It's my job on this first day to climb up on this thing, stand there and point the mic, and pick up the scintillating conversation of whoever the current celebrity guest is. Meanwhile, not allowing a shadow to be cast upon their famous face or, God forbid, let the boom get in the shot. So that's the job on that equipment, and here's what happened that first day:

It was a precious few minutes to airtime.

One of the principals of the show had just spotted that I was a new member of the crew. He stomped over to my boom while I was on it and shook the platform with vigor, with fury—doggedly. I was knocked all around as I grabbed the boom arm which was now flailing about narrowly missing the lighting grid. I grabbed the center post to keep from falling six feet down to the cement floor. As he gripped the platform with both hands and shook it hard, he said, "What are you doing up there? You should be in the kitchen barefoot and pregnant."

In front of the all-male band and all-male tech crew, this was supposed to be a funny joke on his part, but there was dogma in his dogged moves.

I managed to extend my foot, which reached his fingers, and I stepped down hard and said, "Thank you for sharing." Also said, on my part, as a funny joke.

While all the crew was intensely looking on, they now all quickly dispersed, pretending that there was nothing to notice, but not before we all knew that, yes, hazing would go on but, yes, I would push back.

And yes, the hazing did go on. There were many incorrect directives. I was to rush to the supply dock and bring back an AW6240 which is actually a huge eight-by-eight-foot speaker that must be driven into the studio with the crane when what was actually needed was an A63 which is a small lavalier mic. When I got back to the studio with the mic, they were all sitting there expecting me to show up with the crane, so they could think it was so funny.

I didn't catch these anomalies because I'm an eagle-eyed engineer, I caught them because I'm an eagle-eyed intuitive. It wasn't hard to figure out their hazing strategies. The boys loved their shenanigans. I knew eventually it would, pardon the expression, "peter out."

One day Bilge Bittermen came to me bearing gifts. Bilge was the lighting director known to all as the Prince of Darkness. He had the best gruffed-up face you'd ever see, a cross between Popeye and a front-end car collision. He was crabby to all, and he and I got along great. I noticed him looking out for me; only don't tell him I noticed.

One day before call time I saw he had gotten into the electrical supply cabinet and was creating something. He groused and threw things and swore and talked to himself out loud. Whatever he was up to was something important.

Well, it was a gift—for me. It was a plug, attached to an adaptor, attached to an extender, connected to a toggle switch, attached to a socket with a blue bulb screwed into it. Plug it into the wall socket, flip the switch, and the blue light comes on. I was thrilled. One of the very best gifts I have ever received.

I say, "So, Bilge, what's the occasion?"

Wondrously, he opened up to me about his life and told the story of when he started out in lighting. He was an apprentice on Broadway to the only woman lighting director in the business at the time, Etta Betterley. She endured a lot just to keep her job and was a damn good lighting director. He admired her and learned from her, and because of that original experience with a woman in the business he crossed over that attitude to me, the only other woman he knew in the business. I now got to bask in the blue-light glow of her abilities. Thank you, Etta Betterley, for paving the way.

And now I know the occasion of this gift to me. I know that my hazing is over, and I'm now accepted on the team. I ask Bilge what finally did it.

He says, "Remember on Friday when the boys rolled the two-ton crane over your foot?"

"Yes, I recall that," I say with irony.

He says, "Well, you didn't cry."

So that's it—don't cry.

Being a woman in this business means you take it like a man.

After Hazing

I know there's no crying for a woman in a man's job, and yet something interesting shifted in the crewmembers.

Now grown men who wouldn't trust me to figure-eight the cable began to come to me with their most personal concerns— such as getting along with their kids or how to talk to their wives. There was a lot of crying going on. It just wasn't me; it was them. Crew in Hollywood is known to work overtime and golden hours and sixth day and fast turnaround—many are divorced or on the verge of it. Others feel estranged from their kids, yet are making large sums of money, so they fear taking time off while work is coming in. Several have boats, some airplanes, and a few, private islands, with no time to enjoy them or their families.

Within a very short time after my being hazed, I became high counsel for all. I was Carnac on the set.

Between call time and sound check and airtime there were several hours of downtime when we were on call yet not yet on-air. That's when they would find me and discuss their problems. It started with the crew and then as guests on the show finished soundcheck and were not yet called for makeup or wardrobe, we'd sit in the empty studio and talk about the ins and outs of their fame. This is my favorite part of the job because it's not a part of the job at all, but here it is presenting itself to me as life work. I wasn't here to point the camera; I was here to have access to people that could benefit from access to me. These perfectly tender human beings would be before me in their deepest vulnerability, and then an hour later I would view them through the camera lens as they would be on-air across the country emitting their special light that we had just been polishing an hour before.

I thought this had been a lateral move for me just to wait out the writers' strike, but it was more than a blue-light gift to me. Life finds a way to meet you and show you what and where you can place your best service.

In My Blood

One day an out-of-town friend of my mother's came to visit and was desperate to have a private tour of the backstage of NBC. Gail had sore feet, so I got one of the golf carts and took her and my mother around the backlot. She was in tourist nirvana as familiar actors waved as we passed by.

Then I drove us onto *The Tonight Show* set. And she, with her sore feet, makes a beeline for the front row audience seat and sits herself in giddy joy as a super fan. This is not unusual, many "civilians" react this way in the company of star paraphernalia.

My mother and I give her a chance to enjoy her excitement. I lean on my camera and my mother, with natural ease, takes a seat, which happens to be the host's seat. She's sitting in Johnny Carson's chair. Oh, now I know why I am here with such natural ease. I am my mother's daughter.

If Gail had been my mother, I'd just make it to the first row of the audience as a fan.

It's a Wrap
As it happened for me—another strike. I was out of a job again, back pitching writing projects. Hooray for Hollywood. ~

28 Years Old

The Complaint

SOME OF MY writer friends have taken off with phenomenal meteoric success. They are on the writing staff of hit shows, doing great work and making money. It suits them. They are thriving. I'm happy for them.

They have all left their garret rentals in Venice Beach to buy oceanfront condos in the Marina and have left their cars they had to carry to get anywhere for the upgraded latest models with the sports package. They are all talented and deserve their new jobs on great shows. A perfect fit for each of them would not be a fit for me. I'm freelance, yet right now that means free as in not being paid.

Maybe I can look at *their* success and adjust something in what I'm doing so I get *my* success. I'm thinking of the Chinese proverb, "An archer shoots at the target not to hit the target but to be a better archer." Is that me? An archer shooting at the target just to be a better archer? Well, yes, better and better, I feel that.

Something will show up for me. My path is here somewhere very close, any day now. Meanwhile, I'm so happy for my friend Matt, in particular. He's off and running right into his future. He has a dog, a hearth, and a wingback chair and, at twenty-eight, he has taken up pipe smoking. He's proud of himself. He is doing and will continue to do very well. I see what he has is for *him*, not what I want for *me*. (Especially the part about the pipe.)

I know that what is not happening for me is what will take me to what *is* my destiny.

I'm grateful that I'm not Matt, who is at this minute at the studio with people he doesn't care for, working on a show he has no joy about. Those on the writing staff order in food from the finest restaurants because the producer won't let them leave the building until they finish the script.

Eating lobster thermidor at my desk at 3:00 a.m. while being sequestered until I write the best joke to rival my colleagues is not my idea of my dream coming true. But it suits "the boys"—the comedy writing teams of Matt and Don, Michael and Steven, and Robert and Joel. Even though they each could buy time on a Gulfstream G5 private jet, none of them could get out to fly away in it.

Meanwhile, I am wondering what and where the next avenue of revenue is for my rent this month. I'm happy not to be at the studio eating lobster takeout yet . . . where is my cash to buy groceries?

Call Here, Go There. See This One, Can't Get in to See That One

When I look at my journal for last year and the year before and the year before that, I see my heartbreakingly poignant pursuit of becoming—so much sincere working at it, devotion really, for so little response. I am happy I've built my skills. Now I need a little finesse to kick in. I need to regard my needs. I need a paycheck.

What can I do to give myself help with this thing?

When I got off the train on the Fourth of July how many years ago? I didn't know anyone in Hollywood. I didn't know how to proceed. I didn't know it couldn't be done, so I just plodded along. Now I have a Rolodex with hundreds of Hollywood acquaintances from several superstars to studio moguls to many Hollywood hopefuls and every stage and phase between. I have talented friends who are on excellent shows, and I've been in to see every producer on every show that's running. It's not that my material is rejected; it's that there are cancelations and reschedules and whole departments moving projects from here to there.

It's true that all my successful writer friends are males, me the only female. I only know a few other female writers seeking work in the business. Frankie won $25,000 on a game show, so she could go off to write her first novel. She is a very talented writer. Her first book showed great promise, good reviews, and little cash. It could soon be a major motion picture, but meanwhile she's a salesclerk in the purse department of Robinson's.

You can blame a lot on the nature of the times and the nature of Hollywood, yet what is the nature of me that is postponing my success?

Why do I have friends who have all succeeded, and yet they come to me for life advice and counsel on their writing?

Why am I the authority they turn to for wisdom on their Act II structure, or how to navigate around the difficult producer, or how to handle the pressure of fame and sudden money and old relatives who think they are entitled to their new money? Why do I have the easy answers to their problems and not the solutions to my own?

I'm not feeling that I want what my friends have. I *am* feeling that I want what I want. And what is that? To go as far as I can with what I've got. To dig deep into the mother lode and download it to the world, to be of service, to help, to illuminate, to give comfort by my offerings in insight and clarity. I'm aware that nowhere in that do I say, "Please, God, get me on the staff of a sitcom."

I came to Hollywood because it was where the best and the brightest have a platform on which to send out their beacon of light. One of my beacons of light is this book. This is my destiny. Maybe if I had a job on staff right now, my important-to-me-destiny would be derailed. Maybe this is all divinely timed and a great gift of correct and right circumstances. I know that the nature of miracles is that you don't see them while they're forming. You have to take it on faith and keep on building.

This Is What I Know

If you're looking for it to come at a certain time, it won't. It'll come when it wants to. Just keep going one step at a time. I think we all have the idea that we know how to get from here to there in the most direct path. But we don't. Life wants to show us the best way. We fight it, thinking we know better. We don't. Follow life; it will take you there.

Each of us has our own soul-led instructions, so here I am, like it or not, trusting and being true to them.

What Is the Key to "Making It"?

Who "makes it" and who doesn't, and what does "make it mean"? I think you can see it hovering around a person.

It's not hard work or perseverance or talent or being in the right place at the right time, although all those things factor in. I think the whole amorphous state of fame and fortune is your blueprint encoded in you.

Either it's got your name on it, or it hasn't, and even when it belongs to you, you still might have to climb uphill all the way to have it.

Yesterday, when I was at a taping of the hundredth pilot for a sitcom that I would be pitching, I met the stand-up comic who has the job of warming up the audience. It's a terrible job. The warm-up comedian is there to "train" the spectators to be a collective audience together and learn to laugh and applaud on cue. Most comedians would rather slit their wrists than take the job, but they do it because they need the money, and it is good exposure. This fellow today is going to "make it." There's that one-in-a-million spark coming out of him. His style is mocking, yet the audience is somehow in on the joke. They seem to love it. Be on the lookout for him, his name is Dave Letterman. (Another raw talent is Robin Williams—look for him too. I can give you a list. And here's another name, Cap Duckport, but you'll never hear about him. He's out-of-this-world brilliant—a natural wit that all the other comics admire—but he's never going to be known because he doesn't have that simple skill to get to the venue on time with his shoes on. He doesn't have that piece of genius.)

"Making It" Is Different for Each of Us

Since I'm not in demand right now, since no one cares about my contribution, I have the privacy and freedom to develop my writing, my life, and myself. I get to focus on all original material and no contracts, no network, no gun to my head except the one that I'm pointing at myself. The level I'm vibrating at just now is the richest, best life for me to be vibrating at. I am writing this book. This is the sacred job that I am in awe of having.

I feel a recurring survival struggle. If it's uphill, I'm going there. Matt doesn't have that kind of resilience in him. If the wind blows too strongly against him, he'll just go home and play video games.

If you hold an apple up to Matt and ask him what it is, he'll say, "An apple."

If you hold it up to me, I'll probably say "an ingredient that goes in a Waldorf salad," or "a prop in the Adam and Eve story." What if I just keep it simple? Can I keep it simple? Probably not. Letting it be *simple* is probably the hardest thing for me. When I am willing to let it happen simply, it will. Like Beloved. I stepped simply, and tenderly, and gloriously into our love, and it is continuing to be spectacular.

Meanwhile, I've always known that it's crazy making to compare the inside of yourself with the outside of someone else. We all have our very own destinies to follow. The life we have is the one that belongs to us, not somebody else.

And I also know that just because I can't pay the light bill doesn't mean I'm not the light.

~~~

Yesterday, Matt was finally able to get out, and we met for lunch. He ordered a baked potato to go with his à la carte entrée, and the waitress said it would be cheaper if he ordered the dinner so it wouldn't cost the extra two dollars for the potato. She was a mom-type trying to save the boy his money. She had no idea the boy could simply pay cash to buy the whole restaurant.

A Thirty-Eight Share

I know that Matt's current life is the one he wanted, and he's thriving even though he tells me that he wakes up in a sweat at night anxious for a thirty-eight share—that's a rating of how many viewers watched his show last night.

As far as I know, I'm not lusting after a thirty-eight share though I know that the ones on staff want that because it will give them a five-year run of episodes and syndication, which means they will have residuals in perpetuity. Umm, residuals in perpetuity, that would be useful, that appeals to me, but really, right now, if I could just have available cash to order a two-dollar potato. ~

29 Years Old

How I Learned to Be Intolerant to Tolerance

THIS MORNING, I had comatose for breakfast. I think Hollywood has become hazardous to my health. My usual get-up-and-go got up and went.

I'm hoping for energy enough to put my shoes on and get out the door. Today, just to get to my pitch meeting with my favorite producer, it's taking everything I've got to get in the car. Driving there, I notice in the middle of the intersection that I can't even steer the steering wheel to make the turn. How can I be a champion for humankind if I can't even get out of the intersection?

When I do get to the studio, the door is too heavy for me to open. I have to wait for someone to come by who is also going in.

Ever the professional, I do my pitch meeting fine although with less energy than usual. I pitch my favorite producer all his shows. He has five on the air at once. As usual, he says he's "bedazzled by my pitches," but alas, they already have all the stories I pitch in development from other writers.

I say, "The next time you call me, send the stories you want developed and I'll come in with those." I didn't know at the time that I had just promoted myself in the ranks of writers' status.

He knows me personally by now—all the times I've been in here. He notices that my body batteries are running low and asks his secretary to make an appointment for me to see his doctor.

I know clearly, in the spirit of never giving up, I have taken care of myself last.

So, okay, I'll go to the otherwise impossible-to-get doctor appointment. Apparently, you can't get in to see this guy unless you're referred by a five-times-top Hollywood producer. I'll show up at his office tomorrow. I hope I can steer the car.

The Glucose Tolerance Test

This is a big-deal Beverly Hills "Doctor to the Stars." This is going to be expensive—the guy's got Italian leather loafers on ... with tassels!

His nursing staff has instructed me to not eat anything overnight. I already feel "on empty" and now no food to fuel me—not exactly a move toward wellness.

He says he'll be doing the glucose tolerance test, and it will take six hours. WHAT!

It's a good thing I brought along my journal. There are entries in it I want to use in my next script.

I don't realize until we're well into this tolerance test that it means the good doctor has me drink a gooey syrup drink like Coca-Cola on steroids. Every half hour he'll take what seems like a gallon of blood. WHAT! I already know I can't eat sugar. I can get very sick from it. I already know I can't be hungry. I already know I could die of this doctor to the stars. My mind says, *Get up and get out of here and go have a hamburger*. Yet my body remains in the little cold room. I'm aware of using my last bits of brainpower to form a plan.

Each half hour he comes in, and each time I tell him that I need to eat so he doesn't have to complete the test because I already know I'm in some kind of insulin shock, so he can stop already. Each half hour he leaves the room, I'm thinking he's going to come back in with a catered lunch, but no, it's another half hour and then he looks for a new vein and splatters my blood all over my chic and adorable sample designer sundress bought for a fraction of retail. Let's please get to the part when I can eat.

As I read through my journal, it is so sunshine and positive through such big blows from the business happening left and right. Yet amid pictures of flowers and gold stars and happy images, I've written a thousand fortifying one-liners to rally myself along. I call them Inner Axioms. Here are just some from one page:

It takes a lot out of you, but there's a lot in you.

Do the impossible thing the possible way.

Have one idea that does work instead of one hundred ideas that don't.

Be light-hearted instead of heavy-handed.

I'll do what it takes; what does it take?

Keep going; it's here somewhere.

Life itself is Everest.

There must be a missing part I don't know about.

I've got the "keep-going" part. I've got the "be-true-to-your-soul" part. I'm not going to fall down the mountain. But . . . I must be missing something. How does the thing get gotten? Solution, resolution, landing—where's that part? I'm ready for that.

Oh, here's what I wanted to look up. It's an excerpt from a play I wrote about warriors soldiering on, but really, it could be about Hollywood.

> *You're in the trenches, with nerves of steel, and toughing it out. Suddenly you panic, and shout, 'We'll all be killed. We're going to die. This is insane.' And you're right. This will kill you; it is insane; you will die. You're dead right. But once you rant and rave, once you get out the terrible god-honest truth, once you know you're in the biggest trouble of your life . . . you get back in the trenches with nerves of steel and tough it out.*

Frankly, as I am ever the champion of my perpetual cycle of joyous becoming, I've hit the wall. At this tolerance test, it is time for me to be *intolerant* of taking care of myself last. It's time to say, "Enough is enough."

I want to get well of course, but this doesn't feel like the road to it. If an Archangel or someone high-ranking in the etheric field came in right now and says he's got a helicopter parked outside to take me directly to nirvana, I'm not sure I would have the oomph to get up and go. I would be in the frame of mind to say, "Can you guarantee me a roast beef sandwich . . . on rye . . . with a pickle . . . from Nate and Al's Deli . . . just up the street?"

If I keep tolerating, then all I'm going to get is more to tolerate. This has got to stop. To stop is where the power is. To stop is where the healing is. Yes, enough is enough.

Having examined the situation, I get up off the examination table—and leave.

I look around the posh offices to tell the good doctor that I'm leaving. I'm informed that he has gone to lunch at La Scala with one of his movie star patients.

I go down the elevator to the parking garage and hand my validated ticket to the attendant. As I wait for my car, I am feeling progressively not so good. There are band-aids all up and down my arms where veins were opened in "vain," and big splats of my blood are all over my now not-so-chic designer dress. I swing from shivering cold to dripping sweat.

It's a very long time before my car finally is coasted down the ramp. It won't start! Suddenly, the parking attendants can't speak English. Great.

So okay, maybe that's a good thing. I'll go walk down to La Scala myself and find food. I'll order their fabulous osso buco and a nice, chopped salad.

Just then the garage starts spinning, and I fall to the concrete ground, adding axle grease to my once chic designer dress as I gasp and writhe on the concrete. A man comes out of the elevator, sees me, and rushes to help me. He says to the parking attendant, "What's the matter with her?" and the attendant says (in perfect English), "Her car won't start."

Okay, so, comedy relief. There's nothing like a crisis to let you forget your troubles. ~

30s Passage

All Healing Happens

So, *WHAT HAS* to happen for *it* to happen? Are my plans keeping me from my results?

I know that I'm indomitable. If a thing is straight up the mountain, I'll go straight up the mountain. *Who* I am is all I need to be. What is mine *will* come to me. It just hasn't come yet.

So, what is this story that I'm sticking to? That I'll do it against all odds? There are no odds against me. I've got all the goodies to advance myself. Only me can stop me, so I need to stop me from stopping me.

I know that Hollywood is a metaphor. People come here to work out the brick wall in their lives. Everybody's got a brick wall whether you come to Hollywood or not. Your wall can be abandonment or insanity in the family or infertility or some terminal gruel. Everybody gets the privilege of standing in front of their own brick wall to find the way. Find *your* way to break the wall down. It's an inside wall, so you can find any outside obstacle in the whole world to play it out.

Hollywood is great for standing in as the inside wall. It looks insurmountable, unattainable, irresistible. You can look right at it. It's so clear. Now, what are you going to do about it?

I choose to heal that thing that stops me. Heal that and be free.

I swear to you, all healing happens. So, let's go. ~

30 Years Old

The Sledgehammer Approach to Success

TODAY, I'M ON a film crew on a location shoot at Santa Monica Pier. There are amusement park rides and carnival attractions here.

The He-Man Booth has captured the attention of many from our film crew. The object is to hit a strike pad with a sledgehammer so the clapper goes up and hits the bell. Along the way up the shaft, you can see the clapper rise to "weakling," "wimp," "need more muscle," "not quite, "almost," and then "champion."

All my fellow Hollywood crewmates try their muscle to hit the bell. The more they miss, the harder they try, and these are some hard "tryers." None of them have made it all the way to their jobs on this film set without huffing and puffing and blowing something down along the way to get here.

But alas, all are swinging the sledgehammer with all their might, yet few are getting the clapper to rise much higher than "wimp."

This puts me in mind of a quote I like from the ever-adorable comic actress, Teri Garr. She said about her rise in Hollywood, "I scratched and clawed my way to the middle."

Most on this crew are familiar with the scratch-and-claw nature of Hollywood. Some are even teamsters who have come to unload the trucks for today's shoot. All are using brute force on the sledgehammer.

Then it's my turn—I do just like all of them: I bring my biggest manly muscle down on it, and the clapper moves not even to "wimp" status.

The sledgehammer proprietor thinks this is funny. His son, who is maybe twelve, takes over the hammer and hits the bell before any of us see his technique. Ah, so it's not brute force, it's know-how. This is a lesson for life. I'm always up for that. I'm also always ready to apply a new skill I don't yet have.

I see that if I keep hitting it the same, I'll get the same result. How about doing it a different way? How about doing it the way that it works instead of the way that it doesn't work?

I lift the heavy mallet and let it use its own weight as I drop it right on the center of the strike pad.

Bammo! Shazam! The bell goes off, the prize is won. The prize is a new skill to now use in Hollywood. "Beyond Effort" does not mean effort more, it means effort*less*. ~

30 Years and 2 Months

The Climb, Part I

IF YOU'RE THIRTY and still aspiring, it's not a pretty picture.

This is supposed to be the spin-around year; whatever we were doing for the first 30 years now changes up. If we haven't already, now's the time to get a real job, get a mortgage, get a baby. Life is going on. Time's ticking. Bills must be paid.

I think I'm supposed to be *there* by now, living the dream that I have for myself, but *this* time is not yet *that* time. I'm very aware of pushing to be over *there* when I am over *here*. I'm not failing, it's just that I haven't yet succeeded.

So where am I—*who* am I at this auspicious age?

As I drive to yet another promising high-powered meeting wearing my white Armani suit bought at Consignment Couture at a fraction of retail, I know that I'm doing it the hard way. At thirty I've taken the longest road. Still striving, not yet arriving, others are on their track by now, or they don't have a track to be on.

Here's what I know: I'm committed. I'm in for the long haul. I'm not going to give up.

It's not happening. Everything I'm doing isn't getting what I'm wanting.

So . . . here's the third thing I know: I see the need for change to get better results. Change the methods. Get new skills. Rethink, regroup, and regenerate. It will be done! I will prevail! Now that's that! Let's get on with it!

CRASH!

A head-on car just jumped the centerline and hit me smack in the left front bumper.

My car and I are hurled through space and land on the side of the freeway locked in bumpers to the fellow who drunkenly caused it.

First the oncoming car and now as I gather my bearings, the oncoming man is shouting at me. I say, "Excuse me, *YOU* hit *ME*."

As I take down the name and license number . . . what? He doesn't have insurance. Why is it always the ones with no insurance who cause accidents that they then don't pay for?

He gets back in his car, and as it chokes and sputters away, he says, "You can't squeeze blood from a turnip." This must be the uninsured-motorist anthem.

Am I alright? My shoe heel is broken off and my pants are torn, but my leg is not broken. I think I'm all right. I'm not dead. I'm grateful to be not dead.

I realize that I won't be making it to my prestigious, high-powered studio meeting—the meeting to negotiate my major development deal, the meeting that was months in the making. Now what? They'll either miss me so much they'll want to give me a contract, or they won't miss me at all and it's the same old—be dazzling, be passed over. You see my point.

It's time to apply a new set of life skills.

If I can do it here on the road beside my crashed car, then I can do it for my greater good. As goes a small thing, so goes the big.

Here's what we're dealing with: the car is smashed on the side of the road.

I pick up the bumper and put it sticking out the back seat. I put the hazard lights on. I notice that I'm down here in a kind of slump in the road. I'll be able to get out, but while I'm here nobody can see me. The possibility of a good Samaritan stopping is negligible.

I'll walk the half mile to the emergency call box. *Cell phones haven't been invented yet.*

I'm wearing twenty-minute shoes; they are not made for walking on the freeway, especially since one of them has been totaled.

I have flip flops here in the trunk somewhere. Here. Good. Now roll up my formerly pristine white crepe Armani pants. Go for the call box.

Where are the police? Don't they regularly patrol the road and dispatch tow trucks? I hope Mr. Turnip doesn't hit or hurt anybody else.

Okay, I'm going half a mile down the narrow shoulder of the road with cars whizzing by. Maybe a miracle will show up on the way. It's come to this at thirty. Here, on my way to the call box, I find myself an Auto Club wannabe.

This is not a car crash; this is a metaphor—someone has drunkenly banged into me. I am not to take blame, shame, or punishment for it. And I'm not going to get anything out of squeezing a turnip.

This is the conversation I am having with myself as traffic whizzes by—am I asking too much of myself? Am I the one that is taking me through too much? What happens if I don't do that anymore? Am I the one who is stopping more life from happening? Do I realize my power? What's going on here? So much effort, so little to show for it. I better be careful, it's not too late to die young. At this rate, I'll burn up before I get to the finish line. I better pace myself to get what I came here to do done.

Oh no. There's no phone in the call box. It's been vandalized.

Fine! Fine! I'll do this myself.

Now that I'm walking back to my car, it looks pretty bad from here. Its vital juices are trickling out the side. Hang in there, my dear, indestructible, ever-reliable workhorse of a car. We've still got to get me there.

Let's see. If I bend the fender back to its rightful position . . . Well, at least it doesn't look like there's frame damage. The wheel is completely crumpled, and the tire . . . that's a very flat tire. Okay, I'll fix the flat. First, I'll change my Armani for something comfortable from the Goodwill bag in my trunk.

It's getting dark and windy. And the jack is rusty and the car warbles on its pivot as cars whip along. This is not my idea of the ideal life experience. I am never letting this in my life again. And while I'm at it, no more struggle around getting work either. I make the unilateral decision now—*below this line I will not go*. (Notice I underlined it.)

Oh no, tight lug nuts. Am I a tight lug nut? I lay on them with all my might and then more. And finally, it's done—the tire holds, the wheel turns, the engine starts, and there on the asphalt is a plastic fork. Of course, fork-in-the-road. This is a choice point, and I choose. I now go from willing to do anything to now I am willing to do what it takes. Nothing more, nothing else. I now go the shortest distance from where I am to whom I will become. I now move out of surviving to thrive.

I clasp the rusty jack as a baton, a scepter, a diploma, and fling it high into the ice plant alongside the roadway. I drive off, triumphant, clunking and skittering but nonetheless, I'm on my way on the road not yet taken.

All things considered, it's a very good day in the life of becoming myself. ~

30 Years and 4 Months

The Climb, Part II

I HAVE TO look at what is developing while what I am going for is just out of reach. Something is getting stronger from the Climb. I hope.

I wasn't getting the writing jobs that my friends were getting, yet they'd come to me for counsel on their work and their lives now that it happened for them. On *The Tonight Show,* as I was crew, I was also developing a reputation for wise counsel. A celebrity—extremely successful—said that she booked guesting on the show just so she can talk to me. I gave her my phone number to book time directly so she wouldn't have to come on the show to talk to me. She was the first one that I charged for my services.

Something was developing when something that wasn't . . . wasn't. Or was it?

One thing I know about life on Earth. It works. It's designed to work—just follow the current of the river. Where we get into trouble is if we think we have to navigate upstream, push against it all, and fight it. No. We don't have to, so don't do that.

Instead of looking at the door that won't open for me, I look at what is wide open and inviting me in. I am excellent counsel for hundreds of people who are influential in the world. My reason for wanting to write was to be a help to people, and I'm here in Hollywood to get really good at writing, to get the very best writer's chops I could, and I am doing that and that is working too. ~

30 Years and 6 Months

The Climb, Part III

IF A PERSON shows promise—now, the promise has to be delivered, or you start to rot on the vine—Hollywood and Vine.

If there are any questions to ask to get good at something, any mentors to be had, any novice state to experience, I better get to it and get over it by now.

The whole concept of apprenticeship is to put ten thousand hours in on a skill. When you have time in then you have the experience, you are saturated, you have become the thing, and you act instinctually. You are it. Ten thousand hours. Yes, that's about right—fifteen years to be an overnight sensation.

I'm thinking of Rudolf Nureyev, considered to be one of the greatest ballet dancers of all time. An interviewer said to him, "You have a natural body for dance."

Nureyev answered with Russian intensity, "I *built* my body for dance."

Perfect Pitch

I'm going from show to show and pitching episodes. This requires an enormous amount of work. You must develop a story all the way to full blown with each beat and then design the best way to tell it, to sell it, to entertain with your delivery.

I am finally positioned to go in and pitch many shows and get invited to come back anytime with more stories. It is a rare privilege to have this opportunity. Yet it is enormous work to cull it all down to a breezy meeting pitching five or six stories at a time. My favorite producer is Norman Lear who has every top show on the air at once. I am in his offices pitching as fast as I can come up with the next stories. I pitch to him and to all his staff on all their shows. I can hardly keep up.

For one meeting, while I was in the elevator going to it, I was thinking that I hadn't yet fleshed out a particular beat of one of the stories. In the elevator, I noticed myself wishing that the wing of the building where I was going would be in flames and that access to the office was not possible so I'd have to duck into the wardrobe department and sew costumes for a living instead. It seemed like an easier life.

The elevator opened and there were no flames, so I was marching soldier-like toward the office when the wardrobe mistress and her assistant ran out of their workshop after me. They were just having a meeting about how to dress "a woman executive who is a creative type" (that would be me.) They ran after me to ask me to take off my clothes. They wanted to copy what I was wearing. Okay great, at least my clothes are a success. Surely, I would follow. They gave me a beautiful suit to replace mine. I tucked the waist and pushed up the sleeves and then it was my style.

The wardrobe mistress looked at me with surprise and said, "Oh, I guess it's not the clothes, it's how you wear them." Ah yes, a great truth: "It's not the life. It's how you live it." This was probably the flames I was wishing for.

I went on down the hall in time for my meeting. As I pitched my stories to the executives—all males, all dressed any which way—as I pitched to them, I noticed that the beat of the story that I was struggling with got solved as I talked and that was a brand-new level of expertise for me. So now another color in the rainbow of my apprenticeship showed itself. After such a good meeting, and the return of my "creative, executive suit," I went home, back to the drawing board for more.

The more is this: I have always said, "There are two people in Hollywood who are geniuses when it comes to story structure, and Norman Lear is both of them." I admire where his mind is, maybe because his heart is also in the right place. I have been working to adopt the Norman Lear story structure gene for myself. Grueling to get there—yes. Making great progress—yes, yes. Dressed for success while I do it. Absolutely.~

31 Years Old

Triple-Digit Retail

I'M ON MY way to my agent's office for our weekly strategy meeting. Usually, I ask him which shows he has called this week to get me work. He asks what new material I have for him to promote. I'd like today to be more productive, as in, an assignment gotten, a contract signed, appointments made.

Getting a go-ahead to write a script can be very lucrative. If it's a show that will rerun for years, I could have my 401K, annuities, residuals, and set-for-life numbers all rolled into one. Several times, I've had great contracts then an industry strike will happen, or the show gets canceled, or the producer gets fired and all whom he hired are wiped out too. If you think the drama is on the screen, *no,* drama is what happens to *get* the drama on the screen.

Getting the job in Hollywood *is* the full-time job.

It's not lost on me that I continue to use work in Hollywood as my day job to support my work on this book. Lucky me, I somehow will get it done and to you before I leave Earth.

Meanwhile, my agent's office is just at the end of this block. I'm hoping to find a parking spot here on Rodeo Drive.

The parking meters on Rodeo Drive are the bargain of Beverly Hills. You can put a dime and a nickel in and have plenty of time to pop into Gucci's to pick up, say, an $800 keychain.

Oh good, that Bentley is just pulling out in front of me, so I maneuver my Carmen Ghia into the space right in front of a chic little boutique. Oh, and there's time left on the meter. Thank you. I accept the riches of the day; that saves me a nickel and a dime.

I'm a little early for my agent meeting, so I go into the boutique to browse. Hmm. The more expensive the store, the fewer clothes they have on the racks. I find that the rule is—the amount of clothes on the rack is inversely proportional to the price on the hang tags.

I don't really have a relationship with retail. I'm from the Midwest. Committing retail is kind of a crime where I come from. I'm more of the "get inspiration" type of shopper. I see it, I don't buy it, I go home and make it myself.

I do enjoy "just looking." It's part of my luxuriant relationship with abundance in the world.

I am looking at the few pricey things exquisitely displayed and making my way toward the back of the store. (The sale rack is always in the back, so you see the full-out retail items first before you get there.)

And here on the sale rack, there is something wonderful. It's a sweater coat, which means it's two things in one, and it's marked down! This belongs to me. It's been waiting for me. The shop girl is all over it. No one could fit in it; that's why it's marked down. It was too small in the waist, too big in the shoulders for anyone else. For me, it's just right.

It was marked down from high three digits to barely three digits. That would be a bargain for Rodeo Drive where the first hundred is a given.

Perfect for me. Yes, when I get my Hollywood writing assignments coming in. Yes, then I'll be almost ready for retail or at least sale retail.

I walk out.

The shop girl shouts, "You mean you're not getting it?"

Halfway down the street I do "get it." It dawns on me.

This is here to show me how creation gets created. If I wait to have my agent say that I have a contract, I'll never have the contract. If I am willing to demonstrate faith, then I open the space for the contract to materialize. My wish is for the best and highest me to meet the moment. I have been in such waiting, and working at, and struggle, and now enough is enough—let's have what I say I want. Not someday. Today. My "someday" can never come true if I don't *make it true*. It's up to me to create "someday" today.

I go back to the boutique, and I buy it. I commit retail or at least sale retail.

A random quote comes to me. "I wouldn't be having this desire if I couldn't get it realized. I set it to get it." My desire is to book the work, the action is to get the sweater coat to demonstrate faith that I'll get the work.

Being the creator of myself, I now walk down Rodeo Drive in my lovely made-for-me, waiting-for-me, only-for-me three-digit wonder. Definitely couture for sure.

So here is what happens on the street:

A woman rushes over to me to ask where I got my sweater coat so she could get one for herself. I can tell by the packages in her arms she is clearly a lady who shops. Also, she seemed to be wearing an outfit she bought to shop in so she can buy more outfits to shop in.

I point her to the boutique, and she runs to it in her Ferragamo stilettos, undeterred that this was the only one.

A man, walking with a blonde starlet, turns his glance to me. He remembers me from an event at the Academy last week and invites me to a screening of his latest film. (Filmmakers are always inviting everyone they see to a screening of their latest film.)

Two ladies come along the street. I am aware of their breasts sticking way out, unnaturally beyond what would be the silhouette that Mother Nature would have chosen for them. They are talking about their plastic surgeon and what more and what else they can think of for him to do to them. Their goals in life are found under the knife. I've been going about my goals under the gun. As they seek happiness through ever more body sculpting, I seek mine to fulfill my mission of acquiring writing assignments so that I can take care of my needs, develop my potential, get really good at what I can offer the world in help and service, and love. You see how all roads lead to Mecca.

By the end of the block, I enter my agent's building and step into the elevator. And there is an actress I have counseled since we met on *The Tonight Show* several years ago. She is a recent *paying* client of mine. She says she would love to have a consultation. Feeling the magic of my sweater coat, I book her appointment date and time right there before we arrive at my floor. As I step out of the elevator, I realize that my three-digit purchase has just paid for itself with plenty of change left over if I want to stop off at, say, Tiffany's on my way home and pick up a bauble.

My agent greets me with the usual no news. I have the idea to ask him to call the producer I want to hear from. He does call, and *I get the job* of writing one of the first episodes for that new series. Then, I ask him to follow up on a call to another showrunner, and he places several more calls on my behalf, and *I get all those jobs*. Plus, he books an important meeting for me with the head of the studio for tomorrow regarding the development of one of my original projects. Great. I know exactly what I'll be wearing. ~

~~~

P.S. Within the week, several other assignments come in. I have signed contracts.

I've begun. That was easy. ~

31 Also

Thirteen Suits

I HAD A pitch meeting with thirteen executives from the network, from upper management, from New York, from where the cash is. Thirteen suits, all in the room to make a deal with me.

I was brilliant and we all knew it. All they had to do was say yes, and we all knew it. All thirteen were laughing and alive and inspired by my presentation.

I thought, this is looking good, but nothing happens until it does. They said, "Thank you, you'll be hearing from us."

As I left the room, I dropped my Mont Blanc pen (bought at a bargain) and bent down to pick it up, and I heard what they were saying through the door. "She's a talent!" "Never seen anything like it." And even "One-in-a-million."

They all muttered agreement and then the head suit said, "I didn't know whether to laugh at her jokes or look down her blouse."

He was saying this as though it was a positive statement. Is that it, my being female confuses them? Well, chauvinism will not stop me, so it doesn't have to stop them either. Maybe they could use a little help to sort this out.

So, I said through the door, "Hello, this is God . . . Hire her. P.S. Notice that God's voice is female." ~

31 Plus

Development

WELL, I DID get hired. I got a development deal with the studio.

This is unheard of for an unknown such as me. This is a coup. This is no darn fun.

A development deal means that you bring your original material to the studio head, who agrees that they will fund those projects they deem valuable. You get a green light. I bring the script, they put it together with the right director and stars and location, and we engage in the collaboration of the miracle cocktail of what it takes to create the magical amorphous object of a hit movie.

Maybe you have heard of Development Hell. You take your precious ideas and work diligently to bring them to life, then the head of the studio says no, then you bring them another precious idea and they say no, and another. It's like driving up a beautiful street until you hit a dead-end and then drive up another beautiful street and hit another dead-end. Do that all day on all the bright and fresh ideas that you can think of and then have to abandon. No wonder very successful actors and directors and writers who have development deals are hanging out the windows of the studio office building wanting to jump and be put out of their misery. Like champion fighters, these are the best years of their lives for creating and presenting their art, and they are kept in the runaround, the turnaround, the cul-de-sac of creativity, until they are no longer a viable commodity for another studio to give them *their* development deal.

Many of these stars, in the prime of their creating, are referred to me because they can't stand it anymore and they don't know what to do. I'm known for talking people off the ledge. I have a lot more success with that than I have with breaking through on any of my own projects in *my* development track.

I think of all that midnight oil that I expended on that very special Katharine Hepburn film that then became the Shirley MacLaine play that then became the papers in the drawer because both talented ladies went on to other projects having never even known about what was being developed for them. I wonder how many monkeys are typing at typewriters in how many studio offices with development deals, creating for the same stars and not getting anywhere.

But never fear since one of my mottos is "Obstacles are only there in case you care to stop." Just for the record: I'm not stopping. ~

32 Years Old

From Surviving to Thriving or How to Live Beyond Your Pathology

YOU KNOW THAT thing that eludes you. That thing that no matter what, it still shows up on a daily basis? Maybe an issue with your weight, or no money, or people you can't get along with? That thing.

Any current challenge in our life is a trigger for the core wound that we've had since childhood. The harder the current event, the deeper it shows the wound that we want to heal. History repeats itself on purpose. We recreate old patterns from childhood, now that we are adults, because this is the time and place where we can create a better method of living.

Here's my theory: In our early life, we had to get very clever about survival tools. Maybe your family wasn't a safe bunch of folks to be living with, but at four years old you couldn't say, "Later for you, I'm getting my own apartment." You didn't have that as an option, so you had to stay and develop survival tools just to continue to be there. Now, in your adult life, it requires that you put down your surviving tools and pick up thriving tools because if you keep using survival tools, that's all that will happen—you will just stay in survival. Now is your chance to thrive.

Here's the problem with your child plan: You're very, very good at survival tools because they kept you surviving, but you're not good at thriving tools because you don't even know what those are yet. And here you are at a juncture. If you're going to go on in a new and expanded version that utilizes all your talents and character, it's time to morph. It's time to go from surviving to thriving.

I tell you this at thirty-two because I see clients who come to me on a regular basis that are turning this all around in their lives. From crisis mode to self-care is a beautiful thing.

The point of surviving to thriving is pretty much the structure of everybody's story from the beginning. It's the basic human story of becoming. You just keep peeling away what you grow out of as you grow into becoming more and more who you are essentially.

I'll give you an example: A young man, Johnny, came to me yesterday. He's an adult now but continuing a habit he had as a child in a family that was dangerous to him. There was very little food or safety at his house. As a surviving tool, he would run down the block to his aunt and uncle's house when it came time for dinner. He sometimes slept on their couch. Now, as an adult, he shows up at friends' houses at dinnertime and sometimes sleeps on their couch. His surviving tools from childhood are causing him dysfunction as an adult. What was a smart solution as a child in survival now can be solved in a new way for him to thrive. The solutions available to him are much broader than what was available to him as a child. Now he can solve his insolvency. He can get a job.

Surviving requires clever skills to endure an unsafe atmosphere. Thriving shows you how to remove yourself from chaos, danger, escalating drama, other people's anger, or bad behavior. Once you see it, once you are conscious of habits you had to cultivate, you can trade them in for adult actions you can take.

You learn to have boundaries; you see you have needs and you meet them. Rather than having to react to what is going on around you, you can create the outcomes you wish and move toward those. It will become easier for you to know an action to take and take it. The beauty of all that expertise you acquired as a child figures mightily into your new adult thriving self. You bring all those skills into your adult life now with the power of your adult self to turn them into thriving. Try it. You'll like it. ~

33 Years Old

Finding Dad

I HAVE BEEN looking for my father for twenty-five years.

If you have your family intact, you might not think that's an important thing to do. Even my mother's policy was "Let bygones be bygones." I don't think it's a bygone if it lives in my body, alive and requiring resolution. I feel the need to swim in my entire gene pool.

To be free to leap forward, it's imperative to go back to go forward.

I have been looking for him since my mother took us and left. My brother was eleven, I was eight.

Divorce can entangle ten thousand feelings and yet gets reduced to something simple—he drank, he couldn't stop, she couldn't continue with that. We packed a small suitcase each and left. My mother didn't know where or what, but she knew she had to take us and go.

I don't remember a goodbye; I just remember that we were gone, and he was gone from us.

Where was he all my life? I've always felt a small space in my heart that I kept open for him to come back into. I don't need anything from him. It's more that I'm all about story, and that requires a beginning, middle, and end.

There's a government building in downtown Los Angeles that houses all the telephone books in the United States. If you want to track somebody's location, you'll be spending time here. You'll see me. I'm a regular.

Besides the white pages to find someone directly, there are the yellow pages for adoption search organizations, maybe numbers for tracking Social Security. What can I look up next to find out where he worked? Did he work?

I am going on . . . very little.

This isn't the kind of research that is just about the task at hand—there is all manner of emotional triggers along the way.

Seven years ago, I found someone who had taken care of him. The last she knew, his drinking was severe.

I asked if he ever talked about his family and his kids.

She said, "No." One afterthought from her (you hope for the afterthought)—"The sister-in-law knows where he is."

Does she know where I can reach the sister-in-law?

"No."

After two more years, I found his sister-in-law's number. When I called, she was either drunk herself or had some severe mental difficulty. She shouts into the phone, "He's dead. Deader than a doornail. He's dead and you should drop dead, too. Die. Die."

I decide that she really doesn't know where he is either, but not before it dredges up great gobs of emotions.

This runs deep, but I know that whatever happens, I can handle it. All this just shows me is that I'm getting closer. I take time to catch up with myself and then I go on to find out more.

I know why it takes years for people to find the members of their family who are estranged from them. There is every force against it, secreted away, many brick walls. But the real reason it takes years is that you enter this search in layers. It's like the knight's journey across the forbidden land to reach the treasure. The treasure is your own becoming. The territory can get savage. It's hard to prevail. But I know how to do that, I live in Hollywood.

I'm at the Four Seasons Hotel in the city where I grew up. It's been twenty-five years and now I have a precious phone number. It's his brother. I make the call.

The last he knew my father was in a home for drunk men. He hadn't seen or heard from him in years. This man would be my uncle, but there is no uncle talk. He did manage to mention the suburb that the institution was in before hanging up the phone.

I immediately get the number and address from information. Simple, 411.

I sit on the bed in the hotel room. So long and now so easy. I guess I must be really ready.

After so many layers of feelings, now, tonight, after twenty-five years, I know where my father is.

He is in a state-supported home. I think that is a kind of human warehouse for people who are unable to live on their own.

The worst thing I could have heard outside of that he was dead was he was in such a place, and yet I feel elated because it's far less to take than what I've been dreading in my imagination. Reality is much easier than what you can think of to bother yourself with.

So many years, and now as I sit on the bed, I know I must go immediately.

It's raining and it's pushing midnight, and I get a cab and go. And the place—what kind of a place?—is far away, about the longest ride ever.

You know the level of my focus because I don't even ask how much the cab fare will be. I never even look at the meter. Such a long ride, the longest ride. I just look at the back of the cab driver's neck and hear the thump of the windshield wipers, as I manage my pounding heart on this Gothic night.

I know nothing about where I am going.

What kind of a place is this? An institution? Does it have bars on the windows? Is he free to come and go? Is he capable of coming and going? I don't know what I will find. Here is a man who has been drinking for a lifetime, what other toll did that take besides the ones that I know about that were felt in all of us? Will he know who I am? Will he care? Will he be foreboding? Will he even be conscious?

And finally, I arrive. Yes, there are bars on the windows.

I can hardly see through the pelting rain. The building is serious, dark, cold, brick. I take my Four Seasons courtesy umbrella and step out into the storm. I suddenly realize the last time I saw him was when he followed us to California, and he stayed at the Statler Hilton, when I was eight. That's why I've always felt a connection to five-star hotels. It's really a remembrance of a connection to him. There are infinite subterranean sweet spots like that, that we have no idea exist in us. This will open wide millions of those connections.

As I stand here, the cab whisks away on this dark and stormy night. He'll be back when he realizes I haven't paid him yet.

I pull open the huge, heavy wooden doors into an old institutional entranceway. The paint is peeling, the smell is of age and disinfectant.

I pass a patient/resident sitting on his haunches on the floor. He is rocking, rocking, too overlong on Thorazine.

There's a dimly lit reception cage where a dimly lit night watchman sits at a switchboard. Something in me requires the watchman to immediately call upstairs to have my father come down. After so long, after so many obstacles, now finally, so close, nothing can stop this.

I am directed to the hallway. He will be coming down the elevator.

I position myself. I stand as still as still can be and as tall as tall is. Sweat makes its way down my arms and into puddles in my hands and something . . . I have always had a bright, white pillar of light inside me. It has always been there. Now I feel that light shoot up out of the top of my head and down to the center of the Earth, and it aligns and plugs in and sets itself in place, on full power. Oh, this is my light that I am now free to shine.

The elevator doors open and there is my father. I look like my mother except for my eyes, and when the doors open, there are my eyes looking back at me.

We rush to one another, there is no holding back, no pulling away. We just hold each other and look at one another and there is just . . . connection. Maybe he doesn't even know who I am. Maybe he thinks I am my mother. I know this: he has been waiting for me. All those years when I hoped he'd find me, here he was waiting for me to find him. Is that the baton that passes between generations? I'm the adult now.

We continue to look at one another and smile and smile, just experiencing this astonishing feeling.

I see his hands that are just like my brother's, our noses the same, our hair both curly. It's like when mothers see their newborns—there's such familiarity. That space in my heart that I have held open all my life, remarkably, fills in with this missing piece.

I don't know what he understands. He might have had shock treatment—a radical procedure routinely administered in these times. I know his has been a lifetime of alcohol.

Yes, definitely there are my gestures in his hands. My brother will not want to know he looks like him.

And yes, we have curly hair together. But not just curly. That wave that goes that funny way and that little curl that turns the opposite direction both together on my head and his. My curl that always went its own way I now see was the way of our family lineage.

His feet look quite swollen and difficult to walk on. I realize that this is his small world here—from bed, to food, to the elevator up and down.

We both know this is our biggest life moment together. He is completely available for it.

He keeps saying, "You're perfect. You're perfect. I love you." These are the only words he says, and he says them enough to fill the lifespan of years when we were not together. Maybe that's why it took so long to find him. I'm way past needing him to approve of me.

Our visit is just looking at one another and smiling, smiling and hugging and holding one another's hands.

When our time is complete, as I leave, he says, "Do you have enough money for the bus?" It's something my brother would think of.

Yes, enough. It's enough.

I exit the building. The rain has stopped, and the air is spring fresh as though it has been power-washed for the occasion.

And here is the cab waiting for me!

As it whisks me back to the Four Seasons Hotel, I feel my body relax into the leather of the back seat. I expand. I exhale.

In the cab, going back, it is the shortest ride.

I notice a framed photo on the dashboard, of the cab driver with his family. I feel the cool touch of the leather seat. I noticed none of this on the long ride going, and I'm now hyper-experiencing each sensation on this short ride back. I'm aware that the same world is not the same; this has changed everything.

On this cab ride I know two truths unequivocally and forevermore about my family history and my destiny.

It wasn't my fault.

I can do anything. ~

~~~

P.S. Several weeks later, the slippers I sent him were returned marked addressee deceased. ~

34 Years Old

Mother

THAT'S MY MOTHER in the bed, in the hospital, intravenously.

They opened her up and closed her up and threw away the key.

Cancer of the everything. Three months to live.

The morning after her surgery, while she is still in intensive care and not yet awake, I am standing overlong in my closet. I realize that I am thinking, what do you wear to go tell your mother that she's about to die? Not that it matters that I'm even dressed. I grab something bright and as I go out the door, I pick a hibiscus and put it in my hair. At the door of death, greet it with so much life.

We are all here when she wakes up out of the anesthetic. She wants to know immediately, "Did they get it all?" She looks at me directly for the whole truth.

Oh, I thought I was braced for this. It rushes me. Of course, I'll tell her the whole truth. I'm not going to jive her. I don't know where that phrase came from but there it is, I'm not going to jive her. And so, I tell her, "We've got Thanksgiving." And she knows, because today is August.

Ashen

On the first day after the operation comes the hospital walk. They get her up and insist she walk once around the nurses' station. Her gold high-heeled slippers are left on the floor. Her brightly colored, carefully chosen, not-to-look-like-a-robe is left at the end of the bed. Instead, hospital regulation nonskid slipper socks are secured on her dangling feet—feet for the first time without a mind of their own to bounce and dance through the day. The nurses are getting her up now, and she is ashen. She's never been without a tan; even in the depths of Chicago winters, she was the color of life. She's been luminescent from her flashing eyes to the whiteness of her dazzling smile. And now she is staggering on the arm of the nurse, holding onto the

IV bottle that trails on a wheeled trolley beside her. As I stand stoic, my body reels. I am still standing, but I feel myself passing out on the inside. She staggers, ashen, the color of wet cement, and cement dries cold, and then is stone. Hospital-issue nonslip slipper socks, ashen skin, walking in stilted pain—two days later they send her home to die.

It's a peculiar thing recuperating from an operation that didn't do anything to help the situation yet took her down, down. How does she rally from that? What healing can we hope for? Recuperate to get ready to die?

My stepdad can't understand. "Why didn't they fix it?"

Me: "You can't just replace the carburetor when the whole system is shutting down. Totaled."

Him: "Oh."

A car metaphor is easier for him to take. He is so mad at God for giving cancer to the love of his life.

Before all this happened, she was planning a trip to China. My stepdad wants to go right away as if that would cure it. He doesn't want to see that she is way beyond China.

This is the time in her life when she is peeling away from life. No that's not accurate—she isn't peeling away. She is more alive than ever. Her body is rapidly giving way to her spirit, which is now so big, as her body is now so small.

It's as though she is blowing a balloon up and up and it fills with her life force and, soon when it is fully filled, she will let go and the breath of her life will explode out and fill the room with her essence and then she will be gone.

How to Live During Dying

She has long nights of pain. I call the pain management department at the hospital and am put on hold. When I ask for emergency help for her, they say, "Often people with terminal cancer aren't in pain." That is their solution to the problem—the problem doesn't exist.

There's a pamphlet they give families of those who are dying. The motto is "When you get to the end of your rope, tie a knot and hang on." And so, we do, and so we slip down, and so we pull back up and so and so and so. As in other arenas when you look for ways to have a life on Earth, we go over and under and around and through, and then we do it all over again— what we have to do, when we have to do it.

People tend to die in the style that they lived. She would wage yet another night fight with death and live to meet yet another sunrise the next day.

Liquid morphine was not her idea of how she intended to spend her last precious time. And so, she did it her way.

The Pear That Will Save Her Life
If you've had loved ones dying of cancer, you know that's not necessarily what kills them. They die of the ravages, the fight with pain, the totaling of the body, the shutdown of functions, one upon the next. They die of starvation. The body can't take in food. Why would it? To go on? How? Loved ones and well-wishers don't know this. They bring food that sits uneaten. It's a slow death that goes so fast.

She is right here in the family room, sitting up sleeping on the couch in her robe that she never before wore during the day. The day was for places to go and people to discover, adventures to uncover. This adventure is of a different type. My mother, the vibrant one who would feast upon life—now here is her last Earth adventure.

As she is finally sleeping deeply, this is my opportunity to arrange a perfectly ripe pear for her to eat.

I cut it meticulously and put it strategically on her favorite China plate.

I am intensely focused on this task when I realize what I am up to. If I can cut this exactly ripe pear just so and serve it to her prettily, she will eat it and live. I think I'm going to save her life with this pear. When I realize this, I look up and she has died another ten minutes worth.

It's a Long, Short Three Months

It's a funny thing that life goes on, even during dying—like great romance during war times; babies born in the time of famine. I think that at the door to death there is so much life, and part of our lives is always the comedy of tragedy.

I'm not saying that death is a laugh riot, but there is humor in everything and of course we found it. *Dark Victory* was an old Bette Davis movie. She dies by merely lying down across the bed as the music plays and the sun shines even though she can't see it because of her *Dark Victory*. Get it? It's the romanticized Hollywood version of the perfect death. About ten times a day we would say, "This is not *Dark Victory*." Maybe that doesn't seem so funny to you right now; maybe it's one of those had-to-be-there experiences as we were there coping, as her soul is separating from her body so she can leave it behind.

Unfinished Business

Everybody's mind is easier for me to read than hers.

In fact, that's why I can read minds, because hers has not been accessible to me. She had a great joy for life, and also, there was that deep something. That post-trauma from an early time that was there somewhere that I wanted to access and put my arms around. It's the story of our lives together. I was always probing and admonishing and hoping she would finally tell me. But tell me what? She was funny and smart and wise and always found the patch of sunshine to bask in. And, also, there was that *other* part. The part she kept deep and separate. I wanted it out, I wanted it gone, but she'd just say, "Oh don't," and she'd put another deadbolt lock on the matter.

I would continue to admonish her to tell me. "What is it? We can bring it out and love it to healing. It will work. You can be free to be even more so the lightness of being. It's there underneath. Share with me. Let me in. Let me give you all of my love."

She: "No, don't. No."

Me: "Then we are *not done yet*—there is a rush to finish this unfinished business. You're not getting out of here until we do. Time's running out and we're not finished yet!"

All we need is a golden moment where we come to something where nothing is in the way, where our hearts are joined at the hip, ever heartened.

Then in the kitchen, at 3:00 a.m. after a bout of her sheer fight to keep her life force going, when I was hoping she could have the tea I just made her, she told me the story. The one that is a glimpse that tells it all. Here is what she said.

With Papa in the Park

She was eight years old. It was Christmas. There was a heavy snowfall. She was with her Papa whom she dearly loved, and he dearly loved her. It was her mother who was the one who drank, who was the danger to her. I knew her feelings about her mother. I knew some incidents, but only just vaguely. And I knew my grandmother, and I always kept a guard up around her.

This below-zero Christmas when my mother was eight and she was with her Papa, they were in the park, in the snow, *because he was trying to give her away.*

When she told me that, I knew the whole picture. I knew how far it must have gotten for her papa to reach such an extreme measure to keep her from harm. I'm in such awe that she was able to hold that enormous headline fact of her life somewhere very deep and in this moment, in her circumstance it burst out of her and is gone. I have been asking for this and hoping for this and wanting this and now it comes. And it takes all my heart to hold it, to hold her, and let it all go. I know this has been our golden moment.

She finally sleeps in such deep relief; such lightness of being now surrounds her. I think about the way she made good Christmases for our childhoods but must not have cared for them herself. I think about her choice to be an excellent mother instead of what she experienced, and about her strength at every level for as long as I've known her.

From here and now I go back to her eight-year-old self, in the park where no one was there to take her. I give so much love to her. Joined at the hip, whole-hearted.

The Last Days

I take her to the final hospital stay, and in the end, we were all in the right place at the right time doing the right thing. Having been in the hospital room for seventeen hours without leaving, I would say to myself each hour, "If I leave to go eat and she dies while I'm gone, am I ready for that?" I wasn't and I wasn't. And finally, seventeen hours later, I knew, Okay, now is the time. I have to be willing not to be here when she leaves.

I went to eat at the coffee shop next to the hospital, there was an aquarium by my table. I took one bite of my lunch, and all the fish came over to my corner of the aquarium and I knew that she had died.

Here is the conversation I have with the fish in the aquarium: "Tell me."

The essence of them: "It is."

Oh, of course, I accept that. I let her go. She doesn't hurt anymore.

I finish at the coffee shop and walk slowly across the parking lot and back into the hospital room. When I had left the room, so had my older brother to go get a shower at the house, and so had my stepfather—stepped out into the hall talking to other people. That left my younger brother in the room. My mother seemed to be seized out of her body. She grabbed the bed rail, and her beautiful and strong and dazzling teeth chipped in the seizing and landed at my younger brother's chest; with that, he was instilled with her strength and her life force. She did not go gently into that good night without giving her final love, ever the mother.

As with everyone before they leave, there is an orchestration of where the loved ones are and what they are doing. So many people feel so bad that they were not there for their loved one or, if only, or why that way? It is always more elegant than you would think it to be. Of course, she was waiting for seventeen hours for us to leave the room so she *could* die. She did it her way. I understand that. And in the end, it's all perfect.

My stepfather doesn't think it's perfect. He's going to strangle God when he sees him.

After Death

There was a big can of acetone on the stand next to her bed. The nurses had taken her nail polish off so they could monitor her vital signs. Now her vital signs have gone off with her.

After she has gone out of her body, after all that pain has vanished, when it is now over and quiet and we no longer wince at her every fighting breath, after, when her body lies there still, I polish her always-red-nails for her next travels.

Three days later, we charter a beautiful yacht (its first voyage) to take us out to sea at sunset. She loved to travel, now she will have the whole Pacific Ocean to move around in.

We pick her up at the mortuary. We never had to pick her up before. She was a woman who drove herself. I had her ashes box on my lap. I was feeling dizzy from the whole idea when I noticed a sticker on the bottom of the box. It was stamped "rush order." That's hilarious. She's on her way to e-t-e-r-n-i-t-y, there's no rush. It's yet another beat of the human comedy.

And there's more from the ashes box. When the time came, when the sun is setting and the boat is rocking, we can't get her ashes box open. It's a slide mechanism and it's stuck. We are running from the bridge to the main salon looking for a screwdriver. And perfectly, it opens, she is released, the sun sets, as we champagne toast her astonishingly giving life. We look to the horizon and then to our mother, the Pacific Ocean. Latitude 33°36'04" N, longitude 118°15'33" W. ~

35 Years Old

Healing the Hollywood Heart

I conduct a seminar called *Healing the Hollywood Heart*. It addresses why you want what you want from Hollywood and how to have it. (This malaise, this frustration that you might feel about wanting to excel and not yet able to, will find you anywhere. Hollywood isn't the only place you can be confronted with drama.)

Here's some of the ad copy I initially sent out:

> *There's a bumper sticker,* Just Say No to Hollywood. *If you can do that, go now, turn your U-Haul around, and seek your destiny elsewhere. But if you can't, if you must be here, if you're sure to become who you know is in you to become . . . then welcome.*
>
> *History repeats itself—if you experienced abandonment, rejection, or indifference as a child; chances are you are feeling the same lack of response to your work in Hollywood. It's time to change the course of your history.*
>
> *It's not what's in front of you that's stopping you, it's what's behind you that's holding you back.*

What's the story you tell yourself about what happened when you were a kid? Change that story and you change the result that comes to you now as an adult.

There is one demographic group that is particularly successful at getting at the bubbling cauldron beneath their ambitions—young men with an urgency to land on their manhood. They tend to be mid-thirties and feel a strong do-or-die pull to their ambitions. They must break through. They *must.*

I particularly love this group—to the man, they are a son having an issue in his relationship with his father. I like a quote from the photographer Richard Avedon, "With fathers and sons it's never over."

Many are here *looking for Dad in the studio hierarchy*. There's one thing I know for myself because of having an absent dad, I've always relied on my own authority. My father was a good provider because he provided me with the steeliness to provide for myself. Maybe because I was a girl, I could do that readily. It's different for boys. A boy needs his dad and when he doesn't have that, he comes to Hollywood and places his dad's approval in an unyielding studio authority figure who won't return his phone calls.

Because I settled that for myself, this particular category of young ambitious men started ringing my phone. It developed into an intense sub-group for men *Looking for Dad*.

Here's my theory: As kids they see what isn't working for Dad. As an act of love, they take on Dad's dilemma to fix it for him. That's what history repeating itself is—you repeat it to repair it. You recreate their pattern within yourself so you can embody and correct the pattern for them. It was never meant for you to solve *their* life; it was meant for you to create *your* life. Once you *recreate* *their* life in yourself you see why they did what they did in their circumstance. Through the maturing of that, you release, accept, forgive, and allow *yourself*, and now you can go on to have your own freedom to create your destiny.

So many young men are here in Hollywood confronting that circumstance they want to fix in Dad. They want to accomplish the thing Dad couldn't accomplish.

Here are some examples:

Infidelity Dad: You loathe his extra-marital affairs and then you get to the age he was when he did that, and you do it too.

Bankrupt Dad: As he did before you, you go into many promising businesses that all get to a similar plateau and then fizzle.

Absent Dad: You had to be the man in the family when you were eight and now money comes in, but it all goes out to others.

Competitive Dad: He refuses to acknowledge your achievements.

Drunken Dad: You take up drinking too and then must go to rehab to get Dad's alcohol out of your system.

You see, it's not what *he* wants for you. It's what *you* want for him. There are many possible Dad circumstances that a son takes on within himself to fix.

If you have a good relationship with your dad, you fare very differently for your future and yet you might find it hard to surpass his money quotient and his level of success.

Once you clear the *dad circumstance* you are free to go directly to your dream and create it.

I was particularly thrilled to witness two young men not yet in their own driver's seat of themselves, escaping their new high-powered, high paying, highly restrictive Hollywood executive positions for a general romp about in Paris on a four-day weekend. Feeling an existential epiphany coming on and with all the intensity and sincerity that was exploding out of their urgent hearts, they wrote on a placemat, at a French café, the manifesto for the ages.

Be who you are, and accept people and things
for what they are—not what you wish they were.

They unwittingly freed themselves from limits in thoughts and behaviors on the way to becoming their own men.

If you're a woman, there's a whole other set of criteria and relationship with mom. Among other topics, we address *Phantom Mother*, especially around weight loss. You may find that you are carrying your mother's weight on your thighs. With this work, you can completely drop her body out of your body and lose a whole person out of you.

It's such a privilege to have dear brave souls show up in full vulnerability and be willing to connect the dots of their life to see themselves clearly and make new autonomous choices.

For many remarkable people, *Healing the Hollywood Heart* has been wildly successful. ~

36 Years Old

Prelude to Getting Out of Dodge

GOD CALLED THIS morning to ask if I'm tending to great works.

Yes, yes, of course, I am. I'm working on this book you are reading. I am on it every day. So yes, I am tending to great works.

And besides, my work in Hollywood is going spectacularly. Much of my original material has become fast-track, green light, go projects.

And then, too, I have my many seminars and programs that I've developed for those clients who are looking to get into Hollywood, move up in Hollywood, and just as many who would love to get out of Hollywood. Also, I have successful audio programs that I've created for people unresolved around their weight, grief, money, and love. I have healing methods for any issue that eludes a person. The idea is we can shift anything into empowerment.

All this work supports the writing of this book. It's gratifying and a privilege to be of service. While it enables me to do what I want when I want because I want. I've carved out a reality where I am free to do my own work and get really good at doing it. And as ever, Beloved is ever here, ever loved, ever loving. It's a golden life.

And now, I feel in my heart that I am being given the opportunity to step up to the next level.

Just when I finally moved from surviving to thriving, just when it's all going so well, I am invited to jump into the wider world. I know that it's an invitation to take a leap into a larger version of myself. The me that I came in to be I am becoming, and now an expanded part is opening up.

So many clients call me whose hearts can break on a daily basis because of their experiences in show business. I have to remind them that Hollywood is pretend.

Just this week, a design team worked overtime into the night to have the all-important set on location ready by dawn and then had it suddenly scrapped just before the morning light got a chance to shine on it. Going from "the most important thing in the world" to dismantled and thrown in the dumpster—what does that do to the people who pushed themselves to create it? They begin to feel only dumpster-worthy themselves. Hopefully, with tips and clarity from *Healing the Hollywood Heart,* they can crack themselves open to a deeper result.

There is the never-ending line of newcomers that ride into town hoping for stardom but instead get eaten alive. I came to Hollywood to be with the best and the brightest and to be one of them. Alongside brilliant talent doing the height of their genius work, there is also the underbelly of it all—the petty, the fury, the see-you-in-court part of Hollywood. I decided early on to have a higher result from and for Hollywood. Maybe that's why I have so many clients who came here for that same purpose—to enrich with their offering and to be enriched by offering it. That's the part I wish to make more prominent and available to all.

I can do that while also being clear that it's not my job to save anybody from themselves. It's my job to contribute my note to the symphony of life. Everybody else can contribute their note, too.

And now comes this invitation right out of my heart to me that I know to respond to.

I know I'm going up. I know that where I am isn't yet where I will get to.

So, I ask myself what I ask of my clients. Have I fully created the life I want to have? Have I gotten far enough up the mountain to see the view I came to look at? What yet wants to come out of me? What more is in my destiny?

I'm not going to stop here, midway, when there is more *up* to go. How far can I get to? How much more is there to reach? Is there more along the path of becoming? Let's see how far I can take myself and go.

It's not children. I know that I won't be having any this lifetime. I know that I won't be waking up at fifty startled because "I forgot to have babies."

It takes everything you've got to be everything you are and then some to become more. And that's the point—the more. Whatever all-the-way is, I'm going there. The part that I didn't know I had in me, the part that wasn't yet fully realized, I'll go realize it.

In society, success looks like stock options and job security. In life, at least my life, success is following the path to myself. Have I become my whole true self? Have I gone as far as I can go? Is this the best and the brightest experience at this time in this place? Is there more to avail myself of?

It's not new for me to choose the road less traveled. I've always taken that road because that is my road to take. I'm just going to keep following my heart. It knows where to lead me.

(I'm about to take a sharp right turn here. Come along. It might inspire you to feel the larger world call you.)

I have a heartfelt talk with Beloved. He understands that love has a lot of air and space to it. He's a man who knows that a woman has got to do what she's got to do and gives his love for me to go do it. He loves me enough to watch me go and to be here when I get back. This is why we chose each other in the first place.

This night, I pick a place on my globe as far away from Hollywood as I can get without coming back in the other direction. I sublet my apartment, pack up my work in a duffel bag, and light out for Greece.

Ten fingers, ten toes, everything else up for expansion. ~

37 Years Old

Greece

I FLEW TO Malaga, Spain, visited a friend who wrote down how I would get from there to Greece by land.

Here's what was written on the paper:

> *Leave Malaga, get through the South of France and then to Italy, and then on to Greece. To Voghera—leave Genoa 17:00, arrive Voghera 19:00, depart Voghera 21:00 on couchette to Brindisi. Arrive at Brindisi the next morning at 10, take the ferry to Patras, Greece, and then the train, then the bus from Patras to Athens. In Athens take a taxi or bus to Piraeus Zia Marina, and Piraeus Zia Marina go by hydrofoil to Hydra.*

From that piece of paper, I did find my way to Hydra, Greece, and I'm here now.

Before all this started, I had thought I was out on the road just for fine-tuning, just a slight adjustment of something, but *no*...the use of it was to discombobulate me, require me to take care of my every need. Just getting a cup of tea in the countryside in France never happened. I know that I can usually speak money exchange and food in any language, and yet all my other surviving skill sets were knocked around just to get from one point to the next. Forget about thriving.

I know this was all designed for me to let go of everything. This is what I mean by leaving surviving tools to pick up thriving tools. Thriving tools are simple, except for those of us who never learned to use them before. Simple, but they just aren't my "usuals." Such as: Asking for help. Reacting to what is going on with your immediate feelings as in "Oh, s*#t." Learning to kick dirt, which I discovered can be quite useful. Curling up in a ball and checking out for twenty minutes and then totally resetting from there.

The nature of order and chaos is that they are the same. I know this because many years ago when I was about to graduate from high school and go on to college, I was in a bubble bath planning my life, and Einstein came to me on one of the bubbles and said, "Order and chaos are the same." Okay, thank you . . . What does that mean? Oh, I get it, yes thank you—in order for more order to form, it has to deconstruct, reorganize, and then build up further. No wonder I experienced chaos just to get to Greece. Now I'm in a state of empty and ready to fill. Oh, goodie. Progress.

I think the thirty-seventh year is the year of existential aloneness. It's the time in our lives to stand as an island and see what we are, distinguished from the who that everybody else is pursuing. It's also the time to look at all the roads open to us and decide which ones to focus on and which to let go of. I think we all have many talents and many ways to express our one life story. We came to learn and to be what we learn. Here on this island, it's uncanny, there are many expats here—talented artists and writers—who are in varying stages of doing or not pursuing their art. It just makes me ever more pursuant to mine.

At the moment, I'm standing in the bank to open an account. This is a grand, ornate building decorated in gold. A shaft of light is beaming in on me through the arch in the ceiling. I have filled out paperwork that has just been returned to me with a formal and impressive passbook. As you know, in America, on official papers, we give our mother's maiden name; in Greece we give our father's first name and our first and middle name. My father's first name was Woodrow. My middle name is Joy. As I stand here in this ceremonial building with this shaft of light shining on me, my passbook reads "Viki, Joy of Woodrow."

Since I know my father to have been a long-distance truck driver before he married my mother, for years whenever I was on a highway, I would look up into the cab of trucks I'd pass and think, "Are you my dad?"

And here, now, easily, I find him in my passbook, in this bank, on a remote Greek island. The most splendid gifts come when we are completely released from ever expecting them. This is my fortune. I am my fortune.

Do you hear that? It's a Greek donkey letting out a primal scream, all part of the ambiance here. There are no cars on Hydra because there are no roads, it's all steps, so everything has to be carried up by donkey. This morning, one carried up a refrigerator motor and carried down the garbage.

Since this is an island, there are limited resources. If you don't have it, you probably won't be getting it anytime soon. What becomes the most important need—that which you don't have.

The Aegean Sea is straight ahead. Over my left shoulder is the Saronic Gulf where the sun sets over the Peloponnese. This is my office. A friend, one of the expat writers, has loaned me the use of her little Hermes portable typewriter. Most of the other writers on the island write in longhand because the sound of the typewriter is too much after an evening of ouzo. Since I don't drink, I got custody of the typewriter and use it every day at my little Greek wobbly table set up just on the palazzo overlooking the Aegean. As I can view the island, the clickety-clack of the Hermes typewriter can be heard on the port, so I am called Clickety-Clack by the locals.

My Clairs

We haven't yet directly discussed my extra-perceptions. I'm a high-level empath. I have been since I was born. That means that I can access the stories of all the people coming and going on the street. I can read people's deep desires, what they want and need, why they came into their lives, and what they are doing here about why they came. I love that I can know this and can impart information should anyone want to know. And many people do want to have clarity for their lives.

One thing that has happened to me on this trip is that I can't seem to read everybody's mind like I always have. I think this is given to me as a temporary circumstance so that I use my wisdoms on myself rather than always being other-directed. My head knows this, but my heart continues to love to see and feel everybody. I do know enough to leave people alone so they can save their own life. It's a patient practice just watching them get to it themselves.

I love my abilities to see into a person, and also, I see I am to feel my feelings first before I feel everybody else's feelings for them.

I think that's part of the reason I'm here in Greece. I know that I had to come all the way over here to know all about living over there. I think we all come to Earth with many talents. There are lots of possibilities we can develop, and we do. Some of our possibilities fall by the wayside, and some are brought to the fore and focused on. It's like juggling—first throw one ball in the air and get good at that and then throw the other one up there, and then a third, and pretty soon you can keep them all going at once—but not at first. You look at one at a time to get it good and going right and then the others can be integrated into the whole. And that's the point: To be whole. All the disparate parts, you keep wanting to throw out or keep first. Finally, you embrace all your parts so that you are your whole full self.

I think I came all this way to integrate all my departments and allow that they work together to bring something special that only I can bring. That's what I came here to know, and now I do know it and I am willing to integrate my talents together.

I'm at the port just now having a spanakopita made especially for me by Spiro, the baker. The old fishermen are sitting on the dock waiting for their sons to bring the boats into the harbor at the end of the day. Because many of them spent their youth diving for sponges, they have neurological concerns now.

I see one fisherman in particular, Constantine. I can see his whole life and the life of all the members of his family. I see an additional developing health concern for him. I send healing light to him and his family.

My empathy has returned to me. I am in awe to welcome it back.

It won't be long now before I am ready to leave the island.

At a party, at the home of one of the expat artists, I had a wonderful conversation with a prominent international director about world cinema. It was brilliant. Stimulating.

Later, the party host asked me what I was talking about with the director.

I said, "World cinema. It was brilliant. I realized that I've been missing intellectual conversation."

She said, "He doesn't speak English."

Oh, jeez, no wonder I thought he was brilliant, I was doing all the talking!

One thing you learn on an island—know the time of the ferry and know when it's time for you to be on it. Well, it's time for me to be on it.

Travel is so broadening we don't even know what enrichment we get from where, but now that I'm on the hydrofoil leaving the island, I know I've got that enrichment with me. Whatever I came to develop, to shift, to clarify, to empower, whatever I flung myself across the world to do, I did.

I see the island receding behind me. I turn and look forward, filled. ~

38 Years Old

Elevator

ON MY WAY back to Los Angeles, I stop by New York and I'm on the street at possibly the one and only continuing working pay phone.

I was just in the Fifth Avenue library reading *Publisher's Weekly* because I realized that even though I didn't speak Greek when I was in Greece, I'm a little rusty on soundbite, buzzword English. If what I want to do is meet with agents and let them know I'm coming to present my content, I better be able to pitch my content.

So, I got the lingo and a more rapid-fire cadence, and I'm ready to make calls now on the one working street phone.

I make a lot of calls and connect to Connie Clausen, a top New York agent who says, in perfect New York style, "Come over now."

So, I hop in a cab and get there fast.

I intend for this meeting to be a get-acquainted visit in preparation for talking about the book that you are reading now but that won't be ready for decades. I'm starting now since I have no idea how long it will take to make inroads into publishing, maybe years.

The office is on the 16th floor. As I am going up in the elevator, I ask myself, "What would be the best and highest content that I can offer now with the information and inspiration that I have at this moment to give?"

I knew that what was on the tip of my heart was a desire to utilize all that I had culled from the blood, sweat, and tears I had accumulated in my adventures of being a writer in Hollywood.

By then I was somewhere between the 9th and the 11th floors. As I continued to go up in the elevator, the idea for a book came down into me. By the 12th floor, the Inner Movie Method arrived already in me, sitting in perfection, awaiting my permission to start its heart beating.

By the 16th floor, I had organized the pitch, then I knocked on the door, and made the deal for *How to Write a Movie in 21 Days – The Inner Movie Method.* *

Beloved and I will be happy to have me come home now. ~

~~~

*(Note from the future) It turns out that this book becomes an industry standard and best-seller in its field for years to come.

39 Years Old

How to Rest on Your Laurels in Paradise

MY BOOK, *How to Write a Movie in 21 Days: The Inner Movie Method,* is done! I am here on a tropical island to reflect on the experience of writing it. I'm here to take the deep breath after my outstanding achievement in becoming an overnight success in just fifteen years.

Here's the conversation that I am having with myself on the beach:

Life is *big.* Milestones and events that visit everyone's life, such as weddings and babies and grief and love—when they are in *your* life—are a very big deal. To experience them takes everything you've got, and then it takes even more. And it's supposed to! That's the point. It takes you through a cracking open of everything in you to arrive at a more expanded version of yourself. Now you own that bigger territory of yourself that you couldn't reach before. These things that take so much out of you, add so much to you. Expansion expands you.

Writing that book was an enormous force of energy to bring it up through me, to get it done. I'm reeling from its effect. How could such a thing take so much to get between pages? I huffed and puffed up the hill. From "I will do this" to "It is." I did do it. I am here.

Months ago, two dear ones to me, my Beloved and my best friend, Libby, cornered me in the car and did an intervention on me—a writer's intervention. They were worried that it was killing me to get this thing done. Now it is done. I love it. And I'm in paradise to decompress, to rest, to take the way-down-deep breath and exhale. Ah. My book is alive. It has a life force all its own—capable of being out in the wide, wide world meeting millions of readers that it can help. Right now, as I am here rejuvenating, and getting ready for it, it is in New York getting printed and published and put between its beautiful front and back covers and sent on its adventures out in the world. I can hear its heart beating on its own, right next to mine. I bless its great grand life just beginning now.

And me too. Who I was as I was writing it now evolves to who I am having written it. There's someone I no longer am, the one who worked to get here. Now, I am here, someone new for me to get acquainted with. What I aspired to be; I have become. And what I aspire for it to be, it is becoming. Gifts all around.

As I am reveling in this new territory, getting used to the new expanded version of myself and readying to experience my book in the world, there is a familiar figure coming toward me on the beach. It's a long-ago friend from Hollywood.

Years ago, in network television, we partnered on a few scripts, hoping to get work as writers. As I was on speakerphone finalizing the last details of a very big series deal for us, he sat right across from me listening intensely while his eyes jetted away as far from that impending success as he could fling himself. I knew he would find a way to self-sabotage, and within the week he disappeared, never to return to Hollywood. Although friends, I haven't seen him until today.

I find out now that he took up residence in a van on a beach on this island, and he has lived here in the van on the beach ever since. It seems like heaven, but I think there is a piece of private hell in it for him. Can you really find paradise if you leave behind something you were too scared to let yourself have?

As we sit at my condo pool, catching up, I notice him judge and criticize the families enjoying their vacations. The man who is excited about his promotion, and the teen who lusts after the Porsche—to him they are all "losers." He says, "They are sleepwalking the American Dream. None of them know what's what."

So, I ask him, "Well then what *is* what?"

And apparently, he doesn't seem to know either, but he is sure that everybody in and around the beach today is a "loser."

That's fine, I don't begrudge anybody their worldview, and yet he is dissing and simultaneously soaking up the amenities at my pool area. There is an ice case here with complimentary cola of which he has taken several bottles. He has also taken three beach towels. And now he's speaking critically of many of our mutual friends who stayed back in Hollywood when he left. What did any of us ever do to him? I see what we did—we succeeded. We got what he didn't get. He's not feeling his own happiness for the life he chose. He's feeling the loss of the road he didn't take. He wished to be a writer but never wrote.

At one point I mentioned that I was here on the island decompressing after having written my book. I said, "It was huge to get it done."

And he said, "I know," and I knew he didn't know.

It's a private club, the one you are a member of when you have experienced what someone else hasn't. One of the very best aspects of coming through something deep and wide and hard and done is that you know. And you don't know until you do.

You don't know your own strength if you never stretch it all the way to its full capacity. You miss out on what is the magical, wondrous nature of your life force. Knowing your own strength is one of the vital components of a soul's journey. Knowing your own strength is one of the gifts you get for daring to go for it. When you opt out, then all your life force has left is maybe to be mad at everybody else for your missed dream.

My phone rings in my condo that is just off the pool area. I go to answer it and realize that he has followed right behind me and is now in the bathroom and *taking a shower.*

I suppose someone who lives outside without plumbing never passes up an opportunity when they get near hot and cold running water. But really, I would have preferred he at least ask. Why do I even care? Well, I don't care about the shower, I care that he seems to be unresolved about the dream he said he had but didn't materialize.

How much better you feel when you've done something than when you haven't. Yet, I think everybody has their own success. It must have been a big achievement for him to leave the mainland behind. It must have taken fortitude, or something had to kick in for him to accomplish that.

Every soul has its mission. The one they take or the one they don't take. Not taking a path is a path in itself. All roads lead to yourself.

Oh, this is so funny, you're not even going to believe what just happened. He's coming out of the condo after the *very long shower,* and he's taken a banana from my kitchen. Of course, banana envy!

He's welcome to the banana; I claim the world. The man who couldn't/wouldn't doesn't stop me from delivering.

But I don't want to leave it there. I don't want to have the meaning of my accomplishing something wonderful be that somebody else is uncomfortable. I hope that what I put out in the world inspires people to accomplish what they want to accomplish.

I remember that look he had in his eyes when he beat it on out of Hollywood. At least some part of it was the look toward the destiny that *does* belong to him: the destiny that suits him better and fulfills his reason for being. Everybody's got an instinct for their own right life no matter how it may look from the outside. I know his glory is in him. He has his lifespan to divulge it to himself. And anyway, I'm his friend, so I'll get to see it when it appears.

～～

Just as suddenly as he appeared, he now gathers up the towels, the sodas, the banana, and leaves before he invites himself to stay for dinner.

His surprise visit into my life today is there to tell me that even though I wrote my book to help people to get their dream to come true, not everybody wants their dream to come true.

I wrote my book as an invitation for anyone with a heart's desire to give them all the beats it takes to deliver on it, all the beats to have it come true.

In one word I would say that my book is *permission* to stop stopping yourself and keep going through all the ten thousand bumps along the way of any dream you have.

My book offers that despite how hard it is, how scared you are, how distracted you can make yourself; you can still accomplish your heart's desire.

There's a full section in it titled "Embracing the Impossible Obstacles." It addresses such issues as "Psychosomatic Ailments That Only Writers Can Think Up to Stop Themselves", "What to Do about the Heebie-Jeebies." Even "How to Pay the Rent While Paying Your Dues," and a whole chapter on what you'll run into with the family and how to make them your greatest champions. That's called "What to Say to Your Spouse When You Can't Come to Bed." And there's even a chapter that is required reading for your family to know how to cope with you.

I'm all for everyone breaking through whatever is so important to them that it scares them the most, stops them the hardest, and with my book they can find their way through to do it anyway.

You can apply *the Inner Movie Method* to any pursuit in the action-adventure of your life and you'll be sure to come out the hero. If anybody just wants a *very long shower* and a few amenities—well, okay. To each his own. There's nothing like that good feeling when you do the thing you wanted to do. ~

39 Years, Later That Day

Lifting the Veil of Invisibility

As I WALK along the beach at sunset, I notice people are staring at me. Why are they staring? They must not know I'm invisible.

There is a plane I operate on that is a private stratosphere, a place to create magic without being observed as I continue my self-appointed job of dispensing light and not being seen while I'm doing it.

As I think this, I walk past the condo lobby's full-length mirrors. The sunset is gleaming off my copper-studded, highly reflective, custom-made bikini. Oh, I see, now I am visible. ~

40s Passage

In Full Bloom

JUST BEFORE MY birthday, I asked my photographer friend Riley to take a celebratory picture of me leaping into forty. I got lots of prints of the picture, mounted them on thank you cards, and sent a copy out to everyone I could think of who was in my first forty years. I thanked each person for their particular contribution to my life. It was a beautiful exercise in gratitude to specifically tell each person what they mean to me. Since I sent them out early, I'm already noticing in my travels, as I visit many of the people, that my cards, with my exuberant leap, have landed on their refrigerator doors. When I acknowledged each person, it meant so much to them I am here on refrigerators around the world. What a great surprise birthday gift back to me.

I bring this up because it reminds me that we just don't know our effect and influence on others. At forty it's a good time to get conscious of personal power and manage it responsibly. It's a beautiful time of life to be posted on loved ones' refrigerators.

I'm aware that when I walk into a room, I'm going to change the current of the air. Will I be oxygen for others, or will I drain the life right out of them? At forty my choice is to be the fresh air in my and someone else's life.

So today it's my actual fortieth birthday, and I'm in Cabo San Lucas at the end of the Baja Peninsula at the beautiful Resort del Sol on the beach. I'm here continuing to work on *this* book.

Last night I had a dream in which I built a sandcastle. I did it myself, alone. That's usual. That's pretty much how I operate. Today I decided to build an actual sandcastle on the beach to see what there is to learn between last night's dream and today's reality.

Forty years, and I have gotten here. My methods are I don't give up; I don't take no for an answer; I have been scared but I do it anyway; I decide what I wish to have in my life and then create it. I am the source of my experience.

And now at forty, thanks to the climb it took to get here and the continued love and wisdom from Beloved, I switch from getting there to being here. I am here now. I let the magic come to me. I put in the good ingredients and reap a rich harvest. I proceed, I follow the natural phenomenon. Life happens for me. So, let's see what happens from that.

I show up on the beach and immediately find a child's sand shovel. Let the new castle materialize.

Immediately I notice this castle won't be like the one that I built in my dream.

I discover that the sand is not sandy. It is gravelly with rocks. Here I am on the beach with my shovel but no way that the sand is going to pack and pile. I see it will have to be a stone castle. I start to gather rocks to stack them on each other. Within moments two men show up with curiosity and each with a strong work ethic. We start building together. Our meeting is like kids in kindergarten, we just come together and play as new best friends with no preamble or discussion. We instantly get to work, each of us at our natural strengths. I see that I am the designated supervisor, yet no one has to be supervised. Our castle starts materializing. It seems to know how it wants to be put together, and we just keep a steady pace of doing the next and the next thing.

One of the men, Phil, begins to realize that he has a talent for masonry as he balances one rock on top of the next and creates sturdy walls stacked eight feet high. With the back wall being supported against the bluff, there will be no mortar and no need for any.

The other man, Frank, busies himself dredging a grand moat all around. It's as though we knew this as our mission from ancient times and we showed up on this beach today to do our part.

Now our castle seems to be putting out a beacon of welcome as more people show up.

Those who are strolling along the beach seem to want to contribute. One muscular teen drags several palm fronds to our building site. He allocates them as the roof. A dog brings us the first tennis ball and people bring dozens more to line the bridge that crosses the moat. Kelp washes itself up on the beach to be draped along our gateposts as a welcoming roped entrance.

Little kids come for a pretend tea party. They bring their own furniture, a found beach chair, and a straw hat to hang on the wall. A washed-ashore lobster trap becomes the window frame.

One weathered local said, "Man, I could live in there."

The concierge from the five-star hotel comes out to ask if he can send a photo crew down to take shots to use in their ad brochure. And when the hotel crew comes, they're equipped with soda pop, snacks, and ice water for our working pleasure.

A photographer with his girlfriend uses the site for a bikini location shoot.

An irrigation engineer on vacation is eager to instruct us on how to get the water to the moat. He is so proud to express his knowledge in front of his family.

Random beachgoers pick up random flipflops found along the tide line and drop them off for us to include. We amass quite a few, which I put at the front door. It gives the impression that there is a party going on inside with lots of one-footed revelers.

Some people don't like it—a celebrity who came to the beach for seclusion complains that it is attracting too much attention. A lawyer thought someone could get hurt and the hotel would be liable. His wife rolls her eyes and says, "You're supposed to be on vacation from all of that."

And then, there at the end of the day just before sunset, there it is, a grand stone castle on the beachfront property at the very tip of the Baja Peninsula. Astonishing. Beyond our wildest thoughts yet materialized clear and here.

In the end, it comes back down to Phil, Frank, and me. We use the last of the soda pop to toast our creation. The end product is spectacular. The by-products are the deep feelings of it. Something happened for us in having this experience. We will leave here with more than we came with.

As the tide comes in, pieces of our castle go out. We like that; this temporary structure embeds something within us eternally. We saw it from not there, to being there, to now going back to pieces on the beach. How did all those parts come together to become this grand thing? And then rearrange itself back into pieces? Each rock and flip-flop came together in magnetic connection and then floated off as the palm fronds now float on the waves and travel back down the beach in the direction they came. What is left is the eternal imprint on us. All the best from all the pieces.

Frank shakes my hand and thanks me and chokes up. He says he never experienced anything like it. He says, "It made me feel bigger than I am."

I say, "Maybe it just showed you how big you always have been but just didn't notice before."

Phil says he couldn't explain why but he thought it was the most important thing that ever happened to him.

For me, it is simple arithmetic. All the pieces add up to more than each piece separately. As with everything, its meaning is what we decide it to mean. Even for the lawyer.

That Day at Sunset

After our magical sun-drenched day on the beach and castle building, I am back in my hotel room reflecting on the sandcastle as a metaphor for life. I marvel at all the parts of ourselves that come together and go apart throughout the span of a lifetime. The light of the setting sun fills the room and bounces off the beautiful bathroom mirror—overlooking Baja and the whole sea.

As I step out of the shower, I catch a glimpse of my body in this sunlight. I see that, nude, I have tan marks that appear as though my bikini is still on me. I take the quintessential photo of myself in the beautiful mirror that is reflecting the setting sun.

The photo that Riley took of me jumping into forty, that I sent out to all my dear ones to commemorate being forty, that one was the public one, this photo, nude in the mirror, is my private moment snapped of me at forty. Here I am in full bloom—remarkable. From way back there when I was just conceiving this life to this delicious present moment. Ah, so lovely to be alive.

When I was in my twenties, Beloved used to say to me, "You'll be great at forty."

I would retort, "I'm great now."

And I was and he agreed, yet I see his meaning—now at forty I notice that I am lit from within. ~

40 Years Old

CNN

I'VE BEEN ASKED to be on CNN to promote my book, *How to Write a Movie in 21 Days: The Inner Movie Method*. Yes! Thank you!

The studio call was for 5:00 p.m., the show airs at 6:00. The guard downstairs pointed to the elevator and said to go to the Green Room—there would be a sign on the door. That was the last human I saw. The next hour . . . Well, I'll tell you about it.

I found the Green Room. It's bare bones—not exactly a grand décor to bespeak the prestige of this international news network.

In fact, it's just me in here and a huge clock ticking off each minute of airtime as the high-decibel, on-air audio feed blares so loud you can probably hear it right now all the way to your house. I'm reminded that prisoners of war sometimes are tormented by loud broadcasts constantly blaring so it's impossible for them to keep a thought straight. So here I am not keeping a thought straight.

I occupy myself by trying to climb up the wall to reach the speaker to somehow turn the damn thing off. When this doesn't work, I decide to leave and go find someone. The door is locked. I'm locked in!

I knock on the door and then pound on it. No one comes.

Is this the Green Room? Maybe I'm not in the real Green Room. Maybe they're looking for me and I'm not there, I'm here.

There's no phone or emergency alarm or food. No food!

Does anybody know I'm here? Will anybody find my body before rigor mortis sets in? See what I mean about what loud noise does to thoughts?

Okay, since action isn't working, let's move to a Zen approach. Letting the Divine plan unfold. Ohm. Letting the self be at one with the noise. I am in equilibrium . . . I am . . . I am . . . it is . . . Oy Vey!

5:34 They could have put craft services in here—at least a deli tray or a candy machine. (You know how I am—no matter what's going on, I'm fine when there's food available.)

5:37 I try some stretches and a little soft shoe.

5:40 Let's assess the situation. I am alive. Soon, I will want dinner. Sometime tomorrow I have meetings; if I don't show up, will scouts be sent to pick up my trail?

5:41 Maybe if there was a magazine in here or a window to look out of, or jump out of, something.

5:41:30 Unless it's a low-budget TV station you're usually greeted by the producer who takes you around, brings coffee, escorts you to hair and makeup - all points are covered gracious living wise. Not here. Not at CNN International.

As the clock ticks off to airtime—still no one comes.

5:57 still nothing happening. International television, the chance of a lifetime, and I'm a "no show" due to being locked in the Green Room (if this really is the Green Room). It's not even green. Although they never are.

5:58 Maybe I won't be found until days from now when the next person booked on the show will be directed to the Green Room, and they'll find my dead body, but they'll have to go on the air anyway as an expert in their field.

One minute to airtime—still no response.

Twenty seconds to air . . . The door flings open, the floor manager bolts in as directives are being squawked out of his headset. These people like it loud. Except, here is the soundman right behind him. I can hardly hear him as he whispers and pulls at my clothes to put the mic on me as I'm swooped down the corridor at breakneck velocity toward the studio.

Now an earbud is put in my ear and now a sound level check. "Hello, my name is—" I'm cut off. No time to say my name? Do I even know my name at this point?

A release form is thrust before me to sign without reading. I'm now quickly seated and hooked into the completely dark announcement booth. It's a small black padded box. I am rigged in. It's so dark I have to blindly adjust my vision to see the one little red tally light against the blacked-out wall. In there somewhere is the camera lens pointing right at me—when it comes on, I'll be on.

Yikes, here comes on a thousand-watt interrogation light.

If you've ever watched CNN and seen distinguished experts in their field look like deer in headlights, they are in this small dark padded booth with this interrogation light on them, not being able to see the camera, barely hearing (on a delay) the interviewer's questions. Where is he anyway?

Did I mention, this interrogation light is beyond flashbulb bright? It's not just for, say, if you committed jaywalking. This is an interrogation light that would be used for a major crime.

Nevertheless, I'm ever so serene.

This much I know about myself: When there is a crisis or high drama all around, I'll go into a deep calm and kick into constructive action. I am the picture of methodical, assured, effectiveness.

Later, I'll throw up.

Everything in Life Leads You Where You're Going

And now, from locked in the Green Room to international exposure in five seconds and counting,

That's when my life flashes before me, not my whole life, just all the parts I need at this moment.

From years of broadcasting and production, I know to smooth out my shoulder line and sit squarely in the frame of the shot. I wipe sweat off my top lip, so perspiration doesn't reflect in the camera. I clear my throat. I pull off my earrings that I see could be distracting because this set is lit very hot. I hold my head at a slight pitch to let the key light bounce off my eyes instead of making me squint. I angle the lavalier, so I don't pop my p's, locate the lens in relation to the tally light, and create eye contact with the interviewer, who I just find out is in their studio in Atlanta or Washington or New York, or somewhere not here.

Those are some minor things that are second nature to me, having been on-air many times before.

And now, counting.

In three . . .

I think of my eighth-grade gym teacher who had good posture. I'm reminded—when you've got something to say, sit up straight to say it.

The gift of every little thing in my life has a purpose for this moment in my life.

And most importantly, this is a platform I take seriously. I breathe in a focused breath and with high intention—no matter what the question that's asked of me, may the answer illuminate something that comforts and inspires the viewer who is in his recliner chair making a prayer for his eternal salvation.

In two . . .

Out of lockdown and into the wide-open airwaves.

In one . . .

And we go live! I'm in my element, I know how to speak sound bite. I'll talk to you later because right now, I'm on. ~

41 Years Old

Writers Guild of America

I'M ABOUT TO go on stage at the Writer's Guild to speak to an all-seats-filled, standing-room-only crowd of Hollywood working writers regarding my book *How to Write a Movie in 21 Days: The Inner Movie Method.*

Before I start, I am in the bathroom. As I am about to leave the stall, I lean over and the one very big, only button holding my jumpsuit pops off while one of my earrings also pops off and both rush down the drain, gone forever. How curious? Why do you suppose that happened?

I come out of the stall holding my jumpsuit together with both hands and ask the ladies around the mirror if anyone has a safety pin. They, being writers, get into the story of it right away and one, known for her crime drama, goes into high anxiety and crisis mode regarding my current circumstance. Another, known for her Good Samaritan movies, ushers the crime lady out the door to her seat so I can take care of what I have to do to take care of me. A producer just finishing at the sink has a needle and thread that she leaves for me.

Now to attend to my chic silk Rodeo Drive retail jumpsuit—the whole thing was held on by that one big button at the waist. My plan is to make my remaining earring into the *new* button and sew it on securely, so it doesn't burst open in front of the all-seats-filled, standing-room-only crowd.

All I have to do is thread the needle. It's a little dark in here and my reading glasses are already up at the podium. Somehow, the thread has to get through the needle and . . . it *does.* Maybe it is thanks to the ghost of costume designer Edith Head still hanging around Hollywood after her death. I do notice how steady-handed I am. Anyway, crisis averted. I go backstage, ready to go on.

What *was* all that about? Maybe to let me know I am ready.

Wow, it really is packed. I see that this is my moment. It has been a long time coming. Do you notice that in your life, it's longer than you think it should take for you to get where you hoped you were going? But when you do get there, you arrive right on time. As in, I might have always known what I had to say; now, I am whom I have become to say it.

I have a chance to reflect on this backstage because the official of the Guild, who is introducing me, is taking a long time with the introduction. It's almost like a eulogy, like I'm dead, maybe it's death to the climb it took for me to get here.

Manny, Moe, and Jack

When I first came to Hollywood, there were three top producers that I could not get on the phone. You might have heard me refer to them as Manny, Moe, and Jack. I always felt in my heart that I would be working with each on something significant and wonderful, but no luck, no return calls, no dice. It's been a long and winding road from then to now. Here is a platform graciously given to me. Here is how I make my contribution to the goings-on in Hollywood. I had no idea that I would finally be having such a hand in many movies and many lives as I have recently become a part of, shaping and shepherding many film projects into being. My dream came true bigger than I thought.

And so, the long and winding introduction does come to an end, and I step onto the platform.

I look up to the audience to begin and here, in the front row, sitting next to each other are Manny, Moe, and Jack—the three producers I could not get on the phone years before. Astonishing.

Years ago, when I called them, I wanted something from them, and now I see that they come to me because I have something to give to them.

Oh, now I get why my button flew off. In screenwriting, when an earlier scene is revisited later in the script with a new payoff, it's known as a button scene. Thank you, Manny, Moe, and Jack. ~

42 Years Old

Life is Like a Metaphor

By NOW, MANY people in Hollywood have my number. They're calling for wisdoms for their lives. This started way back—well, always. People have always asked me to tell them what's on *their minds*. Strangers on the street, my friends on staff, and now famous people in Hollywood will call with all their personal dilemmas. I seem to be private counsel to anybody with feelings about anything.

I happen to have a class that I teach that's exclusive for twelve people who are luminaries in the movie industry. The class is on writing their scripts. These are successful producers and directors who wish to have a different slant on viewing their scripts and the screenwriters that they are working with. The class is private and takes place in the home of one of the producers. We meet once a week in the formal dining room of his sumptuous Bel Air home.

One evening, one of the women attending, who is an heir in a Hollywood prominent family, asked if we could have coffee after the class. She said that there was something that she wanted to discuss with me.

So sure, we did, and this is what she needed to talk about:

She said that her birthday was coming up and she would be inheriting another million dollars on that day, and she wanted me to help her to figure out what she should do with it.

So, I said, "Well, you can pay for the coffee."

This opened up something quite amazing for me. I helped her to create a foundation and match places and needs in the world that fit her feelings and sensibilities. It started a whole movement of celebrities contributing to helping in creative ways around the world.

I always believed that a star is not known just because they're cute or talented; there is something about them that fans resonate with. They spend years using their energy to "get there;" once they "are there," they can use their energy to lift the world.

For one actress, who grew up on a farm and loved farm animals, we put together a livestock program for remote villages in three different countries. When mother goats have their babies in one village, the babies are brought to the next village, and when they have babies, they go to the next village, and so forth. This develops and expands the livestock for several rural areas.

One director, who had to quit school early when he was a kid, values education, so he is building schoolhouses.

My fondness is for waterworks so communities can have clean water to drink and use for agriculture.

It's amazing what you can do to give a boost to others that turns around and impacts you as well.

To get back to the woman who is from the long lineage of Hollywood achievers but not yet able to own her own worth. She makes movies, but every time she hits any kind of obstacle she goes off to Aspen to ski or Paris to shop. Because she hands the responsibility off to someone else, she hasn't yet felt the personal fruition of any of her projects.

One day I said to her, "Were you born caesarian?"

And she said, "Yes, how did you know?"

"Because you're not letting yourself feel how it feels to get yourself born. You learned to let somebody else do that for you."

She may never have the fortitude to see a thing through, but here's the wondrous part—her foundation helps thousands of at-risk children at childbirth, and that's very gratifying to her.

P.S. If you were born caesarian, this doesn't mean that you have her character. You have a different meaning from your birth.

Call me. We can talk it over.

43 Years Old

The Fourth of July—Twenty Years Later

I AM HERE invited to this beautiful Malibu beach house with a million-dollar view. I see by the exquisiteness of the property that the million-dollar view probably cost about nine million dollars.

Just in front of me is a Bentley pulling up to the valet parking. There's a bumper sticker on its fender, *Walk for the Hungry*. A movie star actress is just getting out of the car. I realize she rides as the well-fed.

It's the Fourth of July. There is a party going on for about two hundred guests.

This is the home of a writer-producer whom I admire. His latest film is a great inspiration to me, and I'm sure the millions of people who will see it will be inspired too. He had his secretary call and invite me here today. I know that I will be offered a high opportunity. This is how business is done at this level. I'm honored to be invited. I see our host is out on the sand with many Hollywood luminaries who also have homes on this beach.

I notice that people are walking around as though this is a model home and they are passing judgment on each room.

I hear one woman say, "I'd never use that shower."

To my knowledge, no one has asked her to move in. The shower is a huge, has-to-be-seen-to-be-believed, glass room. You could pull a small sports car in there and detail it while you're showering with ten of your closest friends.

Another guest says, when he walks into the beautifully appointed library, "This is my taste."

His taste? I think that would be a Naugahyde recliner chair.

I'm as inspired by this beautiful home as he is, as all the guests are. The way there is great-sounding music in each room, the fluff of each pillow, the softness of the lighting on all the art. There's no clutter!

All the little soaps are so perfectly arranged in an abalone shell. The caterer uses a bar towel to keep the Carrara marble surfaces from water spots.

There is constant attention by the waitstaff in picking up glasses and wiping down surfaces. Such quality of materials all around—it makes a difference to have the softest towels. No dust anywhere. There's a light fragrance of freshness like your lungs can take on more air than they've ever had before and are forever expanded. This is just like the broadening benefit of travel to places you've never been. It's giving me the experience to soak up and expand *my* world.

The party moves from room to room. A moment before, I was talking to several interesting people; now, I notice I am alone in the study and realize it is the host's office. I'm always in awe to view where an artist sits to let what comes to them through them and onto the page. It's the most private reverie just between your heart and yourself that develops in the a.m. hours to then go public as a worldwide global feature film. This is probably where he wrote his splendid current film. I look at his bookcase. Oh, my heart just leaps. My book, *How to Write a Movie,* is here right next to his computer, at his desk in an exalted place and it has Post-its throughout.

I immediately think of the hundreds of readers who have said to me, "Your book is my bible." It's such a joy to have written something that can uplift and encourage someone else to do their creating. All highlighted and dog-eared and used as a companion to their creations; such great gratitude I feel in that. And now this man, he's used my book on the movie he's just released that's wonderful and inspiring.

No wonder I was inspired by his film—my book inspired him.

While I am in the study with this lilting music playing, there are fireworks about to take place on the beach.

I'm remembering when I got off the train in downtown Los Angeles on the fourth of July, twenty years ago. I faced in the direction of the ocean and made my wish. Such a little flame on the match I struck, so much noise in this world, yet I was clear. I'm happy how it's turned out so far. I'm happy about my choices. Just because you say you're going to do something does not make it so. Just because you want a thing to transpire does not mean it will. And when you do what you said you want to do, and you are who you said you want to be, then it feels spectacular to be it.

I see a book of matches that is platinum-plated, maybe purchased at great expense from Tiffany's or Geary's in Beverly Hills. And here, etched on the surface in gold— "The best things in life are free."

Oh, and here is the host coming toward me. Time for the next wish. ~

43 Years and 1 Month

The Fourth of July and a Half
As IT TURNED out, the Fourth of July party *was* a good place for business. The host-producer engaged my counsel regarding his next projects. I have also become the creative consultant on films for other writers and producers and directors in town. It's the next place to stand with the next lever long enough to lift the world. ~

44 Years Old

Enough Is More Than Enough

I JUST LEFT my tax accountant's office. While there, I made out my tax check. My heart was pounding in my signature hand.

I am still dazed as I exit the 405 freeway. I realize this is *my* off-ramp. I just paid for it.

When I was five years old, I was on a television show like Art Linkletter's *Kids Say the Darnedest Things*. The man asked me, "How much money is enough money?"

I said, "Enough to pay the taxes."

I just paid my taxes, and, while I was shaking, I did have enough. So I now stop shaking and appreciate my off-ramp. Next year I'll buy the Federal Building that's right here just next to my off-ramp on Wilshire in Westwood. There will always be enough. ~

45 Years Old

My Childhood Neighborhood

I'm INVITED TO be the featured speaker and present a seminar at a conference in Chicago where I grew up.

When I was a little kid, I remember Irv Kupcinet, who was a columnist for the *Chicago Sun-Times*. He had a show on TV at that time, *Kup's Show*, where he interviewed successful authors coming through town. The set for the show was in limbo—a dark background with lights just on the people as they sat on couches around a low table. Irv smoked a cigar. The smoke would waft up into the lighting. I thought it was so sophisticated. I was enthralled. I remember a question he asked a guest: "When did you know you would be all right?" I love that question. I remember thinking that I wanted to be an author on his show. I was maybe seven at the time. Now I'm forty-five, and I'm actually in Chicago, coming into town to lecture on my book. I *am* a successful author.

I'm in my hotel room having a lavish room-service breakfast delivered on a tray with the *Chicago Sun-Times*. And here is Kup's column still going strong. He must be well into his late 70s or more by now and still a city luminary. Surprise, surprise, today in his column he has announced that *I'm* in town with my book and my lecture and my weekend seminar that I'll be starting later today.

Imagine my delight! Thank you, Kup! I'm so thrilled. I put a call in to him at the paper to tell him what I'm just telling you, that he means so much to me. He is great on the phone. We have our own private talk show conversation, about how he inspired my life, and how he's inspired by my call to him. I get to tell him that maybe it all started for me seeing him in limbo lighting when I was seven years old.

Feeling so expanded by our conversation; I decide to visit my childhood neighborhood. It's early. The soundcheck isn't until later this afternoon. The promoter for the seminar must have been the one responsible for getting the mention in Kup's column. She and her team seem to have everything in order, so I decide yes, I'll go. I haven't been back to my neighborhood since childhood when Kup's show was on the air.

The hotel concierge has the map out and concludes that I probably can't make it there and back before evening rush hour. The doorman says you can't get there from here. I think this is funny since most of us can access our childhoods just under the skin. Scratch the surface of any prominent CEO, who wields great power, and he's still the kid who got picked last at baseball. Of course, we can all get there from here because we carry that kid with us. Going on that premise, I catch a cab and I'm there in twenty minutes.

From Michigan Avenue to Mulligan Avenue

How far is it really to reenter your past self? I know how far I had to come out of it to get here. Knowing what I know now about what was going on there, I want to come back and see if I'm okay as a kid. I want to know how that little kid of me is faring. I want to tell me I will make it out okay.

And now, not a moment sooner, and here I am—Mulligan Avenue. It's so small. I think something ironic—it seems to be such a nice little street to raise a family.

It looks as though a Sears salesman has come along and sold the whole block on siding. Is this really it? School that seemed so far away then is just at the end of the block, turn left. The prairie where Pudgy found snakes is just a vacant lot next door to Libby's house. This is where we chased lightning bugs, where we did the bunny hop for Emily's sixteenth birthday, where we'd clear the street at eight o'clock on Monday because *I Love Lucy* would come on. Going around the back, I can feel my mother's morning glories growing along the fence, long gone now. The yard rings a bell in me. We had the only brick garage on the street. There is the unpaved cinder alley that we ran down barefoot to get to Mr. Wingee's tiny store for penny candy. Mary Janes, waxed lips, tootsie rolls, my brother's favorite—bull's eyes. What penny candy did you like? None of us liked Pez. It tasted "ucky," but we loved the dispensers.

I am standing in the alley between time dimensions when a homeowner comes out to empty the garbage right where Patsy Palucci's teeter totter used to be a moment before, or was it forty years ago?

Because the homeowner looks at me warily, I become visible to myself. I realize I am standing in my childhood alley as a grown woman wearing a fashion-forward raincoat I bought this year in Milan that matches Milan more than Mulligan. How did that little barefoot kid become me now?

As I stand here, I give love to the three-year-old child of me in the house. "I hold you so that you know the nature of your future self, so you can get here from there. The light in me salutes the light in you."

This was my backyard. We used to have a swing set. I can almost hear it squeak. I liked to swing so high that the whole swing set would move around the yard, and when I finished my high swinging, I'd push the whole thing back into the holes that were supposed to support it.

There was something about swinging as high as high can be. I think I was teaching myself a skill set for life.

I swing now in my imagination and feel the height of it. I think of Kup's question, When did you know you would be all right? Any life can answer that.

It's when we make that call, or turn our back, or open our heart, or voice that declaration, or get up after falling down, or surrender, or apologize, or forgive, or take a nap, or wake up, or spend the money, or save for later, or get out of there, or ask why me, or decide to get on with it, or let peace in, or be grateful, or allow love, or let go, or hang on, or walk away, or never give up, or stay, or leave, or do the thing that scares us the most, or take the plunge, or go off the deep end, or when we no longer touch it with a ten-foot pole, and finally, finally when our heart cracks open and the miracle comes in.

Dear one on the swing, you are a resilient kid. I'm here to intercede for you, and you are fine. I can let you be, to become who you were intending me to be. I see that I could be trusted all along to be there when I needed me.

I think that the opportunity for any of us to revisit our childhood comes right on time. If I had come earlier, I might have had to brace myself for the memories that would come up. Today, in this moment, my childhood doesn't need me to heal it. If I had come back here any sooner, I might not have memories that include penny candy.

I get back in the waiting cab to speed back to the hotel, my seminar, my life now.

"When did I know I would be all right?"

I always knew. ~

46 Years Old

Beyond Visualization: Feel It in Your Heart, Have It in Your Life

THIS IS YET another year of international lecturing. All this year as I travel, I am also writing my next commissioned book, *Beyond Visualization: Feel It in Your Heart, Have It in Your Life*. I'm writing that one while I'm continuing to write the book that you are now reading. Both have been written on airplanes, in hotels, and at airports. Each book has a life of its own, and both are coming right along.

For *Beyond Visualization* I coined the word *"feelization."*

Einstein said e=mc2 which is energy equals matter. In *feelization*, feelings matter.

Here's how it works.

When we want something, we also want the feeling we're going to have when we get it. With feelization we conjure up the feeling first. As we feel our heart's desire, we materialize the feeling into physical manifestation. Actually, we all do this all the time, but we aren't always conscious of how we bring things from nothing to being. I created this book to point out how it works.

Some chapters are:

"Why Goals are a Crock"

"You Can Have Anything You Want, What Do You Want?"

"If Energy is Unlimited, Why Am I So Tired?"

"The Answer to the Problem that Creates Another Problem is Not the Answer to the Problem"

"What You Want When You Want It All"

"Why Overachievers Feel Like Failures"

"How to Expand Time"

It's a useful book. I'm happy I wrote it. You can get it on Amazon. ~

~~~

Postscript from the future: *Beyond Visualizaton* was reissued as *Feelization: Feel It in Your Heart, Have It in Your Life*. Since I wrote most of this book while on airplanes, I used the metaphor of putting the oxygen mask on yourself before helping put it on anybody else. At the time, I got pushback. People didn't believe that was the way to take care of yourself so that you can take care of others. Since then, the oxygen mask on airplanes is probably the most used metaphor in our culture. Our philosophy has shifted, and it's still shifting as people are developing a new fundamental approach to care. It's a simple example of an important evolutionary step for humanity. ~

46 Years and 2 Months

Now I've Arrived for Sure

ONE OF MY lines of wisdom has landed as a quote on the tea boxes of Celestial Seasoning Tea. I am now quoted on Mango Zinger and briefly on Emperor Green Tea (although quickly replaced by the barcode). Not only am I now immortalized on tea boxes, but the good people of Celestial Seasoning graciously gifted me with a long supply of products.

Of all my quotable lines, I think they picked an agreeable one to complement the act of having a cup of tea. In case you happen to have your own cup brewing right now, here is my quote: "You won't be happy with more until you're happy with what you've got." ~

47 Years Old

Shutters on the Beach

THIS FIVE-STAR HOTEL is known to be a perfect setting for international deal-making on multimillion-dollar movies. I am here as Oracle. I come onto projects early to shepherd them from idea to the launch of the film. I'm here through every small and delicate creation of the content of the story, to the financials, to the nerves of the executives, and the sheer terror of the director on Day One. And we haven't even gotten to the actors yet.

For this movie, I'm here through heated negotiations between the studio, investors, distributor, and the creative team, who are always strange bedfellows, each with their eye on a different aspect of the production. They all want it to succeed, yet they all land in the crosshairs between show and business.

Things are getting confrontational. The project is threatened to never make it to being a movie. There is tension in this beautiful, elegant setting on the beach.

Here's where I come in. I suggest we take a fifteen-minute break. They can hardly agree on that but do go off to their separate rooms for a breather and a bathroom break. (Never underestimate the power of a bathroom break.) The idea is to reconvene serene. I leave my shoes under the conference table and run out the door, across the sand, and down to the water's edge. I want to put my feet in the cool Pacific that can do its alchemy on the future of this film.

How splendid—the sand, the surf, the sun-bright horizon. All is well with my feet, my whole body, my soul, my light.

Ah yes. All will smooth out with the factors on this project. This will be a wonderful film. Look for it at your local cineplex among next summer's releases.

When fifteen minutes are up, I dance back up the beach to the conference room.

There are two men lounging under the lifeguard stand, drinking from paper bags.

As I dance by, one holds his paper bag high and shouts to me, "Keep rockin' in the free world, sister."

Ah yes, my motto exactly. ~

48 Years Old

How to Save the World

IF GOD HAD meant for us to fly, he would have made the seats bigger.

I know that I'm on the road too long when the flight crew calls me by my first name, I've read all the inflight magazines, and I try my card key in the hotel door and realize that it is from three cities back. All these things have happened this week in my traveling life.

I'm out on the road with the last stop being the Forum on Global Affairs. It's a conference for brainstorming what can be done to fix things in the world such as cleaning the water up for drinking, building schools in rural villages, and organizing medicine airlifts.

In my travels I am seeing many of my colleagues, also on speaking circuits around the world, who will be meeting at the end of the week at the Forum.

I see that I'm not the only one who is feeling worn out. We all usually love the road and thrive on it, but we are all looking a little bit bedraggled.

You have to be careful with the road. You can be vitalized by it, but then it can turn on you quickly and you can feel like you're doing the flying while carrying the plane on your back. A storm in Toledo can affect connecting flights to Heathrow, and this week storms all over the world have had us delayed all over the world.

I prefer when my cup runneth over, not when my cup runneth into the ground.

I prefer having plenty of light to spare and share.

But alas, right now I'm scraping the sides of my energy reserves just to get myself through my venues and back on the next plane.

I have had to learn to billow out like a spinnaker sail when I'm on stage and then have the skill to pull my energy back into my body, so I can get on the airplane and be contained. I'm learning it, but I haven't fully mastered it.

The Wisdom of the Bellhop
Several cities back I was dragging up the stairs of the hotel, and the bellhop bounded up the stairs next to me, taking two at a time, and he said, "Can I do something for you?"

And I said, "I could use some of that energy that you've got."

And he said, "If I give it to you, then I'll be flat."

Well, there it is, that is exactly why—"I'll be flat" I gave my energy in twelve cities for the last two months.

I noted to take his wisdom to heart and put myself to bed the minute I got to the room. Which I did. Sometimes when you start to sleep you realize how tired you really are, and you could use another five days uninterrupted. Except that I didn't have the next five days uninterrupted.

The Messenger Deer
Along about Kyoto I had had enough of travel, with two more cities to go before the Forum.

In connection with one of my speeches here, I am looking forward to meeting up with the messenger deer. They live in a herd in Nara, Japan, in the park that surrounds the temple. The mythology is that when you are with them you receive a message—hence they are known as the messenger deer. Well, there I was in their park, and there they were in the distance, and I saw that as tourists approached them with treats, they would poke the tourists in the crotch area, which caused them to drop the wafer biscuits that the deer would then pick up and eat unencumbered by the taunts of the tourists. So much for their sacred status at the holy temple.

As I was contemplating this tainted turn of sacred events, I was eating my own rice cake when the deer came up to me wanting to poke me in my nether area. So, I said to them, "You have plenty. This food is for *me* to take care of *me*. *I* don't have to take care of you."

And there it is. The message from the messenger deer. Brilliant—I only needed to crisscross the world and get really exhausted to get this message. That's the very best beauty of travel. You always get a perfect message for yourself. It's always a very simple, exquisite message just for you that you most need to hear.

The difference between a tourist and a traveler is this: A tourist might visit a foreign place and event and deem it odd and different from home. A traveler gets the wisdom of what he or she is experiencing and brings it back from the road and takes it to heart. I like to recognize its value and incorporate it into my further actions.

Since I've gotten the message from the bellhop and from the messenger deer I need to include their wisdom in my next steps. Now I've got to walk my new talk.

Hmm, I have one more city to go on my itinerary and that's the Forum on Global Affairs.

My speech is on my favorite subject: *How to Save the World.*

The gist of my talk is this: The way to save the world is by saving your own life. The light in me celebrates the light in you. So, if my light is out there's nothing I can give you to help you with your light. If either one of our lights is out, we need to be replenishing. The best way for me to inspire light in you is to continue to be the light in me.

So, the very experience that I've been having is the very theme of my speech: Put yourself to bed when you're tired. Come in out of the rain.

I'm so excited to give my speech. Yet I know that I must be my speech in practice.

As I muse over this, I press the elevator button at yet another hotel to go down to the lobby, to get the cab, to get to the airport, to get on the plane, to go to the Forum. I press the elevator button and a pain shoots through me from my heart and through to all the rest of me. I get the message now for the third big time in as many cities.

That's enough. That's it. Thank you, body, I hear you. I know I've been asking too much of myself. *Time to go home.* Another axiom from my speech is "Always listen to the truth of yourself even if it seems inconvenient at the time."

I get to the airport, reroute my air ticket, reschedule my engagements, and catch the last plane homeward bound just as the other plane takes off in the opposite direction to the Forum.

I call the organizer and say that, as a public service to myself and the other attendees, I'm going home and that I would fax my speech. Would he please present it? Here is the complete speech:

How to Save the World. "Sweep in front of your own doorstep."

~~~

P.S. Later, the organizer called me at home to say that my speech got a standing ovation. More importantly, many of my colleagues whom I had seen on the road took the three hours I would have been talking to go back to their hotel rooms, put on their pajamas, and get much-needed sleep themselves.

Me, too, on the plane, I got much-needed sleep, and then at home in my own bed, days uninterrupted.

Everything takes care of itself when you take care of yourself. ~

49 Years Old

An Evening with Viki King—A Conversation That's All About You

This is an excerpt of an evening arranged for young people who are hoping to break into the Hollywood industry.

~~~

Me: Hello. I'm thrilled to be with you so we can talk about your favorite subject—you.

This is an opportunity to bring up any issues that you are grappling with. We can apply a few basic wisdoms. It can make life easier to navigate.

Let's talk about it. There's the mic. You're invited to step up.

~~~

Peggy: My family fights me on my dream.

Me: What you want, you want. You don't have to ask anybody if you can have your dream. Just let the world know that is what you will have and work with the world to have it.

Here's a poem from Hafiz, "Run my dear, from anything that may not strengthen your precious, budding wings."

~~~

Ariel: I've got that same problem. My family wants me to go to medical school so I have something to fall back on.

Me: Then you'll fall back on it.

If you follow someone else's road, when you arrive, you won't be there, you will still be on the road not taken because you took the road you didn't want to take.

But the truth is that medical school is the road you want to take. It's more important to you right now to please your parents than it is to follow your own direction. Go ahead. Along the way, you'll form your own road to travel.

There is a difference between being your true self and holding onto what keeps you from being your true self. Let your highest desire lead you. You'll get to your right path at your right time.

~~~

Margo: I'm so lost.

Me: Being lost is the way to find yourself. Your heart knows where it is leading, follow it always.

When you are lost you are giving yourself options, Do I take this road or that road?

You'll take the road to meet the you that you don't know yet. You won't find fresh and new and original on the well-worn road. You'll find it in uncharted territory where you let yourself get lost.

~~~

Penny: (Cries) My father died, and my cat died, and my job ended, and I had to move. It's all gone.

Me: Sweetie. Life wants to set you free. There are times in our lives when everything and everyone are shed. We are dropped off in the middle of nowhere because that's the place to develop the next part of our life. When you are ready, you will be thankful for these circumstances all showing up together, that's when it becomes your opportunity.

~~~

Sue:	Is there more of me to become?
Me:	Yes, of course. Always.
Sue:	If I'm becoming then I must not be me yet.
Me:	You are always you. Within the seed is the whole big tree. Just keep branching out.
Sue:	What am I supposed to be doing with my life?
Me:	Who are you?
Sue:	I don't know.
Me:	Well that's what you're supposed to be doing with your life. Find out who you are and proceed with being you.
Sue:	Should I follow my dream?
Me:	You must, that's what it's for.
Sue:	I'm scared.
Me:	Of course you are, because it means the most to you. It's your precious destiny. As it comes up to get you what you want, you'll be scared, that's the point; it takes you to your new territory where you haven't been before. Keep walking forward. It will lead you to that, then that, then that. Being alive can feel so good.

~~~

Trudy:	I moved out two years ago, but I still can't cope with my family.
Me:	You think you are fully realized and then you go home for the holidays. Raise your hand if you know about that feeling.

Hands go up. Laughter.

Me:	Only go back to know to go forward. In going home, you see that you have been decorated out of your old room. It's now the sewing room or it's now the guest room, which means you are now a guest there. You don't

live there anymore. Good. That's done. You're free to go forward.

~~~

Gigi: I have too many problems.

Me: What if there are no problems? What if there are just circumstances that appear to give you a hard time so that you can solve yourself?

~~~

Megan: I just can't cope with some people.

Me: Oh, everybody knows the same people.

Laughter from the crowd.

Megan: They're weird or screwy. I just can't get with them.

Me: When I see some people, I'm happy to think, *Isn't that great that they signed up for that, that they decided to be that over there, so I don't have to be that? How nice of them.* If everyone is weird or screwy and you can't quite get with them, then you can say they have a different mission here on Earth than you do. Thank you very much, that gives me the freedom to be who I am.

I have a motto: On any given day, the human race is just being its precious self.

Megan: What if the weird and screwy people are in your family?

Me: Honey, they are always in your family. That's where they belong; otherwise, you'd never have to associate with them and where's the fun in that?

Megan: But can't they sabotage you?

Me: They can if you want to be sabotaged. They are there for your education. What do you wish to learn? Remember, you are 100%

responsible for your own good time. What can you learn from their behavior? They are in your family doing you a big favor. Let yourself reap the benefits of them in your life.

When you love people where they are, you don't get gobbledygook in your own grid. Oh, that's great. Write that down and make it your life motto.

~~~

Beverly: How do you have a life without getting hurt?
Me: Oh, sweetie, you don't. Getting hurt is part of it. The use of hurt is to deal with it, learn from it, and come out triumphant.

It's not to be endured, it's there for you to make a change in your circumstance. Use it as your opportunity for growth. Are you loving someone who doesn't respect your love? Hurt alerts you to make a higher choice.

~~~

Rayne: I'm having issues with my sister. I thought things would settle down with her now that we are adults. But she always seems so angry and doesn't talk to me. I want to be ok with or without her in my life. But I'm struggling . . .
Me: Struggle implies that you want one thing while you are caught in another. Let go of all control and just love. Love you, love your sister, love the world.

When circumstances are left alone, without poking at them, they transform. It happens every time.

~~~

Dennis: Everything's already been done.
Me: Not by you. What is your talent that's aching to get out while you're keeping it in?

Dennis: Music. But everybody wants to do music.

Me: It's the same notes that have been around for centuries. Mozart used the same notes. Maybe we'd like to hear how you put them together. Wouldn't you like to make your own music?

Dennis: Yes, I have a unique sound, a fusion. Nobody's ever heard my sound that I've put together.

Me: Then let us hear it. If you have the talent to create it, then it belongs in the world. If you don't sound your notes, there will be a gaping hole in the Earth's vibration where your notes belong.

Dennis: Hmm.

Me: There it is, hear it? Don't die with your song in you.

~~~

Rachel: How come I didn't know I was powerful all along?

Me: If you knew you were this powerful, you would have blown up in beauty.

~~~

Sheila: I came to thank you. I have been in the business for nine years, and I have wanted to be a director. No one would give me a chance until finally I did get hired as a director. The producer who hired me said that twenty-five years ago, when he was on a crew, he knew you, and you were the only woman on that show. He said that if I was anything like you, then they needed me on the shoot. He hired me on the spot. So here, twenty-five years later, because of you, he gave me the job. I want to thank you for blazing the trail.

Me: I'm going to give you a name, Etta Betterley.
        She blazed my trail, so I got to blaze it for
        you. Thank you for that. Everybody in this
        room will get to blaze a trail for someone
        next. Don't you love when that happens?
            This is the perfect time to close.
            Let's make a closing circle where we can
        all send our best wishes to everybody else
        here. Go to your heart and access your
        greatest heart's desire. What do you want?
        Know it clearly and let it course through your
        body, now. Let your desire be magnetic. Let
        all the magic that you need come rushing to
        you. Be awake and alert to receive the
        opportunities and take the actions that show
        up for you. Let that good energy flow to your
        friends here and together light the world.
    Applause. ~

~~~

(Continuing Q & A from this evening can be found at https://
www.vikiking.com)

50s Passage

A Woman's Evolution in Shoes

I NEVER FELT the need to go to the ends of the Earth to search for a meaning to life, but I have been known to seek out the perfect pair of shoes.

I have a snapshot of me at five in my perfect pair of Mickey Mouse sandals. Mickey and I are both smiling the same smile. There's something so mighty about that photo. I'm a kid who's got the *step-right-up, stand-and-deliver, one-foot-in-front-of-the-other* gene. You'd bet on me to stand on my own two feet and dance through life.

Walking Shoes and Talking Shoes

When I lecture on stage, say, in Paris. I walk up to the stage wearing hardy, foot-friendly-nevertheless-chic walking shoes, then I change to my oh-so-fashionable talking shoes for the lecture. I can change them back again to grab a cab back to the hotel. See, walking shoes and talking shoes.

Twenty-Minute Shoes

I have a cache of what I refer to as twenty-minute shoes. I'm careful not to wear them past their expiration time.

I remember the day I gave up twenty-minute shoes. I was at Nordstrom's, and I bought my last pair of high heels, and I knew they were my last. This was a transcendent moment.

I've never been a fan of foot-binding, and I always thought that high-heels are a form of that. I always managed to find the one pair of shoes in the marketplace that were comfortable or I wouldn't, couldn't consider them. Now, even though they are comfortable, these are my last pair. From here, I'll find high-end, fashion-forward shoes with lower heels and cushioned insoles.

If you are still in fashion shoes that might be hurting your feet, enjoy them while you want to. I pass along this tip to you. Here's how you walk in them. You glide slowly and in grace directly to the limo. When you get inside the limo, take them off, put them on the seat next to you, luxuriate your feet in the faux fur carpeting while you admire the beauty of your shoes as perfect fashion objects d'art. Put them back on just before you get to the restaurant. Get out and glide in and go directly to a close table. Take them off under the table, wiggle your toes around during your meal. Use the dessert time to find them and wrangle them back on your feet. Glide back to the limo. Go home and put them on a shelf where you can enjoy looking at them as sculpture. Be barefoot. ~

50 Years Old

Power Surge

IN MY THIRTIES, I remember being interviewed for a teen magazine about being an older woman of thirty. I was quoted as saying to the teen girls, "Strut your stuff because later you'll have more stuff to strut."

Now, this is later in *my* life, and I find that *I* have more stuff to strut.

I'm staying at a lovely resort—just now I'm in the lobby boutique shop; there are many resort clothes and a smattering of well-chosen "important dresses," very highly priced.

I feel the shopkeeper having a losing battle with the chocolates on the silver tray at the register. She appears to be all heart yet uncomfortable in her own skin. As I look around the shop—enjoying the inspiration of the beautiful high-ticket items—she offers chocolates to me.

I say, "Thank you so much. No, thank you." I guess immediately that she can't have guilt-free chocolate unless she gets somebody to indulge with her. She was hoping for a chocolate buddy.

I pull an amazing long evening gown off the rack. It's just a slip of a thing. No darts, no architecture, just a piece of cut-on-the-bias fabric that wants to drape across the body. I'm attending a formal gala tonight where Beloved's orchestra will play. This will work and then I can roll it up in a little ball to put in my suitcase. It's marked down from $1,000 to $10. My kind of dress.

The shopkeeper says, "I hate you."

I realize that she's talking to me. "Oh?"

She continues as she eats her chocolate, "No one has been able to wear that dress. I wondered who it would finally fit. And it's you. Not even young girls have been able to wear it. You have to have balls to wear that dress, but if you have balls, they'd show. Now I see it needed someone like you. It needed you. You're old enough to be confident and young enough to have a flat stomach."

So I say, "Actually, I'm fifty today."

She: That's even worse. I'm fifty! This dress wouldn't even fit my left thigh. And besides, there's no place you could wear it unless you're going to a red-carpet event.

Me: Oh, I'm going to the gala here at the resort tonight. I can wear it there.

She: I hate you worse.

Me: Sweetie, it's not me you hate.

She: I know, don't tell me. I feel bad enough about myself. Here comes another hot flash. I can't stand it.

Me: In Japan, they are referred to as the second spring—the ten thousand blossoms of springtime. It's your portal into wisdom.

She: Wisdom schmisdom—the only thing I know now that I didn't know before is that I'm fat and hot.

Me: Have you explored herbs?

She: Honey, I've tried everything. I can't even talk about it.

I think, but don't say, that I know that for some women they have a new respect for muumuus.

When I first had power surges, I was pretty happy, because all my life before that I felt chilly and when power surges happened, my whole inner thermostat went up and I liked the warmer temperature. But I decide not to tell her this because she will feel worse still. She is a lady bereft—overweight and under-metabolized. She's a lovely woman if only she'd feel that way about herself. I give her compliments on her beauty and grace and the décor of the shop. I give her this mantra: "I am responding joyfully to all the miracles that are here for me now. I easily receive from them and bask in the lightness of being."

I try on the dress. We were made for each other. Do I want to wear a showstopping dress? I'm someone who is more about the show must go on rather than showstopping. I decide that for *my* show to go on, I can wear this showstopping dress. It has been hanging here waiting for me to be willing to be ever more visible.

I offer the lady a list of herbs. We hug.

I pay the $10 for the $1,000 dress that waited for me to turn fifty to buy it. ~

51 Years Old

Whose Gift is it Anyway?

I'VE JUST COME From a business dinner on Restaurant Row. It's late and very, very cold. At the corner, I notice that there is a family—mom, dad, and young kids—huddled on the curb. They're wearing just light sweatshirt hoodies. I pull up, grab my blanket out of the trunk, and offer it to them. The dad takes it just as the mom shouts, "There's our bus!" They rush aboard and are whisked away as the dad throws the blanket in the direction of the storm drain. It gets sucked away to the ocean.

What just happened?

My friend Libby would say, "No good deed goes unpunished."

I get in my car and continue toward home. I feel stunned. I feel like I want my favorite trunk blanket back. I decide it is a sign from the gods to mind my own business.

But you know me, there's a further meaning. I am continuing home along Pacific Coast Highway when suddenly in front of me there is a huge car accident that happened just minutes before. It's extreme with possible fatalities. I realize it happened just about the time it took for me to stop and give my blanket away, or I would have been in the crash. ~

52 Years Old

Yet Another Hollywood Extravaganza Celebration

Look at Me, I am leaving the Hollywood Party—a card-exchanging, contact-acquiring, business-dealing, high-powered, industrial-strength Hollywood party. This is where the giants in the business graze, where my fame is going on without me. It's the let's-have-lunch capital of the world. And I am feeling gloriously ambition free.

There's no one I must meet, no project I'm deeply desiring to join. People long to get or be gotten from. I would be the gotten-from now. I am gotten from plenty and relish that it's a privilege. There is no new position I need to jockey; I *am* in position.

I am no longer getting there. I am here. There is nothing that I must chase down or wrestle to the ground.

I'm leaving the party while people are still coming to the party.

When you walk out in the crowd with klieg lights blazing, you can feel the desire in the hearts of the oncoming partygoers.

I did stay long enough to have the stuffed mushrooms—I'm no fool. But now I want out of my twenty-minute shoes. All I can think of is my couch and my flannel pajamas. As the valet retrieves my car, here still coming are the hopefuls, the excited, the would-kill-to-get-ins. I give my invitation to an ingénue who is one of my film students. She's outfitted herself red-carpet-ready. She has come to me for mentoring for the last few years. It's a joy to give her my help up until now, but she has her life to live her way. My wisdom is for me because I have acquired it. She'll acquire her own. It's just a matter of time before she will be here too under her own power.

I slide comfortably into my car. I have accomplished what I set out to do thirty years ago. It feels so freeing. I drive home to make a great big pot of I'm-Satisfied Soup. ~

53 Years Old

The Stroke of Midnight

My stepfather has had a stroke. We don't yet know the severity, but it's Christmas Eve and apparently, they empty as many beds as they can at the hospital and require patients to be farmed out to care facilities during the holidays and into the new year. I have just hours to find a nursing home and transfer him from the hospital.

It's a peculiar form of Christmas shopping to look for a care facility. From one dreadful place to the other, I hope for better, and each is worse than the last. Finally, after searching all day into the late night, I find a state-run place with plenty of beds, and that's where the ambulance, after several more hours, transfers him. Quite a day, now midnight. Joy to the world.

Thanks to my brother on the other end of the country (it's 3:00 a.m. for him on Christmas), we've had an excellent division of labor through this—he oversees the paperwork tonight. They faxed sixty pages of small print to him. He was going to have to sign away all kinds of rights—you don't even want to know. As soon as all is signed and settled, so is our Pappy, who is now deep asleep. I tuck him in and hold my hand over his heart. Such a strong heartbeat, yet I know this is not something he will come back from. This is the beginning of his last stage of life.

My take-care-of-business-role is over for the night. As I walk out to the parking lot, the chimes from a nearby church ring in Christmas.

As I drive home, I remember that before all this happened, I had been invited to my friend Caroline's house for her annual Christmas Eve party filled with her huge extended family, kids, music, and lots of good food. I wonder if they'd all still be going strong. I call, they are, so I go. The instant I walk in the door they put the new baby of the family in my arms.

His heart beats against my heart in syncopation. As our Pappy is entering into his last part of life, this baby is joining his new life to come. At the doorway of entering and exiting, the life force passes the baton. ~

53 Plus

The Last Residence

By NOW OUR Pappy has been moved from the care facility and is now lodged at the VA geriatric ward. He's safe and comfortable while he is experiencing ever-diminishing consciousness.

I am so grateful that my brother got him in here. He had to go to the VA in person to get through a mile and a half of paperwork. It was not looking possible that Pap would be admitted. A doctor overheard my brother, with the clerk and the papers, and took an interest. When he saw the coding number that our dad had as a veteran who experienced combat, the doctor qualified him to be fast-tracked into a bed in the geriatric ward. He authorized the papers and left the building. We didn't know if the man really was the doctor in charge or maybe he was a patient who wandered off from the psychiatric ward.

Lo and behold, he *was* the doctor in charge of it all, and our Pappy was admitted.

The geriatric ward is the place where vets check in but aren't expected to return home. We were informed that it's on average about an eighteen-month stay. For the moment, Pap's condition is that he is on a slow decline. His body seems strong, yet his awareness is diminishing.

We are so grateful that he can be here at this special time in his life. They are very, very good to him. It's a lucky miracle. ~

54 Years Old

Different Strokes for Different Folks

SHORTLY AFTER PAP had a stroke, my Beloved had a stroke.

All strokes are not created equal. For Beloved, there is a high probability that he will not live through the night.

First Days

We are hoping after such trauma that his body fires up again and decides to go for more life.

Just now, there are immediate urgencies—the small things that mean everything, such as being able to get a deep enough breath to breathe.

We don't yet know what is affected, what will come back, what never will. At the hospital, they are using the word catastrophic.

He has his speech, the stroke did not affect that, but he is paralyzed in half his body. Walking again—maybe never. Continuing to live tomorrow—maybe not that either.

His diaphragm as a musician was so very strong. It is now paralyzed. He can talk, but there's no volume for him to be heard. He developed his expert musicianship over a lifetime. It is now gone.

At the moment, conditions are at the absolute basics—can he breathe, can he chew, can he swallow? His life depends on it. The assigned doctor tells us that Beloved will have another stroke within the next seventy-two hours and die. This is said just outside his room where he can hear it. You wait all day for the doctor to come and when he does, his behavior is subpar. He said, "To me, he is just a man, they are all the same."

What? That's not true about *any* man, and you definitely don't know *this* man. As we are out here in the hall, he is in there pulling himself up on the bed bar to affirm his spot in continued living.

This is a man in his prime artistry as a world-class musician, now never to play his instruments again, but we can hardly think of that today.

We overhear a visitor in the next room talking about his brother who had a stroke and "was back up on the ladder a week later."

I'm getting educated in the individual effects of stroke—it's a vastly varied result for each person. Some may be able to recalibrate within the week and come out of it healthy, others within the same week can turn their face to the wall and not recover.

Ah, progress, here comes the rehab team. They put a goal sheet up on the wall to measure progress for the week. My heart takes a nosedive when I see that the first week's ambition for him is to chew, and they are not sure if he can even accomplish that. We soon discover that rehab is physically so basic, yet monumentally heroic when he can get one good breath in.

Here is a man who had made his way from a modest upbringing to performing on world stages and all along has been admired for the measure of his character. Now just getting from bed to bathroom takes all he's got to pull himself out of this deep abyss and live.

His mind wills his body to move, while his body is unable to get the message. He is a man who knows how to succeed; he will have to find a way to do that in this circumstance.

The early goals for the first weeks: to chew, to swallow, to roll over, to blow his breath into a plastic tube and hopefully raise the bouncing ball with his air pressure.

As a musician he has built his breath to sustain the long notes, he had such strength in his breath—now the goal is to blow in the plastic tube, the equivalent of blowing out a candle for hopefully a next birthday. The wish is, can he just have a strong enough breath to raise the ball in the tube an eighth of an inch? This achievement is weeks in the making.

The Impact on Us All

Little sweet granddaughter has come to visit her grandpa. One minute she is coloring on the bed tray, the next minute . . . Where is she? I run out into the hall. Not there.

I know how the circumstance of his stroke feels for me and all the family and friends and orchestra members. It is all that we can handle. What about this little child who adores him?

They have had such a great closeness since she was a baby. They would play the piano together. Yesterday we talked about what a stroke is. How it's not his hand that doesn't want to move, it's the signal in his brain that isn't getting to his hand and leg. And she says, again for the third time, "But why can't he?"

She is under his hospital bed sitting cross-legged in front of the wall where she has drawn a sunflower with a smiling face pointing up toward where grandpa's head lies.

It's been a few weeks, and I notice the skirt I've been wearing each day as my hospital uniform seems to be falling off me, bigger than it was last week. Am I not eating? Or maybe I am but it's not taking.

I chose rubber-soled shoes because they are best for pushing the wheelchair down the hall and transferring him from bed to chair. The feel of the hospital floor through my shoes is cold and hard with no give to it through thin industrial carpet over concrete. It's a floor he will never walk on.

I don't notice during the day, but I feel these things at night. I realize that I am carrying Beloved's emotions that he hasn't been able to get to yet. I realize that, and then I must take the conscious action all day *not* to feel his feelings for him.

My mantra is this: "The life force is a renewable resource. The life force is a renewable resource."

I travel from the VA geriatric ward for Pap to the downtown hospital where Beloved is. As I drive from one hospital to the other, it is clear to me that not just the road is going to be a long haul.

I've been getting through with the strategy "Keep on keeping on." It's not the best plan—not a viable plan. Sitting here in traffic, I need to come up with a sustainable strategy. I settle on "Respond to what is." Life now for all of us is brand new. Something developing each day. I step one foot after the other, releasing our lives as we knew them, stepping into what life will be now. New life unfolds. I meet it where it is, not where it was.

Then I get a call from a dear, young relative who is in Aspen skiing with friends. She did not ask about our Pappy or Beloved, she called unhappy because she said she had the sniffles and couldn't be on the slopes skiing with her friends, so she was at the lodge, by the fireplace having cocoa, and choosing to be miserable.

When I hang up the phone, I think how grateful I am that I don't have her life

The Visitor

A gentleman we didn't know came blithely into the hospital room and brought a magazine and wanted to be sociable. He was visiting from the normal world. It was completely unrelatable to us in this outer space place that we have been flung into. The magazine is sitting on the bed far from possible next to Beloved's one hand that can't hold it. The visitor said it could pass the time. Beloved has no time to pass; he is in the fight of his life to win every precious moment of aliveness. Overwhelmed. Laborious. Ponderous. Tumbling. Tumbling. No faculties to read *People* Magazine. Not now. Maybe not ever.

Beloved, who was always ever gracious, making every fan feel special, is now blank. He is fathoms away in a deep hole working, working to come out of it. We are happy for the visitor to leave. He can return in a year if Beloved is alive then.

For now, there is no casual visiting to be done. No time to pass or chit to chat. This visitor from the normal world made us see how far from the center of life Beloved is presently. Tomorrow he may be closer or tomorrow may be his last.

A Lovely Happenstance

We were able to get him moved to a hospital with a great brain trauma unit. Here's the sweet miracle of it: Last year, coincidentally, Beloved did a fundraising concert for this very hospital. It was a major event that raised a lot of money for this specific brain trauma unit. As he is rolled in on a gurney today, the staff has put up photos on the bulletin board from that fundraising evening. They proudly roll him past the photos. It made us feel like we had come to the right place. Now he can get down to the business of coming back alive.

Cognition

It appears that he has all his marbles. It appears that the problem is physical paralysis, but he is here in the brain trauma unit. This is a brain injury and it's complicated.

You can massage the hand and will it back to life, but it's the circuitry in the brain that just can't give it the message to move.

Also, since it involves brain wiring, we're starting to see the extent of what's really been affected.

The physical paralysis and what we could see are overwhelming enough. Slowly it dawned on *my* brain that the deeper effects of this haven't even revealed themselves yet.

What decision-making abilities will return to him, and what now must be decided for him? In rehab, I learn not to push the wheelchair and instead let him move himself along, banging into walls and sitting trapped in the elevator. It's becoming clear that other aspects of his independence will never return. Now there is the matter of when to step in and when to let him do it for himself.

He has been the master of his life and the hub of the wheel in his world. All the people, places, and magic around him—he created.

Now, how much could he still do? What parts had to be doled out to the team to do for him? What kind of team had to be assembled?

Each day another new development shows itself.

Award Banquet at the Beverly Hilton

It was the first outing from the trauma unit. He hadn't left there for a month. Just getting his suit pants on with the belt and dress shirt to be buttoned all the way up was an odyssey. A man visiting in the next room was the one who helped manage the tying of the tie as it brushed Beloved's paralyzed hand. And this was the first time I would be transferring him from wheelchair to car. We had practiced it the day before. Pivot don't lift. Swing him over to the seat on a sling. Bend your knees, don't lean. Use leverage. The chair, the pedal, and the cushion all must be loaded in also, in the right sequence, so it all fits.

We are going to an award banquet where he will be honored. Many a time, he's played concerts at this hotel in this ballroom—it's the go-to Hollywood ballroom for award shows.

Since he's performed here a thousand times, we enter through the kitchen, like he's done a thousand times before because he had instruments to unload. Now we enter there because of the wheelchair access to the stage. The waitstaff has always known and admired him. He always treated each one with respect and kindness. Now, seeing him for the first time since the stroke, they all stop what they are doing and stand in silence as he is rolled onto the lift. As the lift ascends to the stage, their stillness erupts in an ovation for him. It is one of the unbearably beautiful moments of life.

From that emotion, we now enter the stage. It feels like a distant foreign world. I understand what it must mean to be institutionalized—you're so happy to get a break from the hospital yet almost fearful to be without it. This room was built for celebration and festivities. The hospital is built for those remaining in sickness.

I wheel him around to the head table on the dais and park his chair next to a prominent man, a judge, who is here to honor him. While I adjust the brakes, the man says, to him, "How crazy does it make you to know that you'll never play your instruments again?" Like a lioness protecting her cub, I want to lunge at the man and dismember him into small pieces for pointing out the elephant in our room.

That night when we arrive back at the hospital, with him back in pajamas, we both fall into an exhausted sleep.

The next morning, we get the news his friend, also a prominent musician, who had a stroke last week, has died. In a way it was hopeful when Jerry had his stroke too. Maybe they could do this thing together. But he has died. A double death really; now Beloved was even more alone in the possibility of coming long and far back from it.

The Home Visit with the Rehab Team

We are all here at the house, three weeks before he will be released from the hospital. The rehab team has done this before. They know how emotional it is for a person to visit his old life and be hit with the reality that it's going to be all different from here forward. Just that little bump at the front door now becomes a major obstacle. All this before we even get into the house. In the kitchen, we see that it will be impossible for him to access the refrigerator. There's no way for him to be able to use the can opener. The simple necessity of feeding himself is now just beyond his abilities.

Everything is different now—an independent life is now dependent. I see him notice neighborhood kids running on the sidewalk. Noticing how easily they move. He sees their freedom that he no longer has. He's coping, and then the trap door opens, and he falls through to a whole new set of rude awakenings.

Nibblers on Wilshire

The day he gets out of the hospital—freedom. Once the life-or-death question is settled for the moment, the top priority is the freedom of being alive. That's what we have today—the sheer joy of it coming right out of us.

We go to a restaurant we've been to a million times in our former life. This time we are in nirvana here.

We laugh and swoon over the glorious green beans as I feed them to him one at a time.

Liberated from the pall of hospital food, he rejoices in each crispy, wondrous French fry, every delicious piece of meat, juicy and savory down to the last bite, and then the sheer rhapsody of each spoonful of ice cream and chocolate syrup. We are laughing and holding each other close.

A solitary man, reading his paper at the counter, finishes his meal, folds up his paper, and walks over to our booth. The man sidesteps the wheelchair and looks to Beloved's half-paralyzed face and says, "You're the luckiest man in the world." ~

54 Plus

Yes, Someone Did Die

IT WAS OUR Pappy. He didn't die without a last great hoorah.

This is what happened.

While waiting at physical therapy for an orderly to come and get him and bring him back to the geriatric ward, he took it upon himself to take the golf cart for a drive all over the sprawling VA grounds. They had to chase him down. They wanted to throw him out.

My brother was called in, he being the parent now. He asked Pap, "Did you take the golf cart?"

We hadn't seen much connection from him for a while, but now his personality came proudly to the forefront. His eyes reverted to their clear blue twinkling selves, and he was overjoyed remembering this last great joyride of his life. He would definitely do it again if he had the chance. We were happy about that since he loved to drive, and he hadn't driven since he was in this place. Where's the fun in that?

But then there was the matter of having to deal with the administrator who wanted him out of there. My brother asked the man, "How was he able to take the cart?"

The administrator said, "It was sitting there, and he just got in and drove it away."

And my brother said, "You mean the key was left in the ignition where any patient could have access to it?"

The administrator, possibly fearing liability, after a long pause said, "Er . . . well . . . never mind. He can stay."

He did stay until his very last dance on a Thursday afternoon when the volunteer big band would come into play from noon to one. Dancing for him consisted of pulling him up from sitting to a standing position so he could sway to the music as I held him. One of the patient's wives took a picture of us doing this "dancing" when the light was coming in strong from a high window. It came to us like a direct beam that went all the way through me and enveloped him. When I saw the photo, I knew he would be departing soon. That was his last dance. He died before the next Thursday's big band performance. ~

55 Years Old

Hoping and Coping

THIS IS THE year for Beloved to come long and far back from the brink.

I am bringing his favorite takeout. The door is locked, and my arms are full. I look in through the glass. He is on his new recliner chair, the one that comes to a standing position by remote control so he can get out of it. He is sleeping deeply. What faraway land has he gone to in such deep, deep sleep? And then suddenly his body balks into a seizure. I drop the takeout, crash the door, and rush to him. I hold him as the paramedics are on their way.

Is this a new sign of things to come? More doctors? More hospitals? More what? Is this how it is going to be? I move now to another way to live with this circumstance. Let go of improvement and embrace gratitude for what is.

And "what is" does include the medical world—a whole city block of medical buildings with walkers and gurneys and pharmacy and those who are sick and those family members worried.

And next to it all, across the street, is a 99 Cent store. I leave him in radiology and run over there. Here is my chance to refill all those necessary things that have been on empty for weeks. The dish detergent and laundry soap and my reading glasses side mount is broken off. I can stock up on those, too. In great glee, I step into the store and stop cold. This is a foreign universe. I realize immediately I have lost my talent for shopping. I can't even begin to go in. Everything bombards my senses. I become, or finally notice, my enormous fatigue. My brain, so long a guest on the brain trauma unit, is having its own time coping with this new world. It's called the 99 Cent store because ninety-nine senses are coming at me—too many when I already have the set of ten thousand sensations brand new since Pap's stroke and Beloved's stroke.

I brave forward—if I can cope with all that's happened so far, I can surely cope with shopping. I wander in—a stranger in a strange land. Unable to focus on dish detergent, I walk out realizing I have my own new hippocampus to enroll in.

The medical world is back to its old tricks, saying, "He could be dead any minute."

Well, I can't get too excited about that. We can all be dead any minute. And excuse me for saying, but he's not dead yet and he has already outlived several of his friends and one of the doomsday doctors.

Meanwhile, whole areas of his brain function that we can't see are altered—tiny, small aspects, so many, one hundred million changes.

You easily see the physical ravage but there's more, much more, and we are seeing those each day.

Catastrophic—yes, no area of life left untapped.

For Now, We'll Just Do It Our Way

We sit together with the fireplace crackling and music on the radio. (In fact, it's his music playing on the radio.) And it's in beautiful harmony with the rhythm of the flames dancing. Is there anything pending or anything due? Have we said all our "I love you's?" We live in appreciation of these precious and maybe last moments, brimful and enjoying what we do have—this moment. The next moments, we don't know about and no longer force-feed those with our hope. Being here now—what a rich way to live, and so we live it. And there is a good surprise in this way of living. We find such depths. We find that's where eternity is. ~

56 Years Old

How a Caregiver Cares for Herself

How are we doing? Thank you for asking. Here are a few events from this week:

Beloved, ever the champion of fundraisers, participates in a foundation that arranges annual programs for families with stroke. We were in their big festival this week and raised a good amount for the foundation.

Also, for this association, I wrote *The Caregiver's Guide to Caring for Yourself*. It's a short book because caregivers don't have time to read. In fact, I recorded an audio version so that it could be listened to in the car when caregivers are transporting their loved ones to the doctor. Any one of the tips I suggest can make all of the difference if only you let yourself take a deep enough breath to let it in. I remind myself to take my own suggestions on a regular basis.

At one fundraising event that Beloved spearheaded, they took a picture of us to put on the cover of their magazine. There are two things noteworthy about this photo—we never looked worse because of all that we have been through, and it is our favorite photo because of all that we have been through.

Meanwhile, I'm a pundit for one of the local news channels. They call me for sound bites on current news events.

Yesterday I ran around to get half-dressed for the news crew. I say half-dressed because I only made myself camera-ready from the waist up. I remember my friend Abigail who said that when her kids were little and she needed to rush and get them to school, she sometimes only managed to get one eyebrow drawn in as her makeup regime.

We may all think we are masters of multitasking, but really, we are doing one thing at a time really, rapidly, continually interrupted by twelve other things. I want to rethink the whole idea of multitasking, but I only have time to think about it while I'm doing something else.

The Pitch

I have an important call coming in from the network in New York. There is just enough time to get Beloved his shower and dressed and breakfast so I can take the call quietly and focused. But . . . NO! They called early—they were all in the conference room, all ten "suits," and they had to do it now. I was in the bathroom with Beloved, who was already wet, soaped up, and ready to be hosed off. I gave the suits pushback, negotiating for them to call at the time we agreed to but no, it was going to have to be now while everybody was together.

While Beloved sits quietly on his shower chair, they were across the country in New York all in the conference room. It was up to me. A sure sign of caregiving—you can't do one more thing but there it is to do, so you just do it. So, I went for it.

I grabbed a roll of tourniquet gauze out of the bathroom cabinet and wrapped my cell phone around my head so I could hear/talk and be hands-free as I continued Beloved's shower while pitching the show in question. Picture this—me with a cell phone tourniquet around my head, Beloved wet and soaped up. On the other end of the phone, on the other coast, ten "suits" in the conference room listening to it all. I catch a glimpse of my hilarious self in the bathroom mirror and notice that I am speaking with great authority to be heard three thousand miles away over the rush of water as I rinse off Beloved and transfer him from the shower chair to the wheelchair where he drip-dries. I leave him wrapped warmly in a temporary towel while I finish my pitch with just enough flourish and flair to bring home the concept and close the deal.

Beloved, now dry, powdered, and puffed comes slowly out of a morning medication stupor to appreciate the surreal and comic nature of the circumstance.

The conference call wraps, the shower wraps, and it's quiet. I sit on the wet edge of the tub, undo the tourniquet, and turn off my phone.

Well, that was sure evidence that I am running on empty. Everything takes everything I've got—a sure sign that I'm sleep-deprived and asking too much of myself.

I jumped right to heroics instead of being a wise woman and arranging a smarter way to handle that. How could I have handled that? I can't think about that now. The ten thousand next things are lined up and awaiting my attention.

P.S. I did get a call back from New York. They want to go forward with the idea I pitched—now, if I can only remember what it was . . . ~

57 Years Old

Hawaii

I MARVEL AT Beloved's "stroke of genius." He was an independent, dynamic man who now must accept help for the simplest of needs. He handles it all with seamless grace. He knew immediately to cultivate a tone of appreciation. It makes his care efficient and a joy. It's easy for people to eagerly line up to do things for him in a way that boosts each of them.

I am aware that we are in slow quicksand. All our energy goes to maintaining. Time to get on to thriving!

We arrange for his care here, and I book a plane to go have much-needed rest in Hawaii. I know that the island has a way of taking me in and gifting me with exactly what I need. And what I need is sleep. I decide to put myself to bed to sleep until I am finished sleeping. So that's what I do. I sleep for *five* days! A few times I get up for the bathroom, to open and close the refrigerator, and then right back to bed, which is unruffled. I just lie across it without moving. Dead sleep. Five days and nights. Then, when I finally do wake up, everything is in right alignment, the world in all its glory, birds, ocean waves. I could even hear the sun shining. And still lying across the bed, still not moving, I am all back, all real, all ready, feeling so liquid, so fluid, so infinitely possible.

A bee buzzes on the lanai. Ah yes . . . Be. A directive from the gods—Be. It's amazing what a little rest will do. Okay, a lot of rest.

Meanwhile, back on the mainland, Beloved is doing so much better too. Of course, when you point your boat in the right direction, everything flows.

When I finally do wake up and get up, I eat the refrigerator.

And then I proceed to line up back-to-back clients on the island, create a documentary, and enjoy friends who had a reception for me at a lovely hotel to introduce me to others who also become my clients. Life works all on its own when we are out of the way of it.

Beloved and I have managed to make room to thrive, and so we are thriving.

As he feels stronger, it allows for all the other random life events with other members of the family to show up when they need to. And of course, they do. ~

58 Years Old

How to Love an Addict; Every Family Has One

ACTUALLY, FAMILIES ARE known to have more than one addict among them. Addiction runs in families like eye color or talent for singing. It comes as a package deal with the scapegoat, the enabler, the codependent, and the next generation of addicts.

It's like a chess game. There are only so many ways you can move on the chessboard. Are you the pawn, the rook, the child of an alcoholic that gets educated by substance abuse?

I remember when I was a kid going over to Jeannie Fay Farley's house to play. We were laughing, jumping, and dancing down the street when she stopped cold. Her body went rigid. Her dad's car was parked out in front. He was home early. She knew that meant he had been drinking, and she would be the one in harm's way and hardly able to get up for school tomorrow. How many times can a body go from carefree to rigid before it's stuck on closed?

Several years ago, I had a friend, Allison, who casually decided to date a man who was a known alcoholic. I said to her, "You mean you know he drinks, and you still want to pursue this?"

She laughed lightly, having no idea what a toll that takes on innocent bystanders.

With Allison, it very quickly rocked her to the core. So much so that she couldn't think straight or take careful action on behalf of her own care. In very short order she was unable to access her own strengths, and *she* is a free-choosing adult who could have stopped seeing him anytime and still it shook her.

Imagine the many millions of children who know full well what it means to have a family member addicted.

Children, who live under the influence of a parent under the influence—what does that jeopardize in their safety and security and sanity and worldview?

I appreciate the enormity it takes for a child living in an alcoholic environment to somehow make it out alive and keep on going.

It's been at least three generations that alcohol goes back on both sides of my family. I'm grateful I didn't follow in the alcoholic's footsteps. I knew not to be the addict, and now it's the next generation and here is another one in our family who is hard at it.

There were those Christmases when I could see it escalating. When we had all those concerns and hopes for him not to hurt himself or anybody else in his unbridled act of over-celebrating the holidays. Seeing his kids wait patiently, before the presents, having been trained by habit to wait for their dad to show up. Making him a plate of food that he's not going to eat. Awaiting his arrival yet knowing that when he arrives, *if* he arrives, he will be drunk.

And now it's gotten to this. We don't know where he is.

He was the golden boy, the bright light of love for all of us. Now he is the man who doesn't wish to be located.

He doesn't know this is love we have waiting for him. He doesn't want it. He can't bear it. With families, it is such as this.

All of us who have a family member who continues under the influence, we are way beyond having tried everything. We know we will get the phone call. We know and will not be surprised, yet we hope the call is from our loved one directly who is now clean and sober. That is what we hope.

And with our golden boy, so in trouble with alcohol and now also with drugs, the family team pulled together our last-ditch effort to extend a hand—not just a hand—our hearts, our hope, our love, our money, our time—invested deeply. I lament amassing the two-inch file of help we arranged. I lament it because it was the wrong move. Our help is no help at all to him. Everybody's got their way to go, and that's the way they are going. To love does not mean to fix. To love is certainly not to judge. The heart knows where it's leading itself. Everyone has their own reason.

Our guidance system misguided him because we were looking through our own filters thinking we have simple answers to someone else's complex life.

We would prefer he didn't have keys to a high-horsepower car. We would prefer that his children are safe. We would prefer our wonderful wonder boy back with us in peace.

I ache with losing his bright light, and our special bond. I still hold the bond but now, not knowing where he is, there is no way of contacting him. He doesn't want to be found.

You can try over and under and around and through and all over again. Nothing settles it, so you carry it and carry on. And that is where I am now.

I am in an anonymous city on business. I just emerged from a speaking engagement wherein I was a great help to many hundreds of people. I help thousands of strangers. It's not mine to help him.

It is just after the last grand effort my brother and I have made to help him. I feel the grief in my whole body.

This is that moment I know unequivocally that my help does not help. I can't pull him up by *my* bootstraps.

After my success at this speaking conference, I decide not to get on the plane.

I need to find a new way to love my loved one going forward from here.

Saying no now is a yes.

I will let my heart break, and it will break open.

I have a hotel room with a big tub that overlooks the city lights at night and the sun-drenched mountains by day. I decide to sit in the bathtub and look out at the day and night until I can let go of the grief in my body and let it down the drain. I won't get on the airplane until this is addressed and released.

I remember before he was born, and we were so excited about his arrival. The fun of him, the joy of him, the brimful love. Now he doesn't want to talk to any of us in the family.

I surrender my desire and expectation for him. I allow that he be free to follow his own way. I radiate all my love to him. I grant myself soft love and know that my deep work here must be for *my* care.

I know that at some point the phone call will come and whatever the news and conditions, it will be right and true. I accept. I pull the plug and let the big tub drain.

The next day I take the next plane out.

It's an anonymous city where I leave this weight behind. It's possible to do and it is done.

As I board the plane, my body can breathe. I feel the lightness of life unencumbered. Ten thousand fresh floating ideas come alive—such freedom, such joy that was there just under the weight of the thing. It has lifted and life shows up.

It is lifted, and now as the plane lifts off the ground, this is my prayer:

I love you with a transparent love, not influencing you with my emotions, desires, or plans for you. I love you with neutral love. I love you where you are; I just won't help you to stay there.

I am free to feel my own feelings and make my own choices about how I wish to live. And you are free to choose your choices. I love you. I release you.

We are both free. ~

59 Years Old

On-Call Oracle—Location Shoot

I'M HERE EARLY—6:00 a.m. It is really cold. I have on several layers of plushy warm clothes. It's still cold.

No one is on the beach because it is definitely not a beach day. Except here come all the trucks to set up for our movie shoot. Here are the set decorators putting beach blankets and sun umbrellas and ice chests in random patterns around the lifeguard stand. The crew is hard at work making the pretend version of a real beach scene.

All on the crew are bundled up because, did I mention, it's really cold. And here come the actors in swimsuits.

This puts me in mind of another location shoot I was on recently. Here's an excerpt of that memory:

It's dawn. We're shooting in a cemetery. It's bone cold. The catering truck is as near as we could get it. There is piping hot everything in the truck. It helps a little, but it's cold. It's corpse cold.

The actors' faces are so cold they can hardly form the words they have to say.

As a public service to all on the crew, I run back to my on-location accommodations and have a glorious steaming jacuzzi. Just ten minutes but my body temperature goes up for the whole crew. I come back and distribute hot chocolate to all and dance each person to warmth. We raise the dead.

Location shoots are always exhilarating, arduous, rewarding, educational, and remarkably thrilling.

I want to tell you the amazing thing I have heard from *every* director on every movie that I have ever worked on. It happens somewhere around 3:00 a.m. when it's below zero, and the hardest shot to get is not working. Every movie gets to that moment, and every director I've worked with has turned to me and said some version of, "I'm having the time of my life." ~

60s Passage

Blooming Dales

Hᴏᴡ ɢʀᴇᴀᴛ ᴛᴏ experience our age when we are that age and then move to the next desires in the next decade and experience that.

I am at Bloomingdales in the purse department (just passing through to get to the bathroom).

Here is a purse—$7,600. This is a dead cow with zippers. I know at least two things,

1) I can buy this and still make my monthly bills.

2) I don't want it.

I see several young girls looking at several purses here the price of a small down payment for a condo in the Valley. They are lusting after them. I'd rather put that money in my retirement fund.

I love my little purse that carries just the things I need, unencumbered, free and tres chic. The girls would look at me askance except that I don't think they see me at all.

As I get in the elevator, they too come rushing in with their adorable bumptious behinds and bustier tops with goose bumps on their arms. They are feeling cold in order to look hot. Comfortable is not the point. They want to turn heads. They want to be . . . hit on. They are . . . advertising. This is part of being a member of their club at their age. *My* club is sublime comfort. I don't leave home without it. I'm practically militant about that.

We get in the elevator together after I see that they have strutted their stuff to the young men with hip-hop jeans down to there. When the elevator doors close, they giggle and are excited that they made the boys see them. They step down off their platform shoes and ready themselves for who might be on floor number three of today's being-hunted-and-gathered expedition.

Meanwhile, I walk unto the next floor feeling so satisfied to continue to be In Full Bloom. ~

60 Years Old

Ode to Mother

As OF THIS year, I am older than my mother. She died when she was 60, and now I'm surpassing that. Even though it was her last year, and this is my "surpass" year, I wonder what family patterns will prevail. What will come out of me when I am beyond where my mother got to be?

As I go forward into new territory that my mother never got to, her influences are with me, as I am about to find out.

Today I am at a five-year-old's birthday party. One of the dads was designated Safety Captain, watching all the kids in the pool. We were talking side by side while our eyes were watching the kids. I asked him if he had a memory of when he was five, and he told me about liking crafts at school. He asked me what I remembered, and I told him when I was at a summer lake, I ran into the water and stepped on broken glass and blood billowed up in the water. My mother grabbed me, as blood gushed all over her. It was a holiday (Fourth of July). There was no doctor around, no hospital. My mother held me in her arms. I remember experiencing her heart pounding hard. *I knew she didn't know what to do, but I knew she would do it.*

And she did. She figured it out, found a doctor, and got me stitches. Since that time, I have not always known what to do, but I knew that I would do it too.

I wondered why I told the man that story. I hadn't thought about it or relayed that incident since it happened. Within moments, the man's little boy went from swimming to drowning. The dad dove in and pulled his boy out. Maybe he felt that same parent feeling of not knowing what to do but immediately doing it. He focused and began compressions.

911 was called—all the other kids were whisked out of the pool area by the other parents. Now there are just a few of us that are hands-on. The little boy is unconscious. His dad continues steady compressions. The fire truck is on its way, and the ambulance is coming. Still, his dad keeps up compressions,

still, the little boy is unconscious. Just as the first responders are rushing in, the boy's lungs let out a gush of water and he takes in a gasp of air. We too gasp in relief, but not yet fully. He continued to be unable to respond to questions from one of the moms.

"Hey, little buddy, are you on the team at school? Are you in Mrs. Simpson's class?" More questions. No answers.

And questions to us from the paramedics. How long had it been, one minute, or was it an eternity? We knew it was fleeting, just moments, between swimming and not coming up for air. Moments, our eyes were right on him.

Now hooked up to gages for vitals—air pressure, heart, everything measured, not blue now but not yet back.

More questions to pull him back into life. "When is your birthday? What were you for Halloween? What's your favorite toy?" He's far, far away from answering. Where is he? Will he be able to find his way back? And then the next question for him, "What present did you bring to Harley for her birthday?"

And then . . . from him . . . his first words. "It's a surprise."

As easily as he had slipped away, he is back. He is here.

Such a relief to the dad. You might have felt that you didn't know what to do but you did do it.

Years from now, when this little boy is man mourning the loss of his dad, what will come out of him in response to today's dad action? We mourn the loss of loved ones and miss their presence in our life, yet their presence is embodied in us. What we choose to carry from our lineage, carries on the lineage.

As for my mother, she always found the patch of sunshine to be in. That's where I got it from. ~

61 Years Old

Taking the Not-Been-Thanked-Enough Part of You to Dinner

AT SIXTY, THERE was talk among my loved ones of giving me a big birthday party for throngs of my closest friends. As it turned out, all throngs were busy, and my birthday came and went without the party. That would have been a certificate-of-merit birthday. One where everyone could say, "You did this and this and that. Good for you, hooray."

But I was busy doing this and that, and all my friends were also busy doing their own this and that, so my sixtieth birthday came and went without us and that was perfectly fine with me. And then when sixty-one came around, all the friends said, "Oh, we didn't do that last year so let's do it this year and I was now beyond the certificate-of-merit birthday, perfectly fine to be perfectly fine for it to come and go without me."

The truth is I don't use the word party as a verb, as in let's party. It's not my style.

Now that I'm sixty-one the thing I wanted most to do for my birthday was to come to Guido's, a favorite restaurant of mine with Beloved. This is the restaurant I referred to in my *Feelization* book (*Feel It in Your Heart, Have It in Your Life*) in the chapter *"Take the Not-Been-Thanked-Enough-Part-of-You to Dinner."* Many people, since reading that book, have done a pilgrimage to Guido's to eat and think of all the ways they can start to be kind to themselves. You don't have to come here to start that in your life. You can start right where you are and treat yourself the best way that you can where you are. And yet you might want to come here because the food is Italian; it can't go wrong.

So, what am I feeling at sixty-one? I know that I can handle anything. I also know I don't have to like it, yet I will prevail. Of course, I knew this earlier than sixty-one. But do you notice that the next tall mountain arrives, and you climb that one, taking everything you've got to get over it? And there's more to you than you knew was in there, and still more to come—more to life, more. One thing I know now that I didn't think that I knew before—each time you climb thinking this will do it, this will clear it, you'll be over it once and for all. I know it's not once and for all when the next annoying pesky thing can come up immediately just as you're triumphing over some other pesky thing that flies in your face and surprises you because you think you've now got it all handled. Well, here's the difference: It—all of it—still will continue to happen, and some events can take you to your knees, but you're fine on your knees. It's part of the whole fully loaded life package. "I've come a long way, baby" happens constantly.

In gathering and accessing all the wish lists I've ever made; I see not everything came true. But, glory of glories, *I* came true. Here is where I intended to be and here is where I've gotten to. As in, there was a me I intended to be, and this is who I have become. Since I'm the one who chooses the things that got me here, I see that I chose wisely. Who I planned on becoming I am.

I love being my age, now that I've gotten here. I wondered if I thought it would be this good. As a younger woman, I thought sixty-one was old. Now that I'm here, sixty-one is not old, it is perfect. Life is getting better as it progresses.

I am a fully realized human being. I know this because I can voluntarily visit relatives for Thanksgiving, and *I* prevail. Maybe they are in therapy getting over me. ~

62 Years Old

Possible Answers to Life on a Random Tuesday

A JOURNALIST CAME to interview me for a magazine. After he asked the questions for the article, he wanted to stick around and ask life questions for himself. His ambitions have not yet come to fruition, he was anxious to figure out his life, and maybe I had answers that could help him. It's always a good time when you can hear the heartbeat of someone wishing to grow himself.

Here is some of our conversation that ended up on the recording at the end of the interview.

Q: Why is it that some people's dreams never happen for them?

A: Because of what we think of ourselves, we keep ourselves from who we can be. Sometimes the problem is not that it doesn't happen, it's that you didn't let it happen, or you didn't want it to happen.

    We all have our deep reasons, and they are unbeknownst to us. Look at what is appearing on the outside of yourself, and you'll see what is being created on the inside of yourself. You can have what you want; what do you want?

Q: What constitutes a dream anyway?

A: It's that thing that's across the road and you getting there takes you through all the psychic shenanigans you must let go of, to get it; that's the perfect dream because it gets you clear. The dream isn't the prize, you are.

Q: Why are dreams so hard to come true?

A: Your dream is the hardest thing you have in your life that you don't yet have in your life. If it weren't the hardest thing, it wouldn't be your dream. It's the hardest because it means so much to you, and it's the simplest because it utilizes all your natural-born talents and great traits. It scares you the most and you love it the best. Why? Because it's the one thing that is sacred to you. Be in awe, it has every meaning for you.

Q: What can we do about fear?

A: Fear is overrated. It's got no power over you. It's just there for you to expand yourself beyond it. Take it as your partner and go.

Q: Can you give an example?

A: I was at a crisis point in my life, and my brother said to me, 'What are you going to do?' And I said, 'There are three options that I see. Option three is the one that scares me the most, so I'm going for option three.'

Q: Why would you do that?

A: If your greatest fear occurs, then you are free of your greatest fear.

Q: Are you afraid of anything?

A: At breakfast this morning I was afraid of gluten. I know I'm not afraid of fear. Fear is there so you know what to be bigger than. It's just there to keep your adrenaline going in the right direction.

Q: How come I don't know what's going on for me?

A: This is the part where you're still working it out, finding out. You don't know. To know happens after this part. It happens at the end of this story you're telling yourself. The 'don't know' will move you to where you 'do' know. Let it, in its own way, come gently to you.

Q: What would be your wish for humankind?

A: Allow space for the spontaneous occurrence
      of miracles.
Q: And lastly, if you could say anything to your
      fourteen-year-old self, what would it be?
A: Two words—compound interest. ~

63 Years Old

The Crawl

IT STARTED OUT at the optometrist's office. I have eye drops to dilate my eyes for an exam. I didn't realize that the time required to "un-dilate" before driving would last overlong, so I went next door to the mall.

I am having a most splendid time because I am rarely at a mall, and it happens to be Christmas time so there are lots of added bits and festivities.

I notice that Santa has a lull in kid traffic, so I sit on his lap and ask for world peace.

He says, "The truth is everybody has to get that for himself or herself."

Wow, be peace within. I never took Santa for a Zen Buddhist. I'm in awe.

Since my eyes are not yet "un-dilated," I treat myself to a mall lunch. Not the best culinary repast, in fact, the minute I come out of the restaurant I start feeling . . . not so good.

I want to go home immediately and lie on my couch; except how do you get out of a mall? It's like casinos in Las Vegas—no windows, no exits. Once you get into the maze, it's designed to keep you there, buying.

By now I'm dizzy and zigzagging my way from one restroom and then the next to finally get to the parking lot. I'll just go out the first exit I can get to. Now if only I can get to it. I'm really not interested in passing out on the escalator.

And finally, sweating from the effort, hooray, I am outside in fresh air and sunshine. But alas, the sunshine, which I normally love, is at odds with my dilated eyes that are still dilated. I scavenge in my pocket for the temporary, wrap-around, polarized sunshield the optometrist gave me.

By now I realize I'm turning kind of green and the possibility of passing out is getting very close.

Somewhere in this car park, my car is parked. Two new goals: Don't pass out and get to my car—fast. A security guard in a golf cart comes up, "Are you, all right? I can take you to your car." And so, he does. He asks me a thousand times, "Are you sure you're all right?"

I never told him that I'm sure I'm all right; the truth is I'm not all right. I'm sure of that. I did mention to him that I ate at Benito's Confetti Café.

He said, "Oh, don't eat there." Too late.

I'm so thankful to be in my car and so happy to be in my own environment by myself. If I need to pass out here, at least I am semi-home.

This doesn't feel like food poisoning, this feels like . . . well, death. You laugh now, but I'm sure you've had that time in your life when first you're sick and are desperate to feel better, then you're sicker and you're pretty sure you'll die, and then you need to die right away just to get some relief. On a scale of one to ten—yes, this is definitely tottering on the brink.

Why am I telling you this? I think it's because of what my friend Terri said when she had a serious car crash. Of all the things that could have really scared her about her circumstance, like never walking again or disfigurement, the thing that scared her the most was that she wouldn't be able to take care of herself anymore. That's it. That's what this is for. It takes me just to the edge of being unable to care for myself— the precursor to "I've fallen, and I can't get up."

With still-blurred vision from the eye dilation and body eruptions compliments of Benito's, I know I have to get home and fast.

It would be the smartest plan to rest in my car until I get my equilibrium and then proceed slowly and cautiously home. But no, I get behind the wheel of my giga-horsepower car and beat it on home, in the fast lane, all the way. But yeah, verily I am mindful enough to call upon the spirit of race car driver Mario Andretti to steer the wheel and get me home. I figure since he is an all-time expert on getting a car the fastest across the finish line without crashing, he's the one to call on for help.

After pulling over several times to leave more of Benito along the roadway, and after taking off pieces of my clothes along the way—such as my belt, and my jacket, and all my jewelry, and opening buttons and unzipping everything unzippable, and shoes off, I arrive home.

Home. I'm home. Thank you, Mario, for getting me here safely, I was way too dizzy to walk. Now I can barely open the car door to get out. I slide against the car to make it to the tree that I hold onto, and then make it to my door.

I'm home, but my couch is up the stairs. I need to get there to get grounded. It takes a v e r y, l o n g time to get there.

Once in the door, I really take off every piece of clothing. I am soaked in sweat, now cold, now hot, swinging back and forth, now shaking, now sprawled on the stairs unable to pull myself up.

Here's where *the Crawl* comes in. I crawl one stair at a time, all the way up. Shivering, I fall into a deep sleep at every third stair. This can be for ten minutes each or is it the next day? I don't know.

Meanwhile, I had the presence of mind to bring the Trader Joe's shopping bag out of the trunk and have it with me for further "deposits."

My goal is the couch; I'm getting up the stairs. I'm rooting for getting to the landing.

This is the level of sick it is when you go quickly from "God, don't let me die" to "Beam me up, Scottie."

Now I have thoughts of every airplane meal and frozen pop tart I ever ate. Maybe this is detoxing from all the food I ever ate, ever. From all the street food from third-world countries to all the careful health tonics and the three-hundred-dollar dinner I once had at Providence in West Hollywood; that memorable gallon of fudge-ripple ice cream, farmer's market organic greens; every non-gluten, no fat, low sodium, no-GMO choice in recent years way back to Kraft mac and cheese and top ramen in college; as a preteen, Mrs. Paul's fish sticks on Friday's even though we weren't Catholic; that questionable Twinkie when I was eight; at five, penny candy from Wingee's grocery store; and all the way back to mother's milk—all now in the Trader Joe's shopping bag sitting heavily on the stair next to me.

Hello, help, please. Is a team of angels here with me? I call upon the White Brotherhood; they are a group of light beings available to help with healing anytime we remember to ask for their help.

Archangel Michael, you're welcome too, and the school nurse who once held my hand when I was sick at school until my mother could get there to take me home.

All of my life I've been throwing up all over the world. Just now—I don't want to anymore. I want to be comfortable and peaceful.

Is this because I asked for world peace for Christmas? This is the answer. Settle peace in your own intestinal tract?

Landing

Just two more stairs. I can almost reach my hand to the landing.

There's a gift in this somewhere. What is the hidden opportunity? Too soon to look for it now. It will have to come to me once I'm feeling better.

It's imperative that I make it to the couch to get to the business of coming back alive if that's what I am going to do— an inch at a time, one breath at a time.

Finally, I crawl onto my couch, I am naked except for my temporary, wrap-around, polarized sunshield for dilation protection given to me by the optometrist. I cover myself with my splendidly soft down comforter. I am home—I am at one with the couch. It will hold me. Now I can heal.

I lie ever still until the world stops spinning. I find myself deciding to never venture off my couch again. No, don't decide that, not while your body is feeling this way. Make your defining decisions when you're upright and can feel the joy of unlimited possibilities, then decide if and what, and when.

This is not presenting itself for me to stop and limit myself. This is an opportunity, an invitation for me to decide to go on and in what way to go on.

As the active creator of my reality, I am mindful of my creation here forward.

I give myself over to wellness. I allow the couch to hold me, and I fall into a deep sleep.

I wake to the night sky. I am soaked and cold—now hot, now cold—I sleep some more. I wake to the bright day. I know I am on the mend.

And then hours later, I am at peace. So quiet within. It's over. I unwrap the wrap-around sunshield, and I bask in sun-drenched joy. My body is quiet now. Such peace. Benito and his confetti have left the building.

There is nowhere I have to go, nothing I have to do. Here on my couch, I am capable of expanding the universe. I am the most there is to be, and then I drop through and there is more to join with and be.

This feels transformational to me. This is a change point.

What are my needs here forward? What will it take for me to continue to take care of myself?

Thirty-five years ago, when I was on *the Climb*, it was me stretching, reaching to the best and highest I could be. Now, *the Crawl*. What more, what else do I want to experience? What still needs doing so I can do it?

At twenty I had a plan. So grateful I did what I did when I did it to leave the now to be free. I know that longevity was never my goal. Quality of life for the rest of my life, that's always appealed to me to practice.

There's a vastness in small things. It's very rich being very quiet. I'm so happy in my home, so happy in my life.

This mall attack has given me the opportunity to decide my future. If there's anything else or anything more, it's time for me to get to it. What do I want for my future? More? Or "Thank you, that's enough."

I see it's a lovely blend of both. A tender surrender of rhapsodic joy in the quiet moment and all the skill required to continue with more.

Just this week, I've been invited to do a lecture tour in Europe. I enjoy the idea to go or not. I'm just as happy being here now or being there if I feel like it.

Oh, I'm so hungry. Thanks to Benito, I'm now on empty. I have a taste for mulligatawny soup. Hmm, I could book a flight to Mumbai or just be here luxuriating on my couch. Either way, I'm at peace. Thanks, Santa—Joy to the World. ~

64 Years Old

Dave

Forty years ago, in my twenties, I was sitting on the beach with a friend. We were writer colleagues working on a TV pilot together. We were having a brainstorming session, ocean front, sitting in two low beach chairs on the sand.

There was something a little bit different this day with Dave. He thought I was funnier that he usually did. One thing that comedy writers do when they hear a joke, they say, "That's funny." They don't laugh. Today Dave was laughing at my jokes.

We were having an unusually great brainstorming session. We were really powering through the structure of the story and getting onto funny dialogue. As we were clicking along, I felt the little screw come out of the hinge of my sunglasses. I caught it in my hand, just in time, before it hit the sand. As we continued, I was getting the little screw back in the hinge.

But there was something up with Dave. I think that morning he must have decided that maybe we could be more than colleagues and good pals. I think he thought, "Yes, of course." It was right in front of his nose. This would be perfect—we already get along. So, this was his chance.

As I'm repairing my glasses, he reaches in through our friendship to become the man in my life and fix this crisis. When he grabs my glasses out of my hand, he immediately loses the little screw in the sand. He also loses any hope of being my hero—there went his boyfriend idea.

We continue with our meeting, never mentioning any of this. I put my sunglasses back on, this time askew on my face. I say the next joke.

He doesn't laugh, instead he says, "That's funny."

The reason I'm telling you this forty years later is because this is a good time to be grateful for all the things that have happened in my life, and also to be grateful for what didn't happen. ~

65 Years Old

Beloved—July

I WAS ON location. I got a call. Beloved was rushed to the hospital.

We've known that the time is getting close for him to be complete with his life. I am kitty-corner way across the city from the hospital that he was rushed to, and it is rush hour traffic just now. My heart wants to leap right to him and yet there is about two hours of distance between us. I get in the car and let go to the flow of how it will go here to there. Surprisingly, all go lights; miraculously, no traffic. I notice I am weaving my way across the city that we have lived in for our forty years of history. Our history is here. Many of our favorite restaurants, concert theaters where he played, hotels where I lectured, the park where we had his last birthday, the hospitals where the grandbabies were born, their schools, Nordstrom's where we had such fun one evening when the lights went out. The Biltmore where he was honored on the day proclaimed for him by the mayor. All the many places he received yet another plaque, too many to have walls enough to display them. And just recently, the community service building that was built and named for him. The doctor said he couldn't go to the ribbon cutting ceremony—"It could kill him." We went anyway, of course, and he thrived on it.

Driving through the places of the times of our lives, some of the hardest times turn out to be the best.

I always hope young lovers give themselves the opportunity to let the thing that crushes them marinate long enough for them to know it was there to crack open their hearts wider.

I'm reminded of many years ago seeing my brother and his wife at their son's graduation from college. They were holding hands. They had done this together. They raised this boy, now a young man ready to go out on his own. History means something—it means everything while you are compiling all the events of your life that later come back wrapped as a beautiful gift of memories.

Now I'm passing the airport. So many times we went all over the world, or we picked each other up or dropped each other off, such good travelers we were together. We had clear divisions of labor, I can speak food in any language, he could ask directions from any local and they always invited us to some wonderful magical exchange.

Events now connecting so clearly, one to another, twenty-thirty years apart.

My heart is so urgent to get there and be with him, yet here is my heart and he fills it here. I see that I'm weaving through the side streets I wove through that first night forty years ago when I noticed myself rushing to see him then. I was surprised by my heart that knew something then that I didn't yet know. I took it on faith. He was the love of my life, and here forty years later as he is completing his life, I know that this is a completing for us.

All the milestones, all the special occasions and the occasions made special because of their simplicity; it comes down to the golden moments—the ones so small, so not planned, and all the more precious when we are in them.

Now feeling each memory in vivid real time. The laughing, the exact words we said, the color of the rooms, what we ate, feelings we felt. Each memory connecting to another and another. All the times of our lives together.

I believe that the impending death of a loved one can be experienced physically within our own body. The energy of him lives on in me. He's readying to depart yet coming closer in to be within me at the same time.

My body is playing the love octave—playing all the notes as in holy, funny, shaken to the core, feelings caught, feelings so big, tender, explosive, implosive, vast, fathoms deep, quiet, still, a crescendo, the sound of a sultry lone saxophone, nothing but its sound all around. The kind of love that's brimful, and then our cup runneth over and somehow the best of times, the worst of times both deepen our history of having a life with each other. We did it. We achieved it. We came together to know the importance of coming together. ~

65 Plus

Beloved—September

HERE IS THE eulogy I gave for Beloved at his funeral.

He had a brilliance for one-minute wisdoms—they were simple, clear, and could go right to the heart of the matter.

For instance, "If you're going too fast, it'll take longer."

Or "Wear the shoe that fits your foot."

His music would even come out of him in his words. There was always a clear rhythm to his wisdoms.

Last week, he said, "Get an idea—go with it today. Tomorrow, get another idea." He was continuing to get good ideas and going with them.

Think of a problem you have and apply one of his simple solutions: "If the ice is thin, don't step on it." Or "Your frame of mind is what makes things happen." Or "Put in the good ingredients." Or one that he said for years: "Look at it like it is." That would take the complications right out of a person's dilemma.

Since you're here, celebrating his life, and you loved him, he probably gave you a wisdom. Think about it now because it shifted something in you. That—right there, that shift—that's where he's alive and well and living in you still. He never let you down. He's going to keep with you, and you're going to make that turn in your road you hoped you could make.

He was the champion of young people to follow their heart. He'd say, "Pick something that does it for you. Do it and do it well." And that's what he did.

He espoused, "Make things better for others." And that's what he did.

And more of his words for those just starting out: "Join hands. Put your part in, whatever it is," "Get on a good road," "Allow yourself to catch fire."

We knew a young man who always got in his own way, and he said to the young man, '"You put handcuffs on yourself and throw away the key." And the young man got it and stopped it.

When he just had the stroke and was in physical therapy on one of the early days, he got up with great effort and got across the room. I asked him what he was thinking, what was that focus? He said, "The body has reaching power." See, he could use his wisdom on himself. In fact, he worked his body like a new instrument he wanted to play.

Take any one of his wisdoms with you today and it can make all the difference. Here's one that can free you, "When you get what you need, that's all you need." Remember the one he told you. Remember it now. Maybe you didn't even notice, like one of the prodigy musicians who came to study with him, who said, "You don't teach us anything, but we learn." Maybe you can just begin to understand the power of his presence that remains in you.

Something so simple as "Give and love and you'll understand what the whole thing is about." It's okay if you don't remember right now what he gave you. As he said, "In music you have that moment to get the air in."

One of my all-time favorite wisdoms from him was, "Everybody's got to be doing something with their time." It was my favorite because he was a man who did something with his time. ~

66 Years Old

Aloha—It Has Come to Me in the Way of Things

WHEN I GET off the plane on my favorite island, I have my procedure. I stop at the beach just up from the airport to sink my toes into the sand and into the ocean. I say a salutation and invocation of celebration. I feel such love for the island. Each time I am here something big materializes.

After my hello to nature, my next stop is at the food store to pick up provisions for my stay. I love this part because, as you know, I love food and must always have it with me. This time when I get to the store, my body is still feeling scattered somewhere in the air zone over the Pacific. In spite of my travel lag, I notice vacationers in the food store experiencing sticker shock. This is an island—that means that everything for sale here has been shipped in. Pick up any random can of anything and it's like investing in a late-model compact.

I notice, while standing in the produce department, I am unable to make a decision regarding lettuce. This is very unusual for me, Ms. Proactive, such as I am.

I then hear a message inside me. "Let the island do this for you." Okay, that sounds good, so I leave the store without any provisions and give myself over to the magic that is surely available to me as soon as I get out of the way.

I drive leisurely and joyously to the timeshare condo, have a glorious moonlight swim, dine on two packets of complimentary microwave popcorn, and go to bed. Tomorrow I'll find food.

In the morning, I am still in a travel stupor. I stand in the middle of the room wanting to get my energy up, yet I am still in slow motion. I need food fuel to get going to get food. When it comes to action, no way can I kick into action. Hmm . . . It's an island, I wonder if they deliver.

Just then I hear a man from the downstairs condo knock on the door next door to mine. He says to the lady who answers,

"We're checking out, and we have so much food. May I give it to you?"

The lady says, "We're checking out too, and we have food to give to somebody also."

I perk up! This is one of those sweet, rare incidents when I know that my whole life brings me to this moment for something important that is about to happen—a turning point. I've just been given a clear and simple choice—left or right, yes or no. It's an invitation for me to step through to some other side of living. It requires me to leave my former self behind. It requires me to let go of "I'll do this myself."

All I have to do is take two steps and open the door. Those would be two steps that change everything. Prior to this, I would fend for myself. I would have been . . . self-sufficient. "I'm fine, I don't need it, I don't want it, I can do it." Now a choice was being shown to me—receive. This was what was meant by "The island will take care of this."

I take the two steps and open the door.

I am rushed with bountifulness. Not only a full box of food from the man. He goes back to his refrigerator *three more times* to bring more to me. The lady gathers up two bags full and a box and three families from downstairs hear our exchange and come rushing with their offerings.

Within moments I have:

1 dozen eggs
1 loaf of rye bread
8 pounds of butter (Yes, 8)
A 13 lb. ready-made roast beef
2 gallons of high-grade vodka
3 bottles of wine
A 6-pack of Ale
6 lb. of shrimp
3 lb. of mussels
3 jars of mayonnaise
2 jars of mustard
2 jars of two kinds of pickles
Every kind of barbeque sauce known to man
1 watermelon

3 kinds of lettuce
Abundant assorted fresh vegetables
5 lb. of blueberries
10 apples
2 cans of tuna fish
1 jar of pesto
3 lb. of pasta
1 lb. of coffee
46 tea bags
1 gallon of lemonade
1 lb. of chocolate-covered macadamia nuts
1 papaya
6 lb. of potatoes
2 bottles of shampoo
Industrial-size jars of peanut butter and jelly
A liter each of olive oil and canola oil
1 gallon of milk
2 containers of whipped cream
2 tins of cookies
5 lb. of sugar
1 box of Tide
48 dishwasher packets
2 seashell leis

Remarkable that these dear people came to the island, shopped, and were all ready to give me their food as soon as I was ready to receive it. And it was delivered to my door.

I am in awe, filled with gratitude, and needless to say, just plain filled—such generosity as they bestow their gifts on me. The man says, "I just wish I could give you more."

And more is what always happens:

I invite people over for lunches and dinners. I go to people's houses and bring enough for feasts. There is plenty to eat, to share, to give, to leave when I leave. I give one of the gallon jugs of vodka to the concierge, who is thrilled to get it. I don't see her for the rest of my stay. I wonder if she drank it all at once.

Life is lush when you let it—a perfect demonstration of the shift from making it happen to letting it happen.

My favorite Hawaiian expression is "It has come to me in the way of things."

The island has always made miracles out of the circumstances I bring to it.

"Yes, please, thank you, mahalo, aloha, Bon Appetit." ~

67 Years Old

The Last of Everything

I was working on the set of a documentary about a high swami. On a break from shooting, he happened to mention to me that I would be leaving the planet within the year. He gave me the date of my demise. Since we were standing at the craft services table at the time, it might have been the moment for me to eat my way through all two dozen donuts, assorted candies, cookies, and industrial-size bags of chips in several ethnic flavorings. Instead, I thanked him for telling me (what do you do in such an instance?), and we carried on with the shoot.

That evening, I was walking into a bookstore and a homeless man at the door whispered the date that the swami had used, I reeled around and asked, "What about that date?" and he said that I would die on that day. Do I have a sign on my back that the set design crew put there as a practical joke?

Steps later, in the bookstore, the proprietor took it upon herself to inform me that I would be dying and gave the same date. Gee, you would think that strangers could keep their opinions to themselves. But alas, throughout the week there were several other indications that there was a clock ticking and an end date looming. So, I decided something: I'm clear that I'm not done with living yet. I'll know when I've completed what I came here to do and then I'll be happy to leave without a fight. I have nothing against death. Just not yet. Not on that date. No.

So here is what I decided: Even though this won't be my last year to live, I'll live each moment as though it is my last and live it as a year of thriving, and that is what I'm doing, living it by the experience of this minute and then this one, every present moment as the one and only moment—now, then now, then now.

You get the idea. The reason I'm telling you this is—I kind of recommend it. There's a lovely sorting that goes on. When you have finite time, do you really want to spend it watching that rerun that you already saw, and it didn't make a difference in you the first time you saw it?

I enjoy looking at everything with a downsizing eye and an expanding heart at the same time. I don't need that. I won't miss that. I'm done with that. That over there was so good and yet that's enough of it. And with other life things, more of that please while it's still possible.

I'm okay with a death of old things. I'm all for releasing what no longer serves me. It's easy to say goodbye to good things that aren't needed any longer. Goodbye also to any limiting story or caught-up belief that keeps me mad or critical of anybody, or anything that's maligned not aligned. My energy is like a rocket ship—dropping off the fuselage that got me this far, so I am catapulted to more, better, higher.

That is what a year of thriving consists of—try it sometime. As I walk in the world, there are two things going on about this experience; one is an incredible appreciation and gratitude for everything and everyone. There's a lusciousness about ringing out every bit of juice from everything. And the other part is that saying goodbye has kept me up to date on every moment. This is good, this is good, this is good. When Beloved had his stroke and was about to die any moment, we lived that way: Anything pending, anything due—are we up to the minute being here in this moment presently? Living that way, we had some of the best moments a human life can have.

If you're going to try this, let me tell you the difference between gratitude and appreciation. Gratitude has an element of dodging a bullet to it. You are grateful that you are here, not there, and whew-that-was-a-close-one and forever-indebted-that-it-turned-out-okay. Appreciation is valuing what it is, where it is, all that it is, as it is, not worrying that it was something bad or wrong and now it's fixed. Appreciation is "as is" awe. When you "appreciate," that makes all the difference.

You'll see that, if you decide to do this, you'll come up with your own way to thrive.

While I was in great perfection of this way to live, I got a call from a dear friend, Marilee. She was inoperable and had a short time to live. We talked about her lifelong hurts and transgressions that she had with her family. She always seemed to conduct her life dwelling on those past feelings that didn't feel good. The present moment never seemed to be available to her, she wasn't able to access the present. I mentioned to her that she might consider having a year of thriving. She was immediately fascinated with the idea and asked for help. For her the deep caldron of hurt that she carried all her life now had a clear urgency to be healed. If she was going to get at the unfinished business and finish it, now was the time. She already said that her family members wanted to come and take care of her and be with her. She didn't trust that it would work out. It was uncomfortable for her to have their help and their love. She agreed to open herself to the possibility of being with them. She didn't have to forgive them yet—just be, just see how that was going to feel for her—just this moment and then the next, and the next, at any time free to make any choice.

I realized that I could give her this practice because she needed a way to have quality of life for the rest of her life that would be ending. Maybe I got the exit date from the swami that really belonged to her. It was just given to me to perfect it and pass it on to her to have the best time of her life this last year of her life.

When we hung up the phone, this is what I knew: I would live on, she would have the best year of her life and leave peacefully. ~

68 Years Old

All Tucked In

Dɪᴅ I ᴍᴇɴᴛɪᴏɴ that I'm lucky in love?

Many people in this world have never been in love, never experienced what it feels like to have a beloved. They know longing rather than belonging. Loneliness can be an epidemic. I'm happy to keep my own company. I'm happy by myself (often better than being with people). I'm filled with the day, the light, the activities, the thoughts, and the good feeling of being. *I've been having the time of my life for a long time in my life.*

Since I've already had the love of my life, I don't have my porch light on, if you get my meaning.

I'm a woman who takes out her own garbage. The man in my life is me. I'm sustainable and maintainable. There's magic in the ability to be self-actualized. I'm free and freedom is a beautiful thing.

And yet . . . if there is any more to love than I know, now is the time to know it. If a new Dear One shows up, he would be a final frontier for me. I know enough to be accessible, to open to love, to be in without my getaway car. But really, do I have to?

Lately, I've had a frustration with those things I don't want to do like taxes and computer learning curves, or the thing on the car that requires that I have to buy something at Pep Boys. My lifelong tune, "I'll do it myself," is starting to change its tune to, "Yes, please, thank you." I could be very happy being served. I could let somebody else take care of that and that, and that would be just fine.

I'm so grateful to feel love every day. It isn't predicated on having a partner. Love is a wellspring from within. Love just oozes out of the air all by itself. And if I want somebody to help with the paperwork . . . maybe I just need an assistant.

If a new Dear One does show up, he will have to be pretty good because my life as I know it, *the life that it took me a lifetime to create*, will change. It will expand and be enriched, but from where I stand now, I'm not interested in changing it. I love the life I created. I'm satisfied with lolling on the couch, watching the night sky over the ocean. You mean he will be here with me as happy as I am without him? I can hardly imagine it since I'm already so full up. Wouldn't having someone around impede my freedom?

I have it exactly how I like it, as I like, when I like, and I like it that way.

I have plenty of loved ones, plenty of friends, plenty of clients, plenty of plenty, plenty good. I don't feel anything missing.

I've gotten to that decade in my life where I clearly know my preferences and have to have them. I know that I like sunrise on the beach without seeing any other human to distract me from my train of thought. I don't go to the Moroccan restaurant because the spices aren't worth the adventure.

I'm aware that once you get it just so, and how you like it, you might think you are fully enlightened, but then the barking pit bull moves into the neighborhood and there goes your enlightenment. I know that it's control that I have. I have the circumstances controlled to such an extent that they wouldn't dare mess with me.

Do I really want to invite love in and open a new can of worms? Aren't I "all tucked in?" Aren't I so very happy to be at one with the couch? If he comes in, would we be at two with the couch? How does that work? And yet, there's more, there's always more.

I remember a friend of mine walked into a room and noticed a man who would later become her husband. The minute she saw him she thought, "S#*t! More growth."

I don't want anybody coming in and tinkering with my heart. It might just knock me off balance. I can live without a "him."

What if a "him" comes into my life and then I can't live without him? I'm not interested in a gaping hole. Where will I be if I need me? Would that be the same place as where I've always been, right here able to continue to tap my own wellspring? Maybe, probably, possibly not. Do I want my tombstone to read, "She lived without him until he came into her life, then she couldn't live without him?"

I can say all is beautiful in my world and I've done it and I can leave now because I've had a fulfilling life. I don't need to stick around for infirmity. I can go now; there's no need to start drooling on a regular basis.

I'm responsible for myself. I provide for my wants and needs. Inch by inch over the decades I cleared my own debris in the road to make my own magic.

When I was four and staying over at my grandparents' house, "all tucked in" meant that Papa would pull the quilt tight over me and tuck the ends in, so I was cozy-safe. He'd say, "Sleep tight, don't let the Wumpas bite."

Now I'm sixty-eight, "all tucked in" has meant something more. As an independent woman providing my own way for my adult life, I find that "all tucked in" means that I've navigated a comfortable place to stand in the world with freedom and calm and everything on the shelves where they belong. I don't find myself in a quandary thinking, "What am I doing here? Who am I? Where am I going?" I've already gone there and I'm back and lying on the couch to savor the evening of my choosing. I'm perfectly happy to walk in the world fully individuated—party of one, non-smoking.

Whatever is needed I can provide. My want these days is to have all my needs met.

As for more stuff—I don't need, say, any more jewelry, but I can get really excited about having the squeak in the brakes fixed. There's nothing like the feeling of filling the gas tank, filling the refrigerator, and paying all the bills. Very gratifying.

This week, my neighbor wanted to talk me into adopting a puppy and plopped it on my lap. My heart turned into a chewy toy, and yet I was "tucked in" enough to enjoy puppy love but decline the offer to adopt it. I'm in a decade where I don't have to be responsible for anyone else's potty activities. A decade from now it might require everything I've got just to take care of my own.

In my forties, I would get a desire for Hong Kong, and I'd book a flight that day, get on the plane and go. It got so friends would call and say into my voicemail, "Are you in town?" Now I continue to be free to travel to any place. How I like to do it now is to be invited to lecture, first-class paid, and bring home cash money in my hand. I make the reservation, pack light (always pack light), and go. A luscious destination—something five-star that includes a complimentary robe, something very comfortable, something where I have handlers to handle the details, where I can make a big impact for others at the conference, something where I can stay "tucked in." I don't require high adventure; I prefer room service.

Once you know what it feels like to provide for your needs, there's nothing that's needed. I've had it all—the dream home, the dream car, the dream clientele, the dream world service, got it, got it all. I have a dozen of everything.

I've long since practiced and been successful at tools of gracious living like getting off the phone from people I don't care to talk to, or not saying yes to events I don't want to go to. I'm free of volunteering for anything, I can have compassion and loving support for everyone yet not worry about anyone. I let people to their own drama and none of it splashes on my fashionable yet comfortable high-end low-heeled shoes.

I know to manage crises far before they materialize—just a gentle adjustment of this action and that attitude. I know to focus so an answer comes immediately because I'm quiet enough to hear it, and I know enough to follow through. As for life mysteries, and global tragedies, my heart is plenty big enough to be brimful with compassion, sending alchemy to transform injustices into love. I've got the life tool kit—the one that rolls me along, the one that tells me to take any tender feelings for a walk. I know that life affirms itself; that I can keep on keeping on, or some days I can't and that's the best choice. I know to make a sacred practice of small things.

Beyond ambition, beyond generating, just at the intersection of "I am who I am" and "make me an offer," as my heart continues to expand, I find that it's all right with me if my "all tucked in" nature pulls out at the corners. There's so much love in here, in me. So much to give that it gushes. I am willing to be as open as open can be. Unraveling, traveling to the outreaches, and then coming back to find I can't, won't, fit back "all tucked in." It's okay with me to disorder my ordered life. It's okay to let the Wumpas in. ~

69 Years Old

The Higher, the Much

I HAVE BEEN known to be the Lone Ranger and Jiminy Cricket rolled into one. It has been a privilege to be a great help to people. This has been wonderful, this has been valuable, this is about to stop. Not because it hasn't been beneficial to all, including me. It has been. It's just that there comes a time in the span of a lifetime when you are given the opportunity to graduate from your expertise. You can immediately sign up for another spin of the same wheel. That's easy. Yet there's an alternative move you can make. When you get to the pinnacle of what you are offering, when you know with your eyes closed how effectively you can serve, that is the moment you can choose to lift off from it. Let it all go and put out an empty chalice. Be willing to no longer be identified with whatever you identify yourself with. When you let it all go, that's when it goes bigger. This is what's known in the trade as a New Soul program.

How you got here to the top of the summit, you got from the ground up. Now you lift off into the ionosphere. All your expertise that built to here, all the reaching, stretching, now gives way to floating, to magnetizing, to connecting from the further, the higher, the place you now become. This place of radiance belongs to you where it is thrilling to play in the field of creation and let next-level wisdoms arise out of you. Now you are in mastery. Oh goodie, more fun to be had. ~

70s Passage

Carrier of the Light

EARLY IN MY life in Hollywood, I stepped onto a stage of a big conference. I was the new speaker amongst many old-guard men. As I was presenting my speech, something began swirling around me. The audience was so enthralled, laughing, applauding, responding in big ways. What was going on here? I realized that the baton was being passed to me—not that the old guard was willing for me to have it. By natural selection, by the order of succession, by the kiss of kismet, when I stepped off the stage, it was clear, I was the new guard. It was my platform, and it was my time to carry its light.

Years later, at the same annual conference, I saw a young woman deliver her presentation. When she came off the stage, I found her in the outside atrium as a leaf was fluttering down off the tree. I caught it and handed it to her.

"This is for you if you get my meaning." And the baton that came to me, I now passed to her. Since then, maybe she has done the same.

I bring this up because in everyone's life is the time when you step into the light you are to carry, and the time when you surrender it to the next carrier. As is true before, during, and after you carry that collective light, you always continue to carry your own. ~

70 Years Old

The High Art of Being Here Now

I'M HERE AT a tropical resort basking in the beauty of the surroundings, enjoying the kids from a local orphanage. They treated me to an impromptu concert with new musical instruments. I am very glad at seventy that I have taken the next road not usually taken.

It's a new life program. Within this year, I found that the methods I used and clients I had, and ways that were my natural go-to ways of life, just seemed to fall away. Life was telling me that something else was about to appear as a great gift to me. So, I let it. I just let it show up and make me an offer. And when I did, I realized that what was waiting for me was all the reaping of what I had sown for the last seventy years.

The very minute I stopped generating projects and making plans, the magic that was waiting for me got a chance to come in, and it did and continues to. I'm so grateful in my infinite wisdom to be smart enough to catch it when it came calling.

This tropical breeze blows through my soul and leaves fresh air in my heart. I find that my very DNA pattern that has been striking the same notes a trillion times since my birth now changes its tune. I hear a part of myself I never knew was in there.

And here, as a nice surprise, on this island paradise, I find Brian Roberts. He is a colleague of mine from the last fifty years as we would offer our expertise internationally. Brian, author of fifty-eight books published in seventy-two countries, is a captain of industry and world success as a business guru. He has given great good in the world. Many thousands of people have been helped by his work.

He's always had a well-ordered life and a full schedule. He worked hard to get it this way, and he's here at the resort heading yet another high-end executive retreat for a big-ticket return. I see him at the pool bar sitting alone; very few resort guests are up and about this early. His breathing is more labored than the last time we saw each other. He seems to be drinking in an attempt to keep up with himself. Seventy for him is not looking promising. He sees me and we embrace hardily.

Throughout the years we have always gotten right to the point, continuing an ongoing conversation that's lasted through a thousand events we were both headlining.

In the VIP lounges in the airports of the world, he always asked for specific wisdom, and I would give it to him in concise directives then we'd dash off to catch planes—his west to my east—weaving the world until our next meet up.

His complaint today is that younger ambitious titans are coming up and cutting into his market share.

Brian: The numbers just aren't there anymore.

Me: Aren't you making your usual seven figures a year?

Brain: Yeah, but low seven.

Me: Low seven—that's an oxymoron. That's one to nine million dollars.

Brian: Well yes, but it's less than last year's number.

Me: How about meeting with the younger titans coming up and passing the torch to them? Let them do the work and you take a percentage. You'd be free to enjoy your own harvest already in progress.

Brian: I don't want something new. I want to keep what I've got.

Me: If all you want is the same thing more so, why do you want that?

Brian: I want to know that I can do it.

Me: You have done it. Maybe there's more in a different direction.

Brian: There is no other direction for me.

Me: Is it never enough?

Brian: Something like that. I want the highest score.

Me: Who sets that?

Brian: I do.

Me:	And you haven't yet reached the score that you set?
Brian:	I have, I just keep moving it up.
Me:	So does that mean that you are competing against yourself?
Brian:	Yes.
Me:	Who wins?
Brian:	I stay hungry.
Me:	Do you ever let yourself feel full? Satisfied? Complete? Content?
Brian:	Complete . . . then I'm dead, and I don't want to be dead.
Me:	Complete as in you begin anew. Or would you rather enjoy being unhappy?
Brian:	I never thought of it that way.
Me:	There's more if you want to change your tune and experience a new song.

I'm so grateful to be having these days be glory days. I invite you to have yours. There are infinite ways to be effective in the world. Lately, I've been stepping in where it delights me to be, and I receive so very much from being there. |
| Brian: | Aren't you afraid you'll lose your grip? |
| Me: | I hope so. |
| Brain: | See, that's why you were always way ahead of any of us smartass bastards.

The difference between you and all the others is that you are the real deal. You never believed your own marketing hype. |
| Me: | That's because I never had marketing hype. You made way more money than I did. I never had a high seven-figure year. |
| Brian: | You would wheel in your small suitcase, give your speech, and they would all fall in love with you, and then you were on to the next |

	venue. We all secretly loved you and wanted you and envied you. You were self-contained.
Me:	Ah yes. I, the Lone Ranger. We all have the life that's right for us. You worked diligently to get a huge following.
Brian:	I was always afraid that people would find me out.
Me:	Doesn't matter what people find out. It matters what you find out.
Brian:	I don't respect myself.
Me:	That's an inside job, Brian, based on your own conduct. I think success is being satisfied—knowing what you did and being happy about it.
Brian:	I'll have sixty books by the end of the year.
Me:	Will that make you happy?
Brian:	Probably not.
Me:	You don't write your books anyway. What's the difference if it's fifty-eight or sixty?
Brian:	Sixty is a higher number.
Me:	That's your story and you're sticking to it?
Brian:	I know, I know, you've always told me, don't be dogmatic about my plan.
Me:	You can't get all the way to your age and be dogmatic. Life shows you long before now to let the flow . . . flow.
Brian:	I don't want the flow to flow. It might take me right to death.
Me:	Or life. It might take you right to life.
Brian:	I'm hanging on to all the moves I know that have worked for me for the last fifty years of my career.
Me:	Are you having a career or a life?
Brian:	My career is my life.
Me:	Yes, I see that. Is that working for you?

Brian:	This life works for me. If I leave it, maybe there's nothing else.
Me:	There's always something else. It seems that if it were really working, you'd naturally move into the next phase.
Brian:	What's that—rocking chair? I don't want the next phase.
Me:	If you keep getting what you've been getting, how are you going to get what you haven't yet gotten?
Brian:	I don't want what I haven't got. I want what I already have that I don't have anymore.
Me:	Does it appeal to you at all to leave behind your expertise and step into simple wonder at the awe of the mystery? The vastness of what you don't yet know might be so much bigger than what you do know.
Brian:	I have no interest in anything. I'll just keep doing what I'm doing.

I hear the kids from the orphanage come running joyfully from down the beach to have me join them. I kiss Brian on the forehead. "Bless your life, Brian. I'm happy for you. Won't you be happy for you?"

His eyes seem so tired, and there is despair in them. My own dogma before I became seventy would have had me single-handedly carry him back into vibrancy. Yet that is not the place he is taking himself.

I run off down the beach with the kids and my life at this age.

When I look back, I see Brian taking a long drink from his glass. I know that the ice jangles in a familiar call to him; the cool-hot alcohol descends down his throat as his body finds comfort in this substitute for being alive.

To each his own.

Postscript—Four Months Later

Brian died. He had a heart attack in a hotel room. He never did get to his sixtieth book. ~

71 Years Old

Birthday Presence

As you know I am an "eat"-seeking missile. If anyone puts food down anywhere near me, I'm magnetically pulled to it.

I mention this yet again because I am at the Four Seasons Resort at poolside for my birthday. Across the pool a Deluxe Premium Double Party Tray has just been delivered to the cabana there. The guests—four women—have barely looked at the feast and *haven't touched it yet*. Beautiful tropical fruits gleam in the sunshine. There are appetizers of lobster and shrimp, and vegetable skewers all healthy bright, with three kinds of breads and two dips and an assortment of imported cheeses.

All luscious wonderful and the cabana women have not started the party. I want to dive in the pool and swim across to come up just in arm's reach of it all. I could order the Deluxe Premium Double Party Tray for myself but . . . I just had one!

I'm so appreciative that I've had a life of abundant eating, and that I can vacuum it all in and still have room for myself in my bikini. The high art of eating, as an art form, has always belonged to me.

And here is Elliot, the server, who delivered my tray and theirs. He knows me from previous visits and asks if there is anything more that I would like. I have a reputation. (I mention Elliot here because he asks to be mentioned as I write this. If you've ever wished for the perfect server, Elliot would be it.)

Ah, feel the sunshine. It's so glorious. My glory days continue. I am feeling them so lavishly. I submerge into the pool and am the only swimmer. You can always tell who's just been in the pool by the wave patterns they leave. Kids tend to create choppy, frolicking seas. Those who do laps usually make rhythmic, even swells. I, now in my seventies, make David Hockney waves, that is, they ripple peacefully and reflect the sunlight. This is what I'm contributing to the pool today.

After my spa day I'm now puffed and powdered and ready for the valet to bring my car. A guest of the hotel rushes out in a hurry. He needs to get to the airport with no time to spare. I tell the valet to get his car first. I have all the time in the world.

"Would you care for a bottle of chilled water while you wait?"

"Yes, please, thank you."

The man dashes off. I leave after him and go in the opposite direction, feeling the luxury of open time.

I get to the canyon and just ahead is a huge and serious car pileup. I pull over and help with getting kids out of car seats and to the safety of the roadside, then direct traffic, then pull a disembodied truck fender out of the roadway. The truck driver calls 911 and help is on the way.

I realize that if the man at the hotel who needed to get to the airport hadn't needed to get to the airport, I would be in this accident now as possibly the third car totaled just in front of the truck.

This has happened to me before. I told you about it twenty years ago when I stopped to give away my trunk blanket. It's another of the ten thousand miracles that we all get; zig here or zag there and a different outcome will result.

Traffic is starting to back up and the best help I can be is to get my car off the road, so I get in and go.

As I continue on my way and feel the gratitude of timing, here come ambulances and tow trucks and a helicopter whooshing loudly as it comes down to land to whisk the most seriously injured to the hospital.

I'm overwhelmed with the milk of human kindness. Humans helping humans.

When the time comes, help comes with sirens blasting to get them there as fast as they can.

The enormity of kindness, people to people—someone crashes and needs help and here help comes. So many hearts in the right place.

May all people in their emergencies feel supported. ~

72 Years Old

The Boat That Doesn't Float

IN THE LAST storm, the high seas tossed a small aluminum boat with a big hole in its hull onto my beach. Its days of being out to sea are over. My neighbors took it upon themselves to drag it up beyond the tideline and give it a new life purpose. They built a sea wall around it and added bright, happy, red-striped cushions and a sun umbrella. It's now an amazing addition to enjoying the beach.

I sit here to write. Always the first thing, I get out my three-by-five cards, and immediately a message that's been waiting to be told to me comes to my mind and I write it down word for word.

As I am sitting in the boat that doesn't float today, I think, "Have I gotten to all the sea adventures that have been for me to have, for this life?" And my boat message for the day comes to me: "The life that you are having is the correct life for you to be having."

I take this to heart because I am so appreciative that I know that and feel that and know my part in making that come about.

In this society of high-achieving and endless self-improvement, many people feel a sense of not being enough. They feel they "Could've been a contender," or "Why me?" or "If only." Of all the myriad of possibilities for our life, this way, this now, this how, is the perfect and correct me for me to be. For all of us, for all the multitude of lives possible for us, none of us was ever meant to be someone or something else. This is it.

This little boat never had it so good as now when it is continually at the ocean yet never again tossed around by the ocean. Its striped cushions have a jaunty sense of joy, and all the beachgoers who come by are enchanted by its presence. Would that we all enjoy the life that comes to us and allow ourselves to live it.

Up until now I never would have liked the metaphor of a boat that doesn't float. It would seem like it wasn't being what it was built to be. Yet now I see it a different way. I see the little boat in the big sea, and it went for the highest adventures and used its full heart in good passion doing it and being it, and it was grand—and now it has a further life, even more grand, even more witnessed, deeper now than the deepest ocean ride.

I see too that all the life choices I made all along the way bring me such awe in where I am now—above the tideline, at one with everything. ~

73 Years Old

The Last Time I Saw Paris

My book, *How to Write a Movie*, was translated years ago into French by the lovely director, Gerard Krawczyk. This year I have been invited, again, to London and Paris to conduct lectures on that book.

I love the bright, independent filmmakers I've gotten to know in London—I so enjoy contributing the one small beat to each of their films to take them to fruition. And in Paris, many new artists to meet.

And yet, to give you a little idea of my frame of mind, while negotiating the logistics of this trip I have been deeply enjoying being at one with my couch—nothing needed, nothing wanted, everything here.

Hmm. Can a first-class air seat compare with the joy of my couch overlooking the whole oceanfront—sunshine, sunset, night sky, moon rise, minus tide—and the all of my sumptuous home experience?

I'm a person who has long had a bag packed in the bottom of my closet. I can be fully loaded and out the door, with passport, in twelve minutes. *And yet* I could just as happily stay here at one with my couch.

I know I don't need anything from Paris except maybe a chocolate éclair. Ooh Lala. *And yet*, I feel that Paris wants to tell me something. So, I go.

And this is what Paris tells me: While I am at the podium, being simultaneously translated, and loving it as always, it comes over me clearly that this is the last time for this lecture on *How to Write a Movie*. Here forward all my presentations will be on my new book, *How to Be the Hero of Your Own Life*.

My Last Lecture

I understand that this is the last time I see Paris for this kind of venue of two-, three-, and four-day intensive seminars. Of course, I'm free to come any time to shop and eat.

There's something profound about a new shift that comes into your life. You know it's coming; you know you'll gain; you don't yet know what leaves for this gain to have room to come in.

When that new life shift appears, and that something equally precious to you deconstructs and leaves to make room for it, that's a surprise. It's not a bargain you meant to strike. I'll give up this to have that. No, you had no intention of giving anything up, *and yet* here it is—my at-one-with-my-couch feeling that I am living, that came because of what leaves.

Now, back home, on my couch reflecting, I'm so happy Paris gave me a chance to have my private goodbye to something that's now okay to leave. I'm so happy to have made an occasion for my last lecture. Because now "I'll Always Have Paris." ~

74 Years Old

Fire!

WILDFIRE IS BURNING all along the coast. There are some very big numbers—ninety-seven thousand acres burning, two-hundred-fifty thousand people evacuating. The only thing between the flames and the ocean now is the coast road. My home sits right there at the beach. If the flames jump the road, they will want to get right to the ocean, right where my house is.

Mandatory evacuation is in place. I secure this book and all of its files in the trunk of the car—that and a warm pair of socks is all that I'm taking. I kiss my house and I go.

(One more thing, I take the tide chart. I always know every day when low tide, minus tide, sunrise, sunset is, when the moon rises and sets and when it's full, and the positions of all the stars in the night sky; that's the precious part of living where I live on the oceanfront.)

Everybody has gone south on Pacific Coast Highway (later I find out they are in no-go traffic on the road for seven hours with flames all around). For some reason I am adamant to go north, even though boulders are crashing on the coast highway. I am the only car going that way. (I think this has made all the difference hereafter. I'm someone who will carry people in a crisis. They all went the other way so there was no one to carry. I was out of the loop of being a responder.)

The last phone call that came in before I left was Amelia, what a friend! She said, "Come here." So, I did.

Getting Out

Okay, I got out through sandblasting winds and flames. I got out with what means the most to me—this book. Now what?

There is no communication—cell towers down, landlines and internet out, no mail delivery service. This is how it goes for several weeks. Not possible to connect with anyone about anything. Not knowing what's burned down, what's still standing.

Being preoccupied with being displaced from my own home, the last thing I want is to be a guest in a friend's house. If you've ever been a guest in someone's home, you know that being a guest is an art form. I hope you know to take out the garbage and wash the dishes and try not to infringe on the privacy of the person whose house it is. If there's a killer dog, right away get him to be your new best friend. Enjoy the experience but remember to get out of there as fast as you can to keep your friend a friend.

After the blasting heat of the fire, it's now unseasonably cold; I can't seem to get warm. There is no sunshine to bask in to get my body temperature up. The thing that would help is if I could just go home where the sun beats in warm and come back tomorrow and go at all the mounting details then, but no, instead it's all happening in midair.

Surprise, the internet is working, sort of. I get an email from a dear client who wants to be positive about the fire. She says, "You are phoenix rising."

I reply, "Don't say phoenix, it implies ashes."

Since I am not of the tragedy school of thinking I use this time to immediately keep my good happiness and get into my sphere of power by taking care of my needs. Privacy, freedom, my own inner rhythm. Of course, that means having my kind of foods available, good water, to be as comfortable as I can get so I can set up my computer and get on with my work.

And if only I can get warm, I'll be able to think straight. I hope I can reclaim access to my brain. It has lists of passwords and account numbers, and mind-bending details lining up for consideration. When I ask it something, it says, "Not now, take a number."

Every day I make the trip to the roadblock hoping that it's opened so I can go home and see what's what.

The roadblock makes for great comic relief. It's the gathering place for the zombie apocalypse. Here hang a lot of people, displaced, who have nothing to do but worry if their home is still there.

The level of dazed, crazed, and stupefied is of rampant proportions.

As you know, on any given day on planet Earth it's easy to notice humans walking around being discombobulated. It's like that here at the roadblock only more so.

Here I'm finding the vaudeville team of Flotsam and Jetsam. Everybody's got their victim story and they are sticking to it. Their thoughts are digging in and spiraling out. Where they stop, nobody knows.

It's not doing anyone any good to hear how bad they fear it can get—no good can come from that, because the truth is, the sun is shining and we're all alive. It's an opportunity to be in a suspended space between what was and what will be—that's a fabulous place to be. How often does that happen? Well actually that happens every day to everyone, but because of this particular circumstance those here are lifted out of their daily patterns so it gives them the opportunity of new choices; that maybe happens just a handful of times in a lifetime. We get to create it all from here. Lucky, lucky us.

Officer Plunkett mans the barricade here. Everybody comes up to him to plead their case why they alone should be let through the blockade. The excuses run the gamut between they have to get home for their medication, or they have to find and feed their pets. Most have their pets and their meds with them at the time. Officer Plunkett is ever vigilant about keeping us all out.

You can't blame people for being a little hyped up, but they are a throng of residents desperate to get through trying every which way to no avail.

The roadblock is in place for two reasons. 1) The fires are still going on, and 2) someone made the executive decision that looting would be kept to a minimum if the road stayed closed. I heard that the house on the beach two doors from mine had been looted. I'd like to know how the thieves got through; they certainly couldn't have made it past Officer Plunkett.

When I think of the zombie apocalypse, I wonder how people will cope if their houses burn down, when they can't handle this part?

I talk to one man who has been sleeping in his car for six days. He is making sure to be first in line to get home. You can just imagine his blood pressure numbers. It's my hope to convey to him that by loosening his tight grip on it all it would be healthier for him. He doesn't want to hear me. *I* hear me. I loosen *my* grip and leave the scene in search of a carwash for my soot-soaked car, sandblasted by the seventy-five-mile-an-hour winds. I drive way past the fire zone up the coast where normal is going on.

Days later, finally, I get intermittent phone contact from a few friends. "Turn on Channel Four."

I do and I see my house burning on the six o'clock news.

Okay, so now a new wrinkle in the scheme of things. Now I can start to make plans. I know that whatever condition my house is in, I'll deal with it. I'm making lists. By now I am up to plan nine. Do I have an image of myself as someone who can carry on? Yes. I do because I do.

Still more days later the roadblock is finally lifted, and I beat it on home.

Going In

The kicked-in front door is boarded up. It's yellow tagged— meaning don't go in there. Nevertheless, I am so happy to be home even though there is no electricity, no water, no bathroom, no roof, no place to cook, or sit, or sleep, or live. I feel like I could figure all of that out and move back home except there is no air to breathe. The air quality . . . there isn't any. Breathing is not an option. I can't be in here for more than a few minutes with the respirator on before I have to go find air somewhere else.

The air quality is unfit for breathing, and yet—did I mention?—I am so happy to be home. Here is the one spot that is mine to stand at the open oceanfront—my ocean, my horizon, cue the dolphins and whales. Mine (although I'm willing to share).

Standing in the middle of the floor on the water damage, debris, soot, and char, all I need is to be able to be here at my ocean and bask in the sunshine. Finally, I feel so warm.

This spot on the entire grid of the globe is mine to be. Here is where I have been the self-appointed holder of the cosmic light for humanity. I have taken my duties seriously and now it's clear that I've been "fired" from my job well done. I did it, done. Everything is conspiring for me to go get this book out to you. This here at the grid of light at the horizon out to sea is not my job anymore.

I enjoy a first-name basis relationship with my heart. We can talk to one another about anything. We can talk clearly, and honestly. I hear my heart say, "Get out."

I say, "Do you mean get out and go walk on the beach for fresh air? Or get out, leave for good, forever?"

The answer: "Yes."

I wonder how long it's going to take me to heed what my heart knows right away. I notice that I stay another hour with the respirator on to make a wish on the setting sun.

Living in the "Don't Know"

This starts the clear-it-all-away phase. This part deals with authorities from the county and random teams of hazmat officials with clipboards. Many authorities come. Many random teams of men, each with their own opinions, come right in without knocking. Of course, there's no door, but it gives me the definitive idea that this is no longer a private residence—it's a construction site, or deconstruction site, or as one random utility worker said who came right in to insult my home, "Too bad it's just junk now."

Then came the contractor Bruno Bustamundo, known as the guy who makes grown men cry. I wanted to hear from him. I wanted the truth. I wanted to know what I was dealing with. I really wanted to be out of the "don't know" so I can make some decisions.

Well, Bruno did tell me the truth. He said at least two years before construction can even start. The whole thing must be demolished. Anything still up has to come down before it can be put back up. Meanwhile, if I didn't believe him, I certainly would when the rains started, which was that afternoon. The whole roof was now dripping down the walls that looked like they could be saved two days ago. Pretty quickly, mold set in.

According to Bruno, "Everything has got to go." He leaves me with boxes of contractor bags, 300 count.

I fill those and need more.

Everything goes.

Debris Removal

There are things to shovel out. There are things that are standing but contaminated, there are things that could go to the thrift shop. My neighbor, Rose, whose place was red flagged (meaning it was completely totaled, nothing left) will be moving to another place right on our beach, so I give her lots of my furniture and pots and pans and chandeliers and art, and I'm very excited to think that at least my stuff will still be here on our beach. So, lots went to her. I had bags designated for friends. Salvation Army came twice. I didn't get the idea until I had already thrown out about fifty bags full, but at bag fifty-one I started to say goodbye to my things. "I'm happy I had you. I'm happy for you to go. Thank you for being in my life." It made me happy; each thing was happy. It was a good idea.

Some stuff ashes, some charred, some soot, some contaminated, some soaked through and now moldy, some just plain had to be downsized. My new motto is "Downsize to upgrade."

Meanwhile, I was offering crisis counseling at the crisis center set up temporarily to help the community. I had finished with my last client of the day when a young man walked in to ask if there was any furniture available. His place burned down, and he was now living in a garage. He said he had a truck.

I said, "Follow me to my house. You can have whatever fits in the truck," and that's what he did.

It felt wonderful that his entire space was now going to be livable. I even found paint and brushes he could use to repaint some of the furniture for it to have a post-fire life. As an added bonus for us, he looked up at the bookcase where several copies of *How to Write a Movie* had dodged the fire. He said, "Are you Viki King?"

"Yes."

It turned out he's a screenwriter and *his* copy of my book burned in the fire, so he went off with a new copy and the furniture and enthusiasm to set up his new life in the garage and write his next script.

Moving

Remember what Ginger Rogers said about dancing with Fred Astaire? She said she did everything Fred did only backward in heels. That's how I feel about this move. Moving at its best, when you want to, is enough of a grind. This is moving with the hazmat suit and the respirator and the gloves on. I filled all three hundred contractor bags and dragged them down the stairs and out. Some things I put in the trunk to go to my temporary place for hot water cleaning and storing until I get someplace to continue living.

Some of the clothes I took and double-washed in a special smoke-clearing solution and then stuffed them all in bags and stored those at my friend Amelia's house.

About the Stuff

It's a good thing that the measure of my life is not about the stuff. I can always get stuff, and I had plenty of it that now I get to dispose of. My real-life bounty is somewhere inside of me, like an eternal light, untouched by outside circumstances.

A Million Little Goodbyes
My friend Ellen asked, "Do you think about your things?" Like for instance, my hat I bought in Paris, the jar my friend Libby gave me that I kept pumpkin seeds in, my luxurious top-of-the-line bed? Yes, each thing comes to me while I'm driving or in the shower, they come to say an individual goodbye. I'm getting to thank all my things little and big. I have the memories of each one, and glory of glories, no clutter.

Meanwhile, as I continue to offer crisis counseling at the center set up to help people through their circumstances, I met a woman who had a fire in her life fifteen years ago and is triggered by this fire and came in to be one of my clients. She had a deep, distant look in her eyes. I see there can be a long-term nature to fire. The flames may be out, but the smoldering can continue.

A reporter asked me, "Is this the worst thing that ever happened to you?"

Me: "No, I don't think that way—worst or best. It just is. What you do with it counts, and you can always do something with it. (P.S. A good policy if you think the worst thing is happening *to* you is to turn it into the best thing that is happening *for* you.) Miracles abound, always."

It's time for me to get the next temporary place to stay. I can then start thinking about where I go from there. Cue my friend Emily. She has a rental townhouse that happens to be empty for three months. She offers it to me.

I hear a voice in me say, "Don't mess with this. Accept it and say thank you."

See what I mean? Miracles abound.

I know all this is going to be a great gift for my life. It's ratcheting up from here. The thing about chaos is that you just have to give it the chance to fall away so it can sort itself out and come into order. Any day or month or year now, this will work itself out.

The Emissary of Light
As is the nature of grief, you repeat yourself, so I'll leave in this paragraph about what I already told you was the one thing that felt like a loss to me but also a significant gift of gain at the same time.

I was being displaced from my loved spot in the world. It's where I had the job of holding the light for all and everything like a self-appointed portal where the sunrise, sunset, open sea, night sky, moon rise, and low tide shone for my witness. It was my job to bask in the sun that beat into my home and then emit it to you.

When my friend Libby used to come to visit me there and the winter sun was low in the sky and would beat intensely into the house, Libby couldn't be in the sun. Not even sunglasses or a hat helped, she just couldn't have the bright sun on her. I can't *not* have it on me. We've all got our glory spot to stand in where our body feels so happy to be home.

Before the fire, I knew something big was coming. I ordered a dozen store-all boxes. I didn't know if they were for reorganizing my body of work and my next books after this one, or for a remodel of my office, or what they were for. I didn't know what, but I knew something was coming. I knew I was gearing up to finish this book. And whatever was coming was designed to help that along and then—whammo!—the gift of fire.

I know I will be in the right place at the right time to carry on. I have been known to tell my clients for years—resist nothing. All is good and right and true. I allow it to set up in a new good way. My old life completing; my new life materializing.

Ha Ha

Of course, if it's life on Earth, it's funny, so that goes on always.

Here are just a couple of funny beats that happened:

I went to check on my lungs from all the breathing I was doing of nefarious contaminated air. I said to the doctor, "I want to get this coughing cleared up so I can get some work done."

And she said, "Plastic surgery?"

Do you notice that people can be hilarious when they don't mean to be?

And on the same day, a woman I know said to me regarding the fire, "You always keep your chin up."

I said to her, "Not all of them."

The next day I was at the DMV for license renewal. They took my picture and there were my chins!

You Find Out Who Your Friends Are

Many neighbors are missing in action. I guess they were spooked by the whole experience, and their places stayed up while mine didn't. We who are red- and yellow-tagged must be like piranha to them. I never heard from some of them. Some other friends were business as usual, semi-checking in yet not really relating to the fire. Some never to be heard from again. Clearing stuff, you also clear "realationships." Oh, look what I just typed. That's a great way to spell that word!

The ones who showed up, showed up spectacularly. Amelia right away, right there, and gracious all the way. Thank you, Amelia. And Emily with the offer of her place for three months. Thank you, Emily. Libby, Amelia, and Emily are sisters and are family to me since Mulligan Avenue when we were kids. Remember, Emily was the one whose hair caught fire at my brother's seventh birthday. Seventy years later, she's the one who had this place for me now.

And SJ—she's in and out of town caregiving her parents, and still she's here as I am for her. Thank you, SJ. And Ellen, we're all about lunch. Thank you, Ellen. And my brother. I am always moved to tears when I think of him. He's the one who sent the hazmat box of disaster accessories. Leave it to my brother to have me suit up for safety. (*Five months later I used the box in my move into my temporary semi-permanent place. A lot happened in between.*) And he's the one who was on email or phone every day strategizing the next and the next actions to take. He's the one who was there and always has been. Thank you, Brother. And who knows how many mighty gods and archangels hovered over it to get us all through it. Thank you. And then to my dear neighbor, now friend, Clarise. We went through the burning part together. Clarise would bring Starbucks takeaway tea, and we would have it on our beach at minus tide then go into our yellow-tagged places, she for restoration and me for deconstruction. The rest of the neighborhood a ghost town of debris and charred trees. And now, Clarise about to be a mom. A baby coming in after so much leaves. I'm going to be the Auntie. Would I be that had we not burned down together?

Landing

Right now, I'm living in the space between places. The next place will maybe be temporary semi-permanent. This could be anywhere in the wide world. Thailand? It's warm there. Kauai? I love Kauai. I have no idea where to go live. I'm not hearing a call to anywhere.

And yet, I'm beginning to feel that it's time to be reunited with my clothes.

I'm invited to dinner with friends who live up the coast at the harbor. They are showing me around their beach. I pay attention—there's something here for me to see. I realize I'm being given a tour of where I could live. There's the ocean, there's an expansive beach, and there's the sunset, available every day for easy viewing.

The next day my dear Clarise, who is so good at the internet, "Zillows" me a place at the harbor. I go over and take it right away. I move in the downsized version of my life. I have a Papasan chair as my couch-for-one. I get a desk and set it up to look out at the boats, the ocean, and the islands beyond. It all falls in place immediately and as house beautiful. This is the place to finish the book.

I am in awe. You see—the gift of fire.

A Regular Day

There is something . . . I can't quite identify it. There, right there. I'm having a "normal day," a day that the whole twenty-four hours is not consumed by fire-related fallout. A "normal day," a fire-free daily life, a regular day with the usual everyday concerns and that's all. None of the above and beyond parts to brace against or follow through or clear up. I'm having a regular day. Wow. What if everything is all right? Wow.

Another month and here came another regular day and looking forward to more regular days.

And my dear friend Ellen, looking around my new place, comments on how great it is that this place happened for me.

"I know. It's because I *happened* it. I am the creator of my soft landing."

The Reporter Is Back Again Asking for a PostScript

I say, "Not to say it is easy. Not to say a laugh riot, but bigger than a pesky-ass annoyance. It runs deep. It burned everything off that was a good thing to burn off. I'm always better off than I was before because that's my policy in life."

Does my heart pang a beat when I go past my former beach on a glorious gleaming day? Yes, I lived there. I always was so happy to sing out, "I live here. This is my neighborhood."

I got to hold the precious lifeforce light for humanity and now, miracle of miracles, imagine my good luck, I live within walking distance to the Dollar Store. Wonders never cease.

And Then There Is the Matter of Gidget

The Malibu Film Society shows first-run films including meet-and-greets with their producers, directors, and actors.

Lately, due to the fires, evacuations, mudslides, road closures, flash floods, and all-around trauma throughout the populous, the film schedule had been interrupted.

Due to the low-slung morale around town, it was decided to show *Gidget* as a feel-good sixtieth-anniversary showing. It was an opportunity for the community to get together with real-life Gidget, who has been a local resident all these years. She's now in her spritely seventies. The plan was to have hot dogs and celebrate as an occasion for conviviality among the locals. *Gidget* was filmed here at our beaches sixty years ago. In the spirit of community support, I went to the screening.

As a kid, I never identified with Gidget, but I did see the film then and I do remember the Cliff Robertson character. He was called "the Big Kahuna." He was the voice of wisdom for the younger surfing kids. He was independent and lived on the beach in a hut of his making. It was aspirational for me at the time. When the film first came out, I was maybe fourteen years old. Now I'm watching it sixty years later. And I notice that as a kid growing up in Chicago, I formed a desire to live in Malibu on the beach and inspire others. It's what I wanted for myself.

I'm making this connection now as I'm watching it sixty years later. As the story winds up at the end of the summer "the Big Kahuna" is dismantling his beach shack and moving on. I realize that I have been called the Big Kahuna by some of the surfers along my beach. I realize that it is my pleasure to impart wisdoms, inspire others, and be a voice of reason. It is certainly my pleasure to live in Malibu on the beach, and now I realize that the beach that Cliff Robertson's beach shack is on is *my* beach. Sixty years ago, they shot that scene here where my current beach home burned down. Way back in Chicago when I was a kid, I instilled in myself all those aspirational desires that I did make true, and on the very beach, it was first shone to me.

Since I created my whole adult Malibu life from a desire I hardly noticed at age fourteen, imagine what I create from here. ~

75 Years Old

How to Be 75 and Thrive

My FRIEND KATE, who is a mere sixty, called me yesterday and said, "No one told me about floaters." (In case you don't know, floaters are pesky little thread-like bits that show up in the corner of your eye, uninvited and annoying.)

I laughed at her. I said, "They'll only bother you until the next thing happens."

And she said, "What next thing?"

And I said, "There's more fun coming."

And she said, "Like for instance?"

So, I said, "Take your pick. You'll find yourself thinking twice before you bend down to retrieve what you have dropped. Or your hip starts to make a clicking noise, or you now only wear long sleeves because your skin looks like crepe paper."

And she says, "What can I do?"

I say, "Take your favorite pan out of the bottom cabinet and put it where you can reach it easily."

She says, "Is there any good news?"

So I say, "There's nothing like going back to bed after breakfast."

But the truth is getting older can be all good news.

You might ask, "Will I be able to handle it?"

Of course, you will. Old age is nothing compared to what it took to get here.

The Summit on Aging

I gave a keynote speech at the Summit on Aging. This was an event put on by an organization of healthcare providers, a group of doctors, and others in the medical field who are finding a need to expand and branch out their thinking about what it means to treat those of us in our seventies and beyond.

They wanted me to come and talk about how I'm being seventy-five because it seems to be working for me. They want to address aging, ageism, and attitudes about age. They want to distinguish if there is a difference between how you think of age and how you actually age, and what correlates or doesn't.

Here are some parts of my talk. If you find anything here that works for you, discuss it with your health team and come up with a plan for yourself.

A Lot to Do with Age is Ageism

My neighbor Richard complained to me regarding his old-age aches and pains. Actually, he's fifty-two. He's had aches and pains for years. It's not his real age that he's feeling, it's double mileage he put on his chassis. His body is feeling the choices he made with cigarettes and alcohol and general raggedy self-treatment. Yet he blames it on age. At any age, the experiences we are having are directly proportional to the choices we have made. People are quick to say when they get old that they creak. When you're any age, you do. That's the life force. Those are not symptoms of age; they are symptoms of being alive. If you have a human body at any age you will snap, crackle, and pop.

Your body is designed to last a lifetime—your lifetime. That could be twenty years old, it could be one hundred and twenty. You get one body for this go-around, and you are in it as your life choices express themselves. If you have something beautiful, take care of it and it will last your lifetime in good shape.

My Body, Myself

My body trusts me to care for it, and I trust it to take care of me. This is an arrangement that took the better part of my life to work out. I've got my back. This is a good place to remind us that you've got your back too. You've been in your body all this lifetime. You are the first authority on how you feel.

Being Your Own Inner Doctor Power

In earlier generations (actually in my generation) people got taught to give their healing power over to doctors, when in fact we are the originators of our bodily circumstances and are the creators of our own wellness.

You hear older people say, "I don't feel old; I feel just like myself at twenty."

Yes, because you are your same self just with maybe a sagging jawline.

My life is how it is because of me. Choices you make in your twenties turn out to impact you at this other end of the life span.

Because I was twenty in my twenties and forty in my forties and so on, I'm in sync with this time in my life now because I did that then, and I can be this now. I love having no pressure. I love navigating under my own rhythm. I love having done what I did so I am here now being this.

Once you are here in upper-digit age, you are not old, you are just yourself who feels twenty.

Many of my contemporaries, being who they always were, are walking around thinking, I don't look it. I don't feel it. I can't believe it.

Eileen, seventy-nine, loves tap dancing and does three performances a week. Doris, at eighty, is a bodybuilder. Imagine what I have to look forward to. I'm *only* seventy-five.

And by the way, it's not a crime to be seventy-five, but it's a near-mortal sin to look it. I don't look seventy-five, but I am seventy-five, so this is what it looks like on me.

I wasn't making life choices in my twenties and thirties to be happy now. I was making those choices because they were correct and good and right for me then. It turns out that because they were correct then it happens to be correct for now.

Life is so much easier when you don't have to discover and choose your preferences because you've already chosen. You know what suits you and then you can just live that. I know I won't be bungee jumping anytime soon. That's a thought that makes me very happy. I didn't know that a life well-lived would be rewarded with such satisfaction at this end. Not everybody gets this part.

Still

At this age, the most heard word is "still." As in, "You've still got it," or "You can still show the young men." I prefer to think of still as being still or having inner stillness.

I highly recommend being in your seventies. I'm happy to be here because I was happy to be all my other ages when I was. Living in the current moment gets you more current moments. If you are always using your time to push toward the future or live in the past, it's out of alignment and frankly not as fun as being here now—where you are, when you are.

I don't have to scare myself with needless pressure. Now is a time to have discernment, to experience simple elegance, to luxuriate. I gear down to savor up, that's where the happiness is. At seventy-five, there's less time to live but more time to live it. I'm still going to die. I might as well live healthy and happy until I do.

My Three Theories of Forgetting

Here's a riddle: What do Hermes Pan (Fred Astaire's choreographer), Pecorino cheese, and the Pillsbury dough boy have in common? In a conversation yesterday, I couldn't think of all three of them or two other names I still don't remember.

I think this business of forgetting is just us clearing our zip drive. We can find solace in that we knew more and forgot what some people never even knew. We're merely relinquishing what we don't need to know anymore to make room for what we haven't yet considered.

Another observation I have in this remembering department: Have you ever gotten in the car, gotten to the corner, and then forgot where you were going? In a split second you remember and go there? I have a theory about the mechanics of that. In the minute it takes you to get in the car and go, you have thought of, say, six hundred thoughts ranging from Burt Bacharach's last hit song to what you'll pack for your trip to New York next week to what galaxy you'll want to visit after you die. Of course, this minute for this trip, to the mailbox, goes way down the list of interesting actions. You haven't really forgotten. It's just a little rust on your wiring.

My third theory of forgetting: Sometimes while trying to remember a word, we rummage in the wrong file drawer. For instance, looking for the word shallot when you mean scallion. Notice that they are from different word files. You can't access shallot in the scallion file. It's not there. So, when you are trying to track a word you can't remember, forget trying to find it and it will come to you.

There's a last little something I want to say about forgetting. I guarantee you that not all readers considering this information are old.

Senior Brochure

I received a brochure in the mail showing senior citizens whitewater rafting. Do they actually think that this appeals to me?

The seniors pictured in the brochure are smiling . . . while whitewater rafting. Why would they be smiling?

The use of you doing what you want to do when you want to do it is that when you get to be seventy-five, you're so happy you did it. And you don't have to do it again.

If my choice would be rafting or sitting on my couch, I'm so happy on my couch. Certainly, if someone at seventy-five wants to whitewater raft or skydive or be in a pie-eating contest, go right ahead. I'm using my time now for what comes with my age—the deepening. Until you get here, you have no idea the wonder of saying no to the community barbeque.

My life is free to do what I please when I please because I please as I continue to have the life force to continue to create choices and fulfill them.

The less doing, the more it seems I am the very essence of aliveness. I cultivate a talent for being right here, right now. I experience expansiveness and vitality. I can sit quietly, and the whole world is within me.

Change Is Just the Way It Is

One of the skills of life is to be willing to go with change. I like a quote from Ram Dass: "Making friends with change transforms the aging process." Be willing to embrace change.

Change is not loss. Change is something to thrive on. Let life circumstances be what they are rather than what you think they should be. Free yourself from comparing your life to how it used to be. You can find each day teeming with new life.

The Doodad Factor

In my twenties if something was missing in my life, I would gear myself up and go get it. Now if something is missing, I don't miss it. In my thirties I wouldn't come home without it, by my forties I had plenty of it, fifties I got more of it or something else, by my sixties I enjoyed it all and downsized. In the seventies if something is missing, it doesn't matter—I am content.

I Subscribe to the Non-Diminishing, Ever-Expanding Theory of Life

I recommend you go at life as a progression, always building upon the last thing. It's a pretty good method.

And yet, here's space for you to choose your own health team and methods. You've been in your body all your life. You are manager of you. Pick out who you wish to have as your support of your health.

How to Live to Be 100

Here's another riddle: How do you live to be one hundred? The answer is don't die.

It turns out that it's not a riddle at all. It's the way to stay alive. Don't die. It's an actual skill. Make the choice in every moment to keep on living. Be alive. You have to want to get up out of the hospital bed and go after a new interest. There's always more. Don't leave the game.

The scientific rule is that life will run down if it isn't fed. Keep fueling your life force and there will be more life force to experience so that when you're done is when you leave, not before.

This might all sound sanctimonious, like I think I'm going to make it out alive. Like I'm not going to have food spots on my gold lamé tracksuit.

In life is everything. If there is an experience our soul would love for us to have then let us have it as all a part of the full story of ourselves.

Or Don't Live to Be 100 If You're Finished Before Then

Being a full throttle, fully loaded, total revolutionary from way back when I propose: When you let it, your body will heal itself, so let it. If there is something that the medical profession does very well that would help, utilize the help.

Probably not in my lifetime but maybe in yours, our society will have no more sickness and no more need for hospitals. There will be no place to go for sickness because the hospitals can be converted to address wellness instead. *It will be a change in consciousness.* Imagine focusing on expanding the capability of your body rather than suffering limitations.

If you are in a decade where parts are wearing out, you can use those changes to slow your pace, relax your grip, enjoy every nuance that comes to welcome you to next ways to be in the body until you leave it.

Maybe, having summits like this, we'll all start to get the idea to take really good care of ourselves and see that it is within our power to do it.

We don't have to get sick in order to die. We're alive now, and someday we'll be dead. Dying is optional. Here's to quality of life for the rest of your life. ~

76 Years Old

The Plot Thickens

DO YOU REMEMBER Richard Peterson, my English teacher I told you about in chapter Fifteen and a Half?

I've known him ever since, and I've always loved him wholeheartedly and dearly. There's a clear, bright light coming out of him, and here he is ninety-one and continuing with that way about himself.

Maybe because of him, I told these stories the way I have because he had a way of telling a story with a light touch to it and a good ending.

Well, guess what, I'm sending him a draft of this book to read. He was my English teacher, and I get the amazing privilege of hearing what he has to say about what I wrote. I'm in awe of how life has a way of always turning out.

Beginning, Middle, and End

One of the joys of living long is that your friendships get to be long too. You get to see each person's lifespan playout miraculously.

Remember in Chapter Thirty-Nine, I told you about my friend who left Hollywood in pursuit of a destiny more fitting to his nature? He did find his belonging in the embodiment of a wonderful beloved. Together they lit up every room they entered for over thirty-five years. He had a good ability to identify in people what held them back and inspire them to go forward. He did find what he came here to do, with people he came here to do it with. And all the while he loved to free-form dance and got a whole community moving, as he generally uplifted the world where he was.

I tell you this because last week he died. We were able to talk briefly every other day until he got way too busy dying and couldn't talk at all. One of the last things he said to me was, "You're my oldest friend."

Because he so loved to free-form dance, at his celebration of life ceremony, it happened that a hundred friends danced the night away on his behalf. ~

77 Years Old

Downward Causation

Between now and the age of my death, I'm going to use downward causation. You might think, What the heck is that? Thank you for asking. Downward causation is this: I am planning my future backward from there to here. I look at now and create what has to happen between now and then to have it come out the way that I choose. We all do this all the time, that's how we have the lives we have—we create our futures with our choices today. We don't always do that consciously. I'm creating my exit now so I can write it here to finish my book and get it out to you before I die. So, when you get to the last chapter hoping I've created a liftoff, that suits me. Anyway, that's the plan. ~

77 Plus

About the Writing of How to Be the Hero of Your Own Life

I CAME INTO this lifetime to do this. I have done it.

Now it's on its way to the publisher. Imagine how relieved I am.

It's like working a one-thousand-piece jigsaw puzzle with five thousand pieces on the table, and you don't know what the final picture looks like until you start putting it together, then the other four thousand pieces go someplace else, but you don't know where and nothing can be discarded.

It's like working a Rubik's cube, behind your back, while balancing on a precipice, in a hurricane, with your hair blowing in your face, and the rent due in two days.

It's like . . . You get the idea. It's like any impossible uphill challenge worthy of our attention when we have to keep going and keep creating the way along the way. And really, why did I do it? Because it is mine to do.

And of course, anyone can pick up the published book and open it anywhere and get something deep and rich for their personal life if they want to. Imagine how good that feels.

In the last forty years, every time I moved, I would have at least a dozen storage boxes of notes, at one point, forty-six feet of notebooks on the bookshelf that were all notes for this book.

It has its own paraphernalia, such as my miraculous mini-cassette recorder: high-end, high-tech, first of its kind in its time, and I was first on the block to get it and use it far beyond the time that it is now obsolete, and all its other tech brother gizmos have taken digital into the ionosphere. It recorded thousands of hours in the car, on the beach, at airports and hotels. I, forever working on it, witnessing life, and recording the details.

From my Underwood typewriter that I proudly bought at the Saugus Flea Market for $14, to the state-of-the-art Selectric typewriter, to the Dictaphone, to #2 top-of-the-line Blackwing Pearl pencils with world-class erasers, to my Tot stapler acquired when I was in high school to go with my Helix stainless-steel ruler for cut and paste, to every color ream of paper, to my electric pencil sharpener—everyone should have one.

The act of bringing it all together—all the iterations from beta to floppy discs, to eight-track, to VHS, to digital, to a dozen computer upgrades from the fifty-pound transportable Compaq, to desktops, to laptops, to iPad, until soon it will all be stored on a pocket crystal.

From ancient messages recorded in scrolls to holographic displays, messages abound and vie for position. There's so much to be said.

And saying it by pulling off the road to write pages and pages just because it comes pouring out at that moment. Writing speed pages while standing at the perfume counter of Robinson's Beverly Hills when the house dick came around thinking I was up to no good.

How many presidents have there been since I've been writing this book? Just now I remember election night for several presidents while I was writing my book. When I was twenty, I was writing this book. I've been actively writing this book for at least sixty years. This has not been easy, but mostly the not-easy parts didn't involve the writing.

Finally, recently, it all came down to and through all the computers and all the iterations and duplications and deletions and finally everything typed neatly, in a single font, in the current computer, in my head, in my heart, in hard copy, on the page, in the file and ready to see what else, what more, what leaves, what stays … finally the full manuscript started to move toward the finish line.

All the wisdom that would come to me for one year, I would gather all of that into the best and highest story for that year, so you could see the progression of a life in each split-second story for each year, and know your own story while you are reading mine.

It took this whole lifetime to get it to me and through me and onto pages and distilled down and expanded out and then cleaned up and cleared and now special parts of it, to my honor, ring like a bell.

Just dripping effort on each page. Year upon year of approaching the desk. So hard, keep going, find it, let it, where did it go, and then clear copy. And somewhere along the way, I left any fear behind. Meant to be my gift to the world, such a gift for me.

An interviewer said to me, "I'm jealous. Why didn't I think of doing something like that?"

And I said to him, "It wasn't your destiny. It's my destiny. You have your own. It's a life choice I made and followed through on for my whole life."

What was it that I was going to know at this end that I didn't know at that end at twenty when I thought I would finish it then? What is it that's different finishing it now?

It's like sculpting a slab of clay. You can't work out the details of one eye in the slab and have that one eye looking out at you until you've brought out the rest of the face so that the details of the eye stay in touch with the other parts of the face. How can I know what the eye can see unless the rest of the face is looking at the world in the same direction? It takes all the parts coming through to bring the whole into aliveness.

And now, as it is alive and well in the world—Glory be. ~

78 Years Old

Update

DO YOU REMEMBER the chapter *How to Love an Addict, Every Family Has One*, where I said, "You hope for the phone call? And you hope that call comes directly from your loved one who you hope is alive and well."

After many years we *did* get the call, and it turns out that our loved one *is* alive and well, and we have him back in the family.

At first, I experienced every rushing feeling—relief, anger, hurt, joy, and then, quickly, to have him back is one of the great treasures of my life. ~

78 Plus

Traveling Light

Y OU KNOW ABOUT packing, it's a pretty intense part of the trip. The better you pack, the better the trip. My policy: Take the smallest of satchels for the highest of adventures. What goes in must be well thought out. Travel light, spread the light, be the light.

In my youth, the policy for packing was to sit on the suitcases to stuff it all in—take as much as you can. And this was before wheels were on luggage.

Now, to me, traveling light means being really good at taking care of my fundamental needs. For instance, I never leave home without my Mickey Mouse socks. Happy feet are a top priority. And always, I have with me my pen and notebook to write my way around the world.

Here's what I refer to as clown-car packing:

Ingeniously choose clothes that all fit with each other— maybe ten items that mix and match to make a hundred variations that you can pull out of the smallest carry-on. I throw in a complete wild card, maybe a brightly colored scarf different from the rest, and I will use it the most. Let what you take be elegantly minimal. Be very, very organized, plan to the hilt, then immediately when you get on the road, let it all go where it will. Be ready to leap off into wonder.

One of my favorite kinds of travel is to be invited for business to conduct seminars, appear in a forum, see clients, or be on location for a film.

Here's a cherished invitation I received to come on my first trip to mainland China.

> . . . *your bestseller book,* How to Write a Movie in 21 Days, *has achieved a level of influence in China that would be impossible to overestimate. Now you've got a huge fan base in here. Some of the solid fans even require books with signatures. They take your book with them every day, it becomes their spiritual food. Considering the need of these fans we have been wondering if you could come here and*

meet them. Lots of the famous Chinese directors and screenwriters will be attending. We would be honored and gratified to receive you and hear you speak.

There's nothing like being invited to a professional venue, being hosted, having handlers take care of your every need, meeting with international colleagues dear to you ever after AND then coming home with cash money in your hand from the job accomplished.

Here are some tips that I use for my travel on my own expense:

Let travel be a wonderful state of flux. Be free flowing so experiences can come into you where you wouldn't let them otherwise if you were at home in your routine.

There await you many fast friends in far places, significant relationships can form. You can be in a charming town for an intense month, or one meaningful lunch in an open café on the port, and then off on the next train north. You can discover people whom you don't know longer than a ferry crossing, yet you can be enriched by your meeting long after.

In questionable locations, it's best to book in at the highest-star hotel you can manage and then go exploring. You can always hail a rickshaw or taxi of some sort back to the known hotel.

Before I go, I always clear up business and straighten up the house. I take what is needed for the journey; I leave what would encumber me. I certainly leave any resistance or story of limitation or fear of, say, soldiers at airports with fixed bayonets. It's a good practice to release any idea of what kind of time you'll have before closing the suitcase to go.

Always what comes up is the next thing to learn on your journey. For instance, reveling in the joy of small moments and being challenged to get out of some others.

The surprises are whom you meet along the way (mostly yourself), and the life question that gets answered by the next train stop.

I like especially knowing clearly what I've learned that I don't ever need to learn again.

Some of my travel memories come rushing in just now:

Still wearing huaraches from just being in Mexico, I climbed the stone steps on the port of Hydra, Greece.

At an invitational dinner of a specially prepared bouillabaisse at a bistro along the Cote d'Azur, my life was forever divided, BB and AB, Before Bouillabaisse and After Bouillabaisse.

I remember marveling at the path the emperor had carved to ride his bike around the Forbidden City in Beijing.

The time, in Corfu, when I thought I would die, I put my passport in my top pocket so they would know where to send the body. It turned out I didn't die, so I went on to Monte Carlo.

In Osaka, Japan, at breakfast, as I stared at the Zen Garden, the entire universe opened and took me to a vast perception of the meaning of the cosmos.

For one trip, someone asked me, "Aren't you afraid to travel alone?"

I said, "No, but I'm a little afraid to meet up with my family in Italy for a week."

The love matters that much.

I especially remember one aquarium at a port restaurant in Positano where the world stopped as I fixated on a turtle as he made his slow way traveling from one end of the aquarium to the other.

In my thirties, in Athens, at the Hotel Grande Bretagne, I picked up an elegant booklet listing the Leading Hotels of the World. I got the lovely idea to go to as many as I could get to in this lifetime. So many coming on the list, so many shifting to other lists. So many yet to go. And oh, here, forty years later, I am writing this at the Malibu Beach Inn, I just realize it happens to be a leading hotel of the world.

I've always been fond of the high-low way of life. Something connects me to a part of myself that feels at home in luxury. I love a five-star hotel, and some other times I'll stay in a hostel that has the warm feeling I like and sunshine beating in.

Always, I've gotten street food at the night market, bountiful food, and yet in other countries, if I landed there late and was so hungry, it could happen that all the food had been put away.

Third-world countries taught me I could go far on oatmeal, long-life milk, and a tin of sardines. I carry a knife that passes at airports, and a fork and a spoon wrapped in my favorite tea towel from Paris. That's my travel kitchen.

Once while I was on a plane coming from Europe back to the US, as we buckled up for takeoff, the man sitting next to me lamented, "Vacation is over, now back to real life."

I said, "Vacation *is* real life."

That sent him reeling into deep contemplation. He didn't speak another word for the entire cross-Atlantic flight, and then when we landed, he found me at the baggage claim where he said, "Thank you," and walked off into his new real life.

In every destination, I am always taken with the light being different here than anywhere else. And the light of the place always goes with the colors of the clothes and the spices in the foods. The music, the language, and the people who are home there all match. Where it's hot and spicy, so are the people.

Many times, at home, I would wake up in the morning and have a taste for foreign places. I'd find a plane that's going today and be on it. Not letting anybody know, maybe faxing them once I arrived or maybe mentioning it when I get back. Maybe not. Hong Kong was that for me. One morning, having a sudden desire for being there, I found a bargain flight that was going that day, I rushed to the airport just in time and went.

That's one idea that changed from travel in my twenties to now. Now I tell people where and when I'm going. It matters to me that they know.

At thirty-seven, in Istanbul, I stayed at a grand hotel on the Bosphorus that had a view of Topkapi Palace and the bridge that connects Asia and Europe—the ancient world to the modern world. Women in burkas and women in western clothes, men in traditional dress and men in suits, crisscross along the bridge. There's something sacred about walking that bridge. You don't just get to the other side, you get to another era, other traditions, and thinking. Another world just there within walking distance of now.

It's where I met Lady Julia, a grand dame in her late eighties, traveling by herself. She had been aboard the Orient Express and had a bad fall and was staying at the hotel to recover. She was ensconced with tea service in a regal setting in the lobby. Her bandaged foot was elevated.

Many hotel guests and staff gave her their attention and comfort. All the travelers, all around, helped her to open her pill jar, or pour her tea, or would bring her a flower from the street market. I saw how she was traveling the world and depending on the kindness of strangers. I remember such grace she had, such joy people showed in giving her their care. I wondered if she was some great guru incarnate, Babaji in disguise, to allow people to have compassion and give them an opportunity to be of service to her.

As fiercely independent as I have been in my life, maybe this is the decade to let people in with small help and offerings. I know how good that will be for all of us.

There are secrets to happy travel besides traveling light. They all amount to this:

Travel the world yet keep close to the bottom of your heart. By that I mean, be open to the whole wide world while you keep your discernment of what you already know to be good and right and true for you.

Sometimes the most meaningful travel is to get out of the house just to empty the garbage.

Let the path unfold and then follow it. What is to be actualized will meet you on the way. Go travel. It's all there for you. ~

79 Years Old

Packing for Heaven

My WORLD TRAVEL is now complete. I know this because as arduous or difficult or joyous a trip, when I arrive back and land at my airport, I always look at all the luggage on the baggage claim carousel and imagine the design of my new, possibly improved, bag. I always know that my travel is to be continued. This time when I returned, I knew that my next big trip—although very far, very different from here—is not a trip that requires luggage.

The closer to leaving here, the more alive I feel. I'm filled with the joy of emptying—I am clear on what to release and what to embrace to be alive in every luscious moment. I feel, as I release and surrender and am done with so much in the physical world, I'm very busy preparing for becoming fully spirit again. I'm packing for heaven—to be in tender surrender and, when it's time, to let the new world come to me.

But not yet! There's more here before going there. I have a checklist. I've got organizing to do. I'm very busy. There's the fun of changing things that have been set in stone for my lifetime. I'm spending money; I'm not leaving for later expressing my love to everybody in my path. I'm following the motto: "If you want what you haven't yet had, do what you haven't yet done."

I always thought anything with "last" in the name seems to catch our interest. There's something so final about "last" that we mortals can't resist, as in the last dance, the last word, the last Twinkie off the conveyor belt. (Although I fear there will always be Twinkies.)

This afternoon I had the last whole bag of potato chips as car food as I drove home from the store. This isn't the first time I decided it would be the last bag. Now, today, maybe this really will be the last one. See what I mean by last? There's something we find significant in the finality. But I think when it's the last day here, it's the first day of forever. Really, there is no such thing as "last" for the soul.

I'm aware of a change in dimension from the human body to the light body to leaving the body. As I am in full release, more life keeps coming my way.

I know that I'll be getting out soon because I did what I came in to do. It's not a matter of health, it's a matter of completion. My body doesn't have to be finished before I am finished with it. I can leave it healthy and just ascend out of it.

When that happens, it's just going to be my time—no cause of death, no breakdown of the physical. It's the expansion of the soulful because I'll be complete. Meanwhile, life continues to show up and I continue to dance with it.

Do you remember the boat that doesn't float that I spoke about several years ago?

I got word that last night's storm sea claimed it. The tide reached all the way up the beach and took it. That's it for our little boat. It won't be coming back.

So, I'm getting the feeling that it's getting close to the end for me too, and because of this new development, there's a whole new expanded universe to explore. A friend of mine, Eddie White, at eighty-four, discovered he had a major talent for writing. He said, "I feel like I got a whole new tank of gas."

Looking at death as the new horizon, I can get ready for the adventure and pack what is useful to take along for the ride. All that which was culled and honed from getting this far, now I get to take a look at it and go from here. I've got a whole new tank of gas.

Recently, a young friend was over and needed to wrap a baby shower gift. She got into the gift-wrapping drawer, and I gasped. She managed to pick out the baby shower wrapping that I realized I had been saving . . . for years. What was I saving it for? The second coming?

What precious belongings am I saving—for what? It's time to wear my good clothes.

As I pack, this is what I sort through—all the usual end-of-life questions. I find that I answered these with my life all along. Questions such as: Have I amounted to myself? Am I whom I hoped I'd be? If there's something I meant to do or be while on Earth, I needed to do it and be it by now. Have I?

Did I learn well what I wanted to learn? Do I know it? Do I feel it? Any regrets I can now release? Any forgiveness I now grant? Am I the embodiment of what I came to be? Is it all accomplished? Yes. I did what I came to do.

When Beloved had the stroke, we breathed each breath with the thought, *Is there anything pending or anything due? Are we up to this minute in expressing our love? Is there anything more, or anything else, that we need to say or be or do?*

As I pack up to leave, I ask these questions of myself and then take care of what might need tending.

I always felt that we all come in to contribute our gift to the world. The secret is that when we do, we are the one who receives the gift.

And so, as I say one-at-a-time goodbyes to the 10,000 things, I am in full appreciation. To the very last. ~

The Last Passage (Whenever That May Be)

80 Plus—Thanksgiving

FOR SOME WEEKS I've known that soon I'll be on my way up and out of life from Earth. Here it is Thanksgiving Day—perfect timing.

I wondered if, when the time came, I would know when I was finished living. I think people certainly know underneath it all. There are many stories we all experience of how our loved ones say goodbye without us directly realizing it at the time. I think we probably all know everything, always, we just keep it from ourselves so we can carry on the human part.

This is perfect—my favorite holiday, Thanksgiving, at my favorite time, sunset, with my favorite loved ones here for turkey dinner.

Why did I know, for several months, that my exit time was upon me? I've been feeling so alive and so conscious that if there is anything else or anything more to do or be or have before I leave, I better do, or be, or have it. And so, I have been very busy with that.

I know that I'm willing. I'm happy to go. I feel excited about being at a rung of the ladder that gets me across to a good landing space. I know I am ever-expanding. And I know that what I came to do, I did. And lately, especially this week, I'm feeling many souls crowding around to ask me their last and final questions for themselves, such as, "Is it really a friendly universe?", "What's going to happen?", "Can I manifest what I want if I think too overmuch about what I don't want?", "How do I?", "Why is that?", "What if?" All the many Earth questions. They ask because I've answered all these questions for myself. Now they can use their lives to answer for themselves.

Today, the gleam of the sunshine is particularly vibrant on the ocean, a whiff of the turkey is scrumptious, and the dressing is looking especially flavorful. Wait. I have to have some. I don't have to leave my body with an empty stomach. Oh, that tastes so good. The turkey is done—all the side delights are ready too. I'll turn the oven to warm. My loved ones will be able to have Thanksgiving after I have left the building.

And here on the counter is my paring knife. The one I got at Ms. Evelyn's yard sale when I was just starting out my adult life.

At that time when I was twenty-four, I didn't know if what I had in mind for my life is what I could create. Now at this end of my life, I am brim full.

If you remember, Ms. Evelyn died alone with no family or friends around her, with no love to send her on her way. I've always thought that I don't mind dying alone, I just don't want it to be two weeks before somebody notices. So, if today is that day, it's perfect. All my loved ones are here.

The Last Heirloom

I wrap Ms. Evelyn's paring knife in a napkin and put it at Arabella's place setting at the Thanksgiving table. I wish Arabella, age twelve, to make a feast of her life. I put the chocolate spoon there too. She is so talented with food.

My heart starts pounding, and I know that I am hearing from home.

I feel flashbacks to earlier times in this life. I feel flash-forwards when I arrive fully in spirit from here.

The family is all out on the beach, flying the kite I brought back from Malaysia. In that culture, kites are flown to celebrate the harvest. There is an art to kite making. The craftsman knows, by touch, to create the exact balance so that the kite is assured a good flight. As the harvest reaps its bounty, the kite flies triumphantly.

I am so happy in my kitchen as I look out to the oceanfront and see the kite in perfect balance. The harvest is complete. You know how I love a good metaphor.

I lie down on my *looking-up-the-coast couch*. I am as still as still can be.

The door that opened at birth and let me in is here opening again for me to easily go on to more light. Imagine my joy.

I feel tender feelings. Just here, just being.

I'm wearing my Ray-Ban Wayfarer sunglasses that I bought early on back when I first came to California and made a practice of being at the beach at sunset. An extravagance at the time, and yet here they are with me now. How many of the possible 29,200 sunsets have we seen together? I know if I missed one here and there, I would apologize to the sun for being elsewhere at that precious moment.

Over time, many people would come to my home, and I would invite them to make a wish on the setting sun. They would wish for the thing they didn't yet have—the house, the car, the baby grand piano—the thing that was sure to make them happy once they got it. The secret of wishing is this: Let your wish be one of gratitude, not for what you don't yet have but for what you already are. When your wish is always thanks for what you *do* have, so much more comes to you.

This is my last sunset, and so beautiful. And my thank you is immense.

Little Laney, who just turned three, has come in from the beach crying with a skinned knee. She goes to the medicine cabinet to get mercurochrome. I paint a heart over her scrape. We nap on the couch together. As I hold her, her young heart is so strong as mine is very still.

Her mom comes in to check on her then tiptoes out when she sees that we are together and sleeping in the sunshine.

As I hold her, I reflect on my three-year-old self. I am in the hallway on Mulligan Avenue on the telephone chair. As my present self, I hold my three-year-old self.

So many times, throughout my life, I would go back and hold my three-year-old self. She knew I was there for her. It has made all the difference for us.

I feel profoundly the heartbeat of being alive. Like a clear bell ringing—the all-together of myself with all and everything. Life is a precious treasure.

I see I am leaving this life alive. I know that I will always be alive somewhere. Life as a progression is always building, ever-expanding, better and better.

That phrase: "You can't take it with you." Not true. You bring along all the love, all the aliveness, all the abundance. I take it with me.

I feel my life review gently upon me. I see all my life, and I've done what I did and what I didn't do I didn't need to. I feel released from all the activities of Earth. I cross my hands over my heart and invite heaven in.

I open my eyes here and then go there and then back here.

It's deeper than a deep sleep. It's a place where I will go and not come back in the morning. I feel that deep sleep and then alert back here and then there and so still.

The shutting down and the opening up, I'm an eternally expanding being.

At birth, I condensed light into matter; at death, I expand matter into light.

As I segue back and forth from here to there, now more there than here, I feel the atmosphere the same. I am vibrating there and here the same. Congruency, alignment, as above, so below. No parallax between here and there. Now I am here and here is now there.

My loved ones all surround me now.

My big, down-stuffed, oversized couch is plenty big enough for the whole family. Everyone is here and Thanksgiving is in the oven.

No panic. No calling 911. They love me enough to let me go forward.

My body is not forcing anything, and I am not forcing anything. It's just time and since no one is fighting this, it is going smoothly. Hey, Mom, look at me, dark victory.

No need for sickness to get me there. It feels gloriously light and bright. And at my favorite time of day—sunset.

I thought I'd be dying alone. The surprise is—all are here.

What did I want it to add up to? It did.

I feel good. I feel ready. I feel the transcendence.

As I lie here, my life force is quieting. Such peace. I deepen further into a relaxed state. I feel a call to be still. Nothing I have to do. It will come and get me.

I go far and deep, and then I'm back here and then go back there. Some of me here, some of me there; each swing back to here, less; each swing to there, more. I see that my learning how to die has come from my knowing how to live.

Thank you, body, for enjoying food as much as I have. Together we were always in agreement that what I wanted to eat you were okay with dealing with once I got it into my mouth. Thank you. You were a splendid body to have. Every year, so beautiful. I appreciate having you. We were a good partnership.

Here is the continuing sun on me as I bask in it. Thank you, sunshine, for always being here for me to revel in. And the beautiful gleam on the water. Always I love that so.

At birth, where I dove through to life, I now lift off to eternity.

This is much easier than my birth. Between birth and death maybe I learned something. Dropping the body expands me. I am leaving alive.

Look at that, my soul knows how to ascend into the higher dimensions, remarkable.

Going forward, between intervals of rest I open my now-clear eyes and, in great joy, report back from where I am going. Oh, the wonder.

They on the couch hear my words. I speak to them from this doorway, cranking it open for them to get a glimpse. I report to them from where I'm going—not yet there, no longer fully here—the door for them to get a glimpse and see it for themselves. This is an exalted passage. I am conscious to lift off, to expand to the highest energy. To enter in full, ready to live. There is *such joy in this passage*. Well-earned. Resting now. Half here, half there. Which is here, which is there?

My heart is open. I feel it ever heightened. It is my last breath on Earth. From human being now back to spirit being.

The sun now setting—a hole in the sky through which the light shines.

And here is the moment when I rise just as the sun sets.

I lift out of my body. I float away from my loved ones at my side. I see my body there on the couch as little Laney sleeps soundly in my arms. I am here at the ceiling. Everyone attending now comes closer and feels the release of me to here. I feel their love as I ascend out the roof.

There is my Replogle globe. It has been with me since I was twelve. It is on an automatic timer and turns on its glow just now at twilight.

As I float above the beach and out to the horizon, my globe descends into the background. Now the Earth is the size that my globe was just moments before, and now the Earth descends into the background as I meld into the sun. It's a bright orange party that's inviting me to come and join it, already in progress. I am now beyond sunset because the sun is perpetual, eternal. I make my wish. I expand from here. I turn to the light of the sun, and I am the light. I am the all and the everything. ~

After

I<small>N HONOR OF</small> my arrival in eternity, there is a celebration. I have said goodbye to my loved ones, and here I say hello. I hear a voice boom out from the sunlight. It's NOBU!

NOBU: Greetings, dear one.

Me: Oh NOBU, I'm so happy to be here. Thank you for that lifetime. Thank you for sending me. I got it. I know how to live a life on Earth. I'm willing to go back right away. Send me back. Send me back.

NOBU: It is complete.

Cue the celestial music. ~

Postscript

I'LL TELL YOU the best part of being dead—I'm having the time of my life. ~~

In your becoming,
the new world becomes.

~ Viki King

Acknowledgements

Whatever you need, whenever you need it, someone or something will show up with the answer that will move you along. That's just what happened for this book.

Rick Ronvik, my high school English teacher, got me started with my own strong writer's voice way back when I was twelve years old, when he gave me a copy of Catcher in the Rye. He's 93 now and he was the first one to do a read-through of this manuscript. Imagine having your favorite English teacher be a dear friend 65 years after school let out. His review, "It's very, very, very good." I think that's like maybe an A. Thank you, Rick.

Writing a book is a solitary experience. Leave me alone for 80 years and I'm a happy writer. I got the book from in my heart onto the desk. Once it was done, I needed help to get it from on the desk to you. That's when I looked for miracles to abound.

Some miracles happen when you don't see them coming. It's a kind of ground force swirl, an alchemy of elements that come together to ignite.

For many years, as I wrote this book, Robyn Wells was a witness to its progress. At one point she even housed two file boxes of drafts and notes for me. And then, with her publishing company, Book of Life Books, she became the publisher. Thank you, Robyn.

Then Judith Arnold appeared from four time zones away to contribute her know-how in the matter of the front matter and the back matter, because it all matters, and the book's interior design. And there's still more fun to be had. You don't let certain treasures go once they come in. Thank you, Judith.

And then there is the lovely Gretchen Martin, who took on the many layers of exacting details in the tech realm and delivered them beautifully. Thank you, Gretchen.

Everyone in the book is a real person. I gave most of them alternative names because I'm really good at alternative names, and also I wanted to keep everyone's life private for them, except Mr. Williams. I didn't change his name because I'm still mad at him from the chapter "6 Years and 6 Months." All the rest, thank you, everybody for being in my book, thank you for being in my life.

The photo shoot – If you need a head shot anytime soon, I highly recommend photographer Nicole Goddard. On the cover shot I'm 79 and a half years old. Thanks to Nicole and make-up artist, Elishah Urbaez, I look just like myself. It was an all-around magical photo session because we shot at Roshanda and Cydney's house; they were the cheering squad. They are also my granddaughter and great granddaughter from my Beloved. Fifty years ago, I was there when Roshanda was born; and 23 years ago, when Cydney was born, and now they are here for my 80-year-old cover shot. You see how this circle of life thing works. Thank you, dear ones.

And more miracles continue to abound because most of the experts in their field that I needed happened to be in my family of friends right here in my friendships, all these years.

The Cover – Visual Effects Artist Steve Hubbard designed it. His credits are many and impressive and innovative. You've probably seen them in feature films you've enjoyed. But he didn't want me to tell you about all that; he wanted me to say, "Cover art lovingly done by a close friend that will always be in my heart." Well, that's true for life. Thank you, Steve.

Kathryn Linehan – Besides being generous-hearted and dear to me, she is always ready with every kind of help, even tech help. When it came time for the book to be put out to people, Kathryn was there with her quick and ready skills. Thank you, Kathryn.

Lisa Schneiderman – another especially dear and longtime friend – also happens to be a top tier publicist. Chances are if you have this book, it's because Lisa made some kinds of connections to have that happen. Thank you, Lisa.

Terri Murphy – Some people are a help just because they are your friend. It also happens that Terri is at the peak of her marketing and presentation skills, so just basking in that talent is an inspiration. Thank you, Terri.

C.J. Cornwell knows something about the spirit of a book. Seeing her bloom through difficult times as she puts forth her own work of art is a joy.

Dianne Skafte – I'm pretty sure that Dianne and I were Oracles together at Delphi, and we agreed to meet back on Earth in the 21st centuries to continue our galactic conversations. (As it turns out she was also a big help with mechanicals on this production such as picking out the quotes that went on the back cover.) She is a great support to me; we are a great support to one another. I'm immensely enriched that we continue with our high-flying work today.

And two more dear friends, Joe Sichta for his early read and testimonial, our precious   beach and sharing soup with the family. And thank you to Ellen Sandler for being Ellen.

Oh, and one anonymous acknowledgement. Years ago, I was on a flight to Kauai and writing the many papers that were parts of this book. Days later, while I was on the island, a woman came up to me to say, "I was on the plane with you. What were those papers you were working on? There was light coming out of them." ~

About the Author

Viki King is well known for her wise counsel to luminaries in the Entertainment Industry as well as to many people, all over the world, in all walks of life.

Viki has addressed various world cinema forums as their keynote speaker in Beijing, London and Paris, and has lectured in the film schools of UCLA, USC and NYU. She is the confidante and visionary to the principals in the creation of many films.

Her book, *How to Write a Movie in 21 days – The Inner Movie Method*, in print for 40 years, has become a classic industry-standard guide and has been translated into many languages. Additionally, Viki is the author of three other books. Her latest work is *How to Be the Hero of Your Own Life – a Unique Autobiography*. It starts before birth, ends after life and addresses all the ages in between.

As one client put it, "Viki has the uncanny ability, with levity and brevity, to get you from in your way, to on your way." ~

Viki can be contacted at

vikikingauthor@gmail.com

vikiking.com

Notes

Notes

Notes

Notes